# The World of the Jinn and Devils

By
Dr. Umar Sulaiman al-Ashqar
Professor, Shariah College, Jordan

Translated by
Jamaal al-Din M. Zarabozo

عالم الجن والشياطين
تأليف: الدكتور عمر الأشقر
نقله إلى الإنجليزية: جمال الدين زربوزو

**1998**

**The World of the Jinn and Devils**
By Umar Sulaiman al-Ashqar

Published by:
Al-Basheer Company for Publications and Translations
1750 30th St. PMB #440
Boulder, CO   80301
U.S.A.

(Note: Not affiliated with Basheer Publications)

©1998, Al-Basheer Company for Publications and Translations

All rights reserved. No part of this publication may be reproduced, stored in a retrieval system, or transmitted in any form or by any means, electronic, mechanical, photocopying, recording, or otherwise, without the prior written permission of the Copyright owner.

ISBN 1-891540-02-5   $11.00 Softcover

## Translator's Preface

Verily, all praise is due to Allah. We praise Him, seek His help and ask for His forgiveness. We seek refuge in Allah from the evil in our own souls and from our sinful deeds. Whoever Allah guides, no one can mislead. And whoever Allah allows to go astray, no one can guide. I bear witness that there is none worthy of worship except Allah, the One, having no partner. And I bear witness that Muhammad is His servant and messenger. O believers! Have fear of Allah according to His right and die not save as Muslims. O mankind! Have fear of your Lord, the One who created you from one soul and created from it its mate and from them spread many men and women. And fear Allah from whom you demand your mutual rights and [do not cut off] ties of kinship. Surely, Allah is Ever an All-Watcher over you. O Believers! Have fear of Allah and always speak the truth. He will direct you to righteous deeds and will forgive you your sins. And whosoever obeys Allah and His Messenger has indeed achieved a great achievement.

To proceed: Verily, the truest speech is the Book of Allah. The best guidance is the guidance of Muhammad. The worst affairs are the innovated ones. Every innovated matter is a heresy. And every heresy is misguidance. And every misguidance is in the Hell-fire.

In the work before you, Dr. Umar al-Ashqar, a well-known contemporary scholar of Islam, has attempted to tackle two important topics. The first topic is that of the characteristics of the jinn. The second topic is the characteristics and methodology of Satan himself.

The first topic concerning the characteristics of the jinn is a difficult topic for many reasons. Foremost among those reasons is that humans, in general, do not have much contact with the jinn and, therefore, it is difficult to gather much information about them. Secondly, the devils are known to be liars. Thus, even when a person does encounter them, he cannot put much trust in what they claim about themselves. Therefore, one must virtually rely only on the statements of the Quran and the authentic hadith of the Prophet (peace be upon him). In this work, al-Ashqar has done a good job of bringing together the texts of the Quran and sunnah such that the reader will have a proper conception of this species that lives in our midst.

The second topic concerning Satan himself is a most important topic concerning which every believer should be knowledgeable. It is no coincidence that Allah has mentioned Satan, his goals, his plots and his allies throughout the entire Quran. This is because Satan is man's greatest enemy. The believer must know the key to defending himself from Satan. Once again, Dr. al-Ashqar has done an excellent job of presenting the information concerning Satan as derived from the Quran and authentic hadith.

I thank Allah for the opportunity and ability to complete this work. I pray that He accepts this work from me and forgives me for any mistakes and errors that have occurred herein.

I completed the translation of this work in the late 1980s. Unfortunately, I have not had the opportunity to publish this work until now. I must express my thanks to Br. Homaidan al-Turki whose encouragement and assistance has helped this book finally see its published form.

Obviously, I must express my thanks to Dr. Umar al-Ashqar for giving me permission to translate and publish this book. That permission was given to me around 1990. I pray that I have not disappointed the *shaikh* by taking too long in finally getting this book published.

After Dr. al-Ashqar gave me the permission to publish this book, a number of its chapters were published in the now defunct magazine *al-Basheer*. I must also express my thanks to the publishers of *al-Basheer* magazine for giving us the permission to publish those articles in this book.

I would also like to express my thanks to my wife Zainab for reviewing the manuscript and consistently encouraging me to publish this work due to its overall benefit.

Many people also assisted in the translation of the work itself. They include Fauzi al-Hesadi, Faraj Sherrima, Mahmoud Misbah, Bashir Shabah, Solaiman Shebani and Faleh al-Sulaiman. I ask Allah to reward them all greatly.

There are numerous others who are always deserving of mention in any of my books. Allah has blessed me by their company, encouragement, help and guidance throughout the years. I pray that Allah rewards all of them greatly. These people include but are not limited to: Nahar al-Rashid, Humaidan al-Turki, Said Lahrichi, Muhammad al-Osimi, Fahd al-Yahya, Hamad al-Shaikh, Ahmad al-Teraiqi, Muhammad Tahlawi and Jaafar Sheikh Idris. Of course, my wife deserves special mention for all of her years of encouragement, help and patience.

I pray that this work is beneficial to those who read it. As always, if anyone has any comments, corrections or suggestions for this work, they should feel free to contact me through the publisher.

Jamaal Zarabozo<br>
January 11, 1998

*The World of the Jinn and Devils*

# Chapter Index

| | |
|---|---|
| INTRODUCTION | 1 |
| 1. IDENTIFICATION AND CLARIFICATION | 5 |
| 2. RESPONSIBILITY FOR THEIR ACTIONS | 53 |
| 3. THE ENMITY BETWEEN SATAN AND MANKIND | 69 |
| 4. THE CAPABILITIES OF SATAN | 131 |
| 5. THE WEAPONS OF THE BELIEVER IN HIS WAR AGAINST SATAN | 169 |
| 6. THE WISDOM BEHIND THE CREATION OF SATAN | 225 |
| AUTHOR'S REFERENCES | 244 |
| TRANSLATOR'S REFERENCES | 245 |
| INDEX OF QURANIC VERSES CITED | 246 |
| TABLE OF CONENTS | 249 |

# Introduction

In the name of Allah, Most Compassionate, Most Merciful

All praises are due to Allah; we praise Him; we seek His help, we seek His forgiveness; and we seek His guidance. We seek refuge in Allah from the evil in our souls and the badness of our deeds. For whoever Allah guides, there is none to lead him astray. And for whoever He allows to go astray, there is none to guide him. I bear witness that there is none worthy of worship except Allah, for whom there is no partner. And I bear witness that Muhammad is His servant and Messenger.

Some people think that writing about this topic is writing about a topic that is from the periphery of knowledge. They approve of humans going over this topic in the quickest of fashions and not giving it much thought. They think that the benefits that accrue from such a study are very limited. Furthermore, they believe that being ignorant of this topic is not harmful at all.

However, I am not delving into something distant. Humans today spend billions of dollars with which they could build cities or countries and end poverty in the farthest reaches the world— and, instead, they spend that money on research to discover if there is life or if life is possible on nearby planets. Scientists spend a great deal of their time and resources on such a question. What about an existence that is known to be living and thinking and that lives right here with us on our earth? They live in our houses and they eat and drink with us. In fact, they even spoil our thoughts and our hearts. These creatures drive us to destroy our own selves and to spill each others' blood. They make us worship them or any other creature so that we will be deserving of the anger and wrath of our Lord. The Lord's anger will come upon us and the result for those who have gone away from their Lord will be a raging fire.

No price can be put on the importance of the texts of the Quran and authentic hadith that have reached us, giving us knowledge of this matter.

Those texts uncover for us the secrets of that existence: the world of the jinn. They give us enough information for us to know about the details of their lives. They also tell us how deeply rooted is the enmity between that creation and man. They also tell us about the extremes and continuous actions that they go through in order to misguide and destroy us.

Following up the numerous verses of the Quran that discuss the jinn and devils should be sufficient for you as an indication showing you the importance of this matter.

The one who looks over these texts knows that the life of a human is nothing but a struggle between him and Satan. Satan wishes to dominate him and take him to his destruction and ruin. The human who Allah fills with His light struggles in order to stay upon the straight path of his Lord and to help others remain on that path. In order to do that, he must fight against that enemy with respect to the inclinations of his soul, thoughts of his heart, and his dreams and aspirations. He must always scrutinize his goals and aims, both close and distant, in order for him to know how close or distant he stands from his Lord and how far he has purified himself from his enemy who is trying to lead him by his neck like a farmer leads his donkey.

I compiled the texts that discuss this topic as well as the statements of the leading scholars in this area. I pondered over what they wrote. The result was this book which is composed of six chapters. The first chapter is an identification and definition of this species: their source, their creation, their names, their types, their food and drink, their spouses, their residences, their animals and the abilities that Allah has given them. In the midst of that chapter, one will find the evidence that proves their existence and refutes those who reject their existence.

Chapter Two explains the goal for which they were created, the means by which they receive the message of their Lord and the generality of the Prophet's message to both jinn and mankind.

Chapter Three is the heart of this work. It discusses the following topics:

(1) The causes for the enmity between man and Satan; the evidence concerning the strength and depth of that enmity; and Allah's warning for us concerning that enemy.

(2) The short-range and long-range goals of Satan.
(3) The methods of Satan in misleading mankind.
(4) His leaders in the battle and his soldiers.
(5) The plots that Satan makes against mankind.

And that chapter is concluded with a discussion of Satan's secret whispering that is his weapon in ruining mankind and planting evil in their hearts.

Chapter Four covers a number of issues by which the devils mislead humans. They include:

(1) Devils appearing like humans and talking to humans and the evil that results from such interaction.

(2) Seances and the conjuring up of spirits; how authentic such things are and their relationship with the devils.

(3) The extent to which the jinn have knowledge of the unseen and the evil that is the result of people believing that jinn do have knowledge of the unseen.

(4) The jinn and unidentified flying objects.

In the fifth chapter, the weapons that a believer must have in his struggle against Satan are defined.

In the sixth and final chapter, there is a discussion of the wisdom behind the creation of Satan.

I ask Allah, Most High, to make this writing beneficial for its writer, publisher and reader. I also ask Allah to grant all of them its reward. I also ask of Him refuge for us from Satan. I also ask that He supports us with His help and care. He is the greatest protector and helper. And peace and blessings be upon His servant and messenger, Muhammad, and upon his family and Companions.

Umar Sulaiman al-Ashqar

*The World of the Jinn and Devils*

# 1
# Identification and Clarification

## What are the Jinn?

The Jinn are a world of their own, different from that of the humans or the angels. They do, however, possess some characteristics in common with humans, such as the ability to think and reflect. Similarly, they also have the ability to choose between the path of good and the path of evil in the same manner as humans. They, though, differ from humans in other characteristics, including one very important characteristic: Their origin.

They are called *jinn* (جن) because they are obscured from human sight,

إِنَّهُ يَرَىٰكُمْ هُوَ وَقَبِيلُهُ

مِنْ حَيْثُ لَا تَرَوْنَهُمْ

"Lo! He sees you, he and his tribe, from whence you see him not" (*al-Araaf* 27).

## Their Origin

Allah has informed us that the jinn have been created from fire as He says in the Quran,

$$\text{وَالْجَآنَّ خَلَقْنَٰهُ مِن قَبْلُ مِن نَّارِ ٱلسَّمُومِ}$$

"And the jinn did we create aforetime of essential fire" (*al-Hijr* 27). In *surah al-Rahmaan* (verse 15), He says,

$$\text{وَخَلَقَ ٱلْجَآنَّ مِن مَّارِجٍ مِّن نَّارٍ}$$

"And the jinn He did create of a smokeless flame of fire." According to Ibn Abbaas, Ikrimah, Mujaahid, Al-Hasan and others the meaning of "*marajin-min-nar*," is "the extremity of the flame," and in one narration it is described as the purest and best (of fire).[1] An-Nawawi said in his commentary to *Sahih Muslim*, "The smokeless flame of fire is that mixed with the blackness of the fire."

In a hadith recorded by Muslim on the authority of Aisha, the Prophet (peace be upon him) said,

$$\text{خُلِقَتِ الْمَلَائِكَةُ مِنْ نُورٍ وَخُلِقَ الْجَانُّ مِنْ مَارِجٍ مِنْ نَارٍ وَخُلِقَ آدَمُ مِمَّا وُصِفَ لَكُمْ}$$

"The angels were created from light, the jinn were created from a smokeless flame of fire and Adam was created from what has been described to you [by Allah in the Quran]."

## When were they created?

There is no doubt that the jinn were created before mankind, as Allah says,

---

[1] See *Al-Bidayah wa an-Nihayah*, vol. 1, p. 59.

$$\text{وَلَقَدْ خَلَقْنَا ٱلْإِنسَٰنَ مِن صَلْصَٰلٍ مِّنْ حَمَإٍ مَّسْنُونٍ ۝ وَٱلْجَآنَّ خَلَقْنَٰهُ مِن قَبْلُ مِن نَّارِ ٱلسَّمُومِ}$$

"Verily We created man of potter's clay of dark mud altered. And the Jinn did We create aforetime of a flameless fire" (al-Hijr 26-27). This verse clearly states that the jinn were created before mankind. Some of the earlier scholars were of the opinion that they were created a thousand years before mankind, but for that statement they have no proof in either the Quran or the sunnah.

## The Names for the Jinn in the Arabic Language

Ibn Abdul Barr said, "The jinn, according to the scholars of the language, are of different types:

1. If one is mentioning the jinn purely of themselves, they are called *jinni* (جني).

2. If one is mentioning the jinn that live among mankind, they are called *aamar* (عامر) whose plural is *amaar* (عمار).

3. If one is mentioning the ones that antagonize the young, they are called *arwaah* (أرواح).

4. If one is mentioning the evil ones that antagonize humans they are called *shaitan* (شيطان) for the singular [and *shayateen* (شياطين) for plural].

5. If they cause even more harm and become strong, they are called *afreet* (عفريت).

## Types of Jinn

The Prophet (peace be upon him) said,

الجن ثلاثة أصناف فصنف يطير في الهواء وصنف حيات وكلاب وصنف يحلون ويظعنون

"There are three types of jinn: one that flies through the air, one that are snakes and dogs, and one which stay in places and travel about."[1]

# There is no room for the denial of the existence of the jinn

A small number of people absolutely deny the existence of another being known as jinn. Some of the polytheists claimed that the meaning of jinn was the souls of the planets.[2]

Some of the philosophers claim that the jinn are the evil inclinations in the souls of mankind in the same way that the angels are the inclination for good in the souls of mankind.[3]

Some of the modern-day people allege that the jinn are the bacteria and microbes that modern science has recently discovered.

Muhammad al-Bahi, in his commentary on *Surah al-Jinn*, says that the jinn are the angels. To him, the jinn and angels are one existence without any difference between them. His proof is that the angels also cannot be seen by mankind. Except that he includes among the jinn those who hide from the world of human beings concerning their belief or disbelief and their good or evil.[4]

---

[1] This was recorded by at-Tabarani and al-Haakim and by al-Baihaqi in *Al-Asmaa wa as-Sifaat* with a *sahih isnad*. See Muhammad Naasir al-Deen al-Albani, *Sahih al-Jaami al-Sagheer*, vol. 3, p. 85.
[2] See Ahmad ibn Taimiya, *Majmu al-Fatawa*, vol. 24, p. 280.
[3] See Ibid., vol.4, p. 346.
[4] Muhammad al-Bahi, *Tafseer Surah al-Jinn*, p. 8.

## Not possessing knowledge concerning them is not a type of proof

The most that these deniers can say is that they have no knowledge concerning their existence. But not having any knowledge about them is not a proof that they do not exist.[1] The mind that denies everything that it does not know of certainly is blameworthy. In fact, that is a reason why Allah blames the unbelievers. Allah says in the Quran,

$$بَلْ كَذَّبُواْ بِمَا لَمْ يُحِيطُواْ بِعِلْمِهِ$$

"Nay, but they denied that, the knowledge whereof they could not compass..." (*Yunus* 39). This thought is a modern invention that no one should be obstinate enough to stick to. Is it permissible for man who has lived hundreds of years to reject their possibility even if a trustworthy person informs him of it? Was our lack of hearing the sounds that go on throughout the world evidence that those sounds did not exist until the radio was invented and gave us the ability to hear and confirm those sounds?

## The truth of the matter

The correct position is that the jinn are a third type of being, apart from angels or humans. They are intelligent and understanding creatures; they are not philosophical accidents or germs and are not like the microorganisms. They are responsible for their actions and have been ordered by Allah to perform some deeds and to abstain from others.

---

[1] They cannot argue by the statement in *Sahih al-Bukhari* of ibn Abbas who denied the Messenger's speaking with the jinn. He only rejected his speaking with them and not the existence of the jinn. Furthermore, Companions other than ibn Abbas, such as ibn Masud, confirmed the Prophet's seeing of the jinn. And whoever knows something is a proof against one who does not know it.

## Proofs for the correct position

**1.** *Mutawatir* **[Undeniable agreement about their existence by different groups of people]**

Ibn Taimiya says in *Majmu al-Fatawa*,

None of the different groups of Muslims have differed about the existence of the jinn, nor in the fact that Allah sent Muhammad as a messenger to them also. The majority of the different groups of the unbelievers also confirm their existence. And the people of the book from among the Jews and the Christians also accept their existence in the same way as the Muslims do, even though one may find some among them who will deny their existence, but in the same way one can find among the Muslims some who deny their existence... like the Jahamiyya and the Mutazila.[1] But the majority of the sects and their leading scholars accept their existence. This is because the reports about their existence have come in a *mutawaatir*[2] manner from the Prophets which necessitates automatic and certain knowledge. It is also known with certainty that they are alive, thinking and acting by choice. They have been ordered to do certain deeds and have been prohibited from certain other deeds. They are not attributes or characteristics of humans or other creatures, as some of the "atheists" claim. Since the matter of the jinn is something narrated in *mutawaatir* form from the Prophets, the scholars and masses know

---

[1] The Jahamiyyah and Mutazilah are two heretical groups that appeared in the history of Islam. The Jahamiyyah, in particular, are known for denying many of the attributes of Allah. The Mutazilah developed their own five principles of religion and accepted or rejected the aspects of faith based on those five principles.—JZ

[2] A *mutawaatir* manner implies that the matter has been reported in such a way, such as by so many people in each generation, that it leaves no room for doubt or question.—JZ

about them and no group that claims any relationship with a messenger may deny them.[1]

On page 13 he also wrote,

> All of the groups of the Muslims acknowledge the existence of the jinn, as do the majority of the people of the book (Jews and Christians), the polytheists among the Arabs and others from the children of Ham (the son of Noah). Similarly, the majority of the Canaanites and the Greeks from the children of Yaafith believe in them. Therefore, the majority of all people accept their existence.

## 2. Quranic and Hadith statements about them.

[There are numerous statements in the Quran and hadith that affirm the existence of the jinn.] For example, Allah says in the Quran,

$$\text{قُلْ أُوحِيَ إِلَيَّ أَنَّهُ ٱسْتَمَعَ نَفَرٌ مِّنَ ٱلْجِنِّ}$$

"Say (O Muhammad): It is revealed unto me that a company of the Jinn listened..." (*al-Jinn* 1). Allah also says,

$$\text{وَأَنَّهُ كَانَ رِجَالٌ مِّنَ ٱلْإِنسِ يَعُوذُونَ بِرِجَالٍ مِّنَ ٱلْجِنِّ فَزَادُوهُمْ رَهَقًا}$$

"And indeed (O Muhammad) individuals of mankind used to invoke the protection of individuals of the Jinn, so that they increased them in revolt" (*al-Jinn* 6).

In fact, there exist many statements about them in the Quran and hadith, and we shall mention most of them in the rest of this work, Allah willing.

---

[1] Ibn Taimiya, *Majmoo al-Fatawa*, vol. 19, p.10.

## 3. Eyewitness Accounts.

Many people of our times and of the previous times have witnessed something of the jinn, even though many who had seen them or who had heard them were not aware that they were jinn. They thought that they were ghosts, spirits, invisible men, creatures from outer space and so forth.

Many trustworthy narrators, of the present day and previously, have narrated events concerning them. The famous scholar of hadith, al-Amash said, "A jinn appeared among us. I said to him, 'What is your favorite food?' He said, 'Rice.' We brought some to him and I would see the spoon go up and down but could not see anyone. I said, 'Do you also have people of desires [and innovations] among you like what we have?' He said, 'Yes.' I said, 'What is the situation of the Rafidha [extreme Shia] among you.' He said, 'They are the worst of us.'"

Ibn Kathir wrote, after recording the above story, "I presented its chain to our teacher Abu al-Hajjaj al-Mizi. He said, 'The chain is authentic back to al-Amash.' Then he said, 'Ibn Asaakeer recorded in the biography of al-Abbas ibn Ahmad al-Dimishqi that he said, 'I heard some of the jinn recite, 'The hearts are in pain until they connect with their beloved and are with Him in any place, in the West or East; They are filled with the love of Allah, and Allah is their lord, they are connected to Allah and not to anything of his creation.'"

I [Dr. al-Ashqar] add: Many trustworthy people have told me about their speaking with the jinn and their seeing them. Allah willing, some of these events will be mentioned later in this work where we will discuss the ability of the jinn to take on different forms.

**4. The source from which they were created.** The messenger of Allah (peace be upon him) has informed us that the angels were created from light and the jinn were created from fire. He made a distinction between their two sources. This refutes the claim of those who say that the jinn and the angels are nothing but one and the same beings.

## Donkeys and Dogs see the jinn

Even though we humans do not see the jinn, some animals, like dogs and donkeys, can see them. It is recorded in *Musnad Ahmad* and *Sunan Abu Dawud* with a *sahih* chain from Jabir that the Prophet said,

إِذَا سَمِعْتُمْ نُبَاحَ الْكِلَابِ وَنَهِيقَ الْحُمُرِ بِاللَّيْلِ فَتَعَوَّذُوا بِاللَّهِ فَإِنَّهُنَّ يَرَيْنَ مَا لَا تَرَوْنَ

"If you hear the bark of dogs or the braying of donkeys during the night, seek refuge in Allah from Satan, as they see what you do not see." This is not strange as many scientists have confirmed that animals are capable of many things that humans are not capable of. Bees can see ultraviolet light and can also see the sun on an overcast day. An owl can see a mouse running in a crowded corn patch on a dark night.

## Satan and the Jinn

Satan, which Allah mentions to us many times in the Quran, is from the world of the jinn. He used to worship Allah at the beginning of his creation. He lived among the angels in the heavens. He entered Paradise. But then he disobeyed Allah when he refused to prostrate to Adam, out of pride, arrogance and envy. Therefore Allah cast him out of from His mercy.

Satan, in the Arabic language, is a general term for any arrogant rebel. It is used, in general, for that one specific being because he was so arrogant and rebelled against his Lord.

He is called *taaghoot*[1] in *al-Nisaa*, verse 76,

---

[1] *Taaghoot* can be understood to mean any false object of worship and submission.—JZ

$$\text{ٱلَّذِينَ ءَامَنُوا۟ يُقَـٰتِلُونَ فِى سَبِيلِ ٱللَّهِ ۖ وَٱلَّذِينَ كَفَرُوا۟ يُقَـٰتِلُونَ فِى سَبِيلِ ٱلطَّـٰغُوتِ فَقَـٰتِلُوٓا۟ أَوْلِيَآءَ ٱلشَّيْطَـٰنِ ۖ إِنَّ كَيْدَ ٱلشَّيْطَـٰنِ كَانَ ضَعِيفًا}$$

"Those who believe do battle for the cause of Allah; and those who disbelieve do battle for the cause of *taaghoot*. So fight the minions of the devil. Lo, the devil's strategy is weak." *Taaghoot* is a word that is well-known to many of the people of the earth, with exactly the same lettering, according to al-Aqaad in his book *Iblees*. He is called a *taaghoot* because he has transgressed the limits, rebelled against his Lord and tried to set himself up as a god to be worshipped.

Satan has despaired of any chance of mercy from Allah and for that reason Allah has named him Iblees (إبليس). *Alabalas* (البَلَس) means he has no good in him. And *ublis* (أبلس) means despaired and lost.

Many of the early scholars have mentioned that his name before he disobeyed his Lord was *azaazeel*. Allah knows best how correct that is.

## Satan, the created

The one who studies the Quran and in the hadith knows that Satan is one of Allah's creation and he has a mind, ability to understand, he moves and so forth... He is not like what some of the ignorant have claimed, "an evil spirit that takes the shape of the evil conscience animalistic part of man, who leads the person when it takes the place of the spiritual, good conscious in the heart."[1]

---

[1] This was stated in *Dairat al-Maarif al-Haditha*, p. 357.

## His origin

We have already stated that Satan is a jinn. Some modern and past writers have disputed this point. They use as a proof the statement of Allah,

$$وَإِذْ قُلْنَا لِلْمَلَٰٓئِكَةِ ٱسْجُدُوا۟ لِءَادَمَ فَسَجَدُوٓا۟ إِلَّآ إِبْلِيسَ أَبَىٰ وَٱسْتَكْبَرَ وَكَانَ مِنَ ٱلْكَٰفِرِينَ$$

"And when We said unto the angels: Prostrate yourselves before Adam, they fell prostrate, all save Iblees. He demurred through pride, and so became an unbeliever" (*al-Baqara* 34). [They also quote] other similar verses in which Allah makes an exception from the angels of Iblees. And they argue that if he is being excepted from a group, it must have been that he was a member of that group as this is the customary mode of speech.

In many of the books of Quranic commentaries and books of history we find narrations from many scholars on this point. They mention that Satan was among the angels and that he was the treasurer of paradise or of the lowest heaven. He was the most noble and honorable of the angels and so forth. Ibn Katheer states in his commentary of the Quran,

> These stories have been related from many of the early scholars. Most of them are from Jewish and Christian legends (Ar., *Israaeeliyaat*) which must be investigated more closely. Allah alone knows the truth of most of these types of reports. Many of them are clearly false since they contradict the truth that we possess in our hands [that is, the Quran and the hadith of the Prophet]. Whatever the Quran contains is sufficient and we need not delve into the stories of the earlier peoples. Their reports have not been safe from changes, additions and deletions. They have fabricated many things in their reports. They did not

have among them those trustworthy people who safeguarded their scriptures and reports from being contaminated by the extremists and others as this nation (of Islam) has had. This nation has had scholars, experts, leaders, memorizers, preservers and pious people who recorded the hadith and scrutinized them, making clear which of them are authentic, acceptable, weak, rejected, fabricated, false. They were familiar with who the forgers were and who were the unknown narrators who should not be considered fully trustworthy. All of that is due to the position of the Prophet Muhammad and the fact that he is the seal of all the Prophets and leader of mankind. Therefore forgeries and interpolations have not been able to be attributed to him and to be accepted by the scholars.

Concerning their proof that Allah excepted Iblees from the angels, it is not a definitive proof. Such statements may be disjunctive.[1] In fact, this is definitely the case as Allah states that Iblees was one of the jinn. Allah says in the Quran,

وَإِذْ قُلْنَا لِلْمَلَٰٓئِكَةِ ٱسْجُدُوا۟ لِءَادَمَ فَسَجَدُوٓا۟ إِلَّآ إِبْلِيسَ كَانَ مِنَ ٱلْجِنِّ فَفَسَقَ عَنْ أَمْرِ رَبِّهِۦ

"And remember when we said unto the angels: Fall prostrate before Adam, and they fell prostrate, all save Iblees. He was of the Jinn, so he rebelled against his Lord's command" (*al-Kahf* 20). Furthermore, it has also been confirmed from an authentic text that the jinn are not the same as the angels or as the humans. The Prophet said, "The angels have been

---

[1] *Al-istithnaa al-munqata* is a case where someone states, for example, "Everyone except so and so," while in reality "so and so" was not a member of the original group. Such a form of speech is acceptable and not uncommon in Arabic. However, such would probably be objectionable if stated in English.—JZ

created from light, the jinn from fire and Adam was created from clay." (This was recorded in *Sahih Muslim*[1]).

Al-Hasan al-Basri said, "Iblees was not from the angels even for the blinking of an eye."[2] Ibn Taimiya said, "Verily, Satan was from the angels with respect to his appearance, but not with respect to his origin and not with respect to him being of the same nature as them."[3]

## Was Satan the origin of the Jinn or was he just one of them?

We do not possess any clear text that states Satan to have been the origin of all the jinn or that states that he was simply one of them. The latter is more apparent from the Quranic statement,

$$\text{إِلَّا إِبْلِيسَ كَانَ مِنَ الْجِنِّ}$$

"Except Iblees and he was of the jinn" (*al-Kahf* 50). Ibn Taimiya is of the opinion that Satan was the origin of all the jinn in the same way that Adam is the origin of all mankind.[4]

## The Food and Drink of the Jinn

The jinn, and Satan among them, eat and drink. In *Sahih al-Bukhari* it is recorded on the authority of Abu Huraira that the Prophet (peace be upon him) told him to get some stones in order for the Prophet (peace be upon him) to clean himself after defecation. The

---

[1] This translator was not able to find this hadith with this wording in *Sahih Muslim*. Instead, there is the hadith that has been mentioned earlier, "The angels were created from light.. and Adam was created from what has been described to you [by Allah in the Quran]."—JZ
[2] Quoted from ibn Katheer, *al-Bidaaya wa al-Nihaaya*, vol. 1, p. 79.
[3] *Majmu al-Fatawa*, vol. 4, p. 346.
[4] *Majmu al-Fatawa*, vol. 4, pp. 235 and 346

Prophet (peace be upon him) told Abu Huraira, "Do not bring me bones or dung." Abu Huraira asked the Prophet (peace be upon him) why he specifically mentioned not to bring those two items. The Prophet (peace be upon him) told him, "They are food for the jinn. A delegation of Naseeb came to me, and what nice jinn they are, and asked me about their provisions. I supplicated to Allah for them that they would never pass by dung or bones except that they would find meat upon them." And it is recorded in *Sunan at-Tirmidhi*, with a *sahih* chain, that the Prophet (peace be upon him) said, "Do not clean yourselves with dung or with bones for they are food for your brothers among the jinn."[1] And in *Sahih Muslim* it is recorded from Ibn Masud that a messenger from the jinn came to the Prophet (peace be upon him) and he went with them. The Prophet (peace be upon him) read to them some Quranic verses. The Prophet (peace be upon him) showed the people the remains of their embers. They asked the Prophet (peace be upon him) about their provisions and he told them, "Every bone on which the name of Allah has been mentioned will have meat on it for you. And the dung are fodder for your animals." Then he said, "Do not clean yourselves with them as they are food for your brothers."[2]

The Prophet also informed us that the devils eat with their left hands and he ordered us to be different from them in this respect. Muslim recorded in his *Sahih*, on the authority of Ibn Umar, that the Prophet (peace be upon him) said,

إِذَا أَكَلَ أَحَدُكُمْ فَلْيَأْكُلْ بِيَمِينِهِ وَإِذَا شَرِبَ فَلْيَشْرَبْ بِيَمِينِهِ فَإِنَّ الشَّيْطَانَ يَأْكُلُ بِشِمَالِهِ وَيَشْرَبُ بِشِمَالِه

"If one of you eats, he should eat with his right hand. And if he drinks, he should drink with his right hand. Verily, Satan eats with his left hand and drinks with his left hand." In *Musnad Ahmad*, the following hadith is recorded,

---

[1] *Sahih al-Jaami*, vol. 2, p. 154.
[2] If we are prohibited from spoiling the food of the jinn, it is must definitely also be the case that we are prohibited from spoiling the food of humans.

$$\text{مَنْ أَكَلَ بِشِمَالِهِ أَكَلَ مَعَهُ الشَّيْطَانُ وَمَنْ شَرِبَ بِشِمَالِهِ شَرِبَ مَعَهُ الشَّيْطَانُ}$$

"Whoever eats with his left hand, Satan eats with him. And whoever drinks with his left hand, Satan drinks with him."

The following hadith is also recorded in *Musnad Ahmad*,

$$\text{إِذَا دَخَلَ الرَّجُلُ بَيْتَهُ فَذَكَرَ اللَّهَ عِنْدَ دُخُولِهِ وَعِنْدَ طَعَامِهِ قَالَ الشَّيْطَانُ لَا مَبِيتَ لَكُمْ وَلَا عَشَاءَ وَإِذَا دَخَلَ فَلَمْ يَذْكُرِ اللَّهَ عِنْدَ دُخُولِهِ قَالَ الشَّيْطَانُ أَدْرَكْتُمُ الْمَبِيتَ وَإِذَا لَمْ يَذْكُرِ اللَّهَ عِنْدَ طَعَامِهِ قَالَ أَدْرَكْتُمُ الْمَبِيتَ وَالْعَشَاءَ}$$

"If the man enters his house and mentions the name of Allah upon entering it and upon eating therein, Satan says, 'There is no lodging for you here and no meal here.' But if the man enters his house and neglects to mention the name of Allah upon entering it, Satan says, 'I have found lodging for you.' And if he does not mention Allah's name upon eating his meal, Satan says, 'I have found lodging and a meal.'" This hadith was also recorded by Muslim. These hadith are clear texts that definitely prove that the devils eat and drink.

In the same manner that it is prohibited for man to eat any meat that has not had the name of Allah pronounced over it, the Messenger of Allah (peace be upon him) permitted the believing jinn to eat any bone that has had the name of Allah pronounced over it. They are not permitted to eat meat over which Allah's name has not been mentioned. All that has been eaten without having the name of Allah mentioned over it provides food for the non-believing jinn who are the devils. In other words, the devils seek as permissible all the food that has not had the name of Allah mentioned over it. This is why many scholars are of the opinion that carrion that have died by themselves are food for the devils because the name of Allah was not mentioned over them.

Ibn Qayyim concludes from the verse of the Quran,

$$\text{إِنَّمَا ٱلْخَمْرُ وَٱلْمَيْسِرُ وَٱلْأَنصَابُ وَٱلْأَزْلَٰمُ رِجْسٌ مِّنْ عَمَلِ ٱلشَّيْطَٰنِ}$$

"O you who believe, strong drink and games of chance and idols and divining arrows are only an infamy of Satan's handiwork. Leave it aside in order that you might succeed" (al-Maaidah 90), that intoxicating liquors are the beverages of the devils. And it is the drink that he orders his patrons to drink, and he participates with them in that action, in its drinking, its sin and its eventual punishment.

## Do the jinn marry and procreate?

It is apparent that the jinn do have sexual intercourse. To prove this, some of the scholars refer to the description of the spouses in paradise. Allah says concerning them,

$$\text{لَمْ يَطْمِثْهُنَّ إِنسٌ قَبْلَهُمْ وَلَا جَانٌّ}$$

"Therein are those of modest gaze, whom neither man nor jinn will have touched before them" (al-Rahmaan 60). The author of *Lawaami' al-Anwaar al-Bahiya* mentions a hadith which deserves a closer look to see at its chain to see whether it is authentic or not. The hadith states,

$$\text{إن الجن يتوالدون كما يتوالد بنو آدم}$$

"The jinn have children in the same way that the sons of Adam have children, but theirs are more in number." This was related by ibn Abu Haatim and Abu al-Shaikh in *al-*

*Udhma* on the authority of Qataada.[1] Regardless of whether or not this hadith is authentic, the verse above is clear that the jinn have intercourse and that satisfies us as proof.

Some people allege that the jinn do not eat, drink or have sex, but that claim is false as we have shown in our clear proofs from the Quran and the sunnah.

Some scholars are of the opinion that there are different types of jinn and some of them do eat or drink while others do not. Wahb ibn Munabih said, "The jinn are of different kinds. One is a pure jinn, and that is like a wind that does not eat or drink, nor does it die or procreate. And there is a class of them that does eat, drink, procreate and has sex and dies. And those are those female demons and desert demons and similar others." This was recorded by ibn Jarir at Tabari.[2]

But what Wahb said is itself in need of evidence and cannot be considered a proof on its own.

Many scholars have delved into the nature of their eating: is it similar to that of the humans, do they swallow or is it by sniffing and so forth. It is a mistake and not allowed to delve into such matters and we are not required to know about such things. Neither Allah or His Messenger (peace be upon him) have informed us of such matters.

---

[1] In the way that the report is being referred to, it seems that it is from the *mursal* reports of Qataada. Such reports are considered weak, unless they are supported through other sources. Unfortunately, the recently published edition of ibn Abu Haatim's *tafseer* does not extend all the way to *Surah al-Rahmaan* to be able to check the entire chain.—JZ

[2] *Lawaami al-Anwaar*, vol. 2, p. 222.

## Marriage between the jinn and humans

One still hears about some man marrying a jinn or some woman marrying one of the jinn or a woman being proposed to by one of the jinn. Al-Suyooti mentioned many such reports from the early generations and scholars pointing to the existence of marriages between humans and jinn. Ibn Taimiya said, "Humans and jinn have gotten married and have had children, this has happened often and is well-known."[1]

Assuming it is possible, many of the scholars showed a dislike for such a marriage. Scholars such as al-Hasan, Qataada, al-Hukum and Ishaaq were known to have shown a dislike for it. Imam Malik could not find any text that would prohibit it but he himself did not like for it to occur and he gave his reason for saying so, "I hate that it would be the case that we would find a woman who is pregnant and we ask her, 'Who is your husband?' and she replies, 'One of the jinn.' Much evil would be the result of that."

A group of people are of the opinion that it is not permitted to marry from the jinn. From the blessings of Allah is that He created for mankind spouses of their own species. Allah says in the Quran,

وَمِنْ ءَايَـٰتِهِۦٓ أَنْ خَلَقَ لَكُم مِّنْ أَنفُسِكُمْ أَزْوَٰجًا لِّتَسْكُنُوٓا۟ إِلَيْهَا وَجَعَلَ بَيْنَكُم مَّوَدَّةً وَرَحْمَةً

"And of His signs is this: He created for you mates from yourselves that you might find rest in them, and He ordained between you love and mercy" (*al-Room* 21). If it could occur, it would not be possible to have

---

[1] *Majmoo Fatawa*, vol. 19, p. 39. [It should be noted that there is no direct evidence for such an occurrence. The Prophet (peace be upon him) never referred to such a practice. The narrations concerning such incidences from later authorities cannot, in themselves, be considered proofs concerning this matter. Furthermore, there does not seem to be any evidence that any children existed that had characteristics of beng partly jinn and partly human. Today, in the United Arab Emirates, there is a clan that claims to be descendant from a female jinn. However, their characteristics are no different from any other human. Hence, it is impossible to prove their claim.—JZ]

that companionship and love between the spouses due to their different species. The goal and wisdom of marriage would not be attainable since the tranquillity and love mentioned by Allah in the Quran would be impossible.

In any case, although people claim that such marriages occur presently and have occurred in the past, if such does occur, it is rare and strange. Furthermore, the one who performs it must seek the Islamic ruling concerning it. It could be the case that the one who does it is, in a sense, overpowered and has no way to escape that situation.

And what points to the possibility of marriage between the two species is the mention of the female companions in paradise. Allah says about them,

$$\text{لَمْ يَطْمِثْهُنَّ إِنْسٌ قَبْلَهُمْ وَلَا جَانٌّ}$$

"Whom neither man nor jinn have touched before them" (*al-Rahmaan* 56). And this verse points to both the jinn and mankind being equally suitable for them.

## Do the devils die?

There is no doubt that the jinn, and the devils among them, do die. The following Quranic verse applies to them,

$$\text{كُلُّ مَنْ عَلَيْهَا فَانٍ ۝ وَيَبْقَىٰ وَجْهُ رَبِّكَ ذُو ٱلْجَلَٰلِ وَٱلْإِكْرَامِ ۝}$$
$$\text{فَبِأَيِّ ءَالَآءِ رَبِّكُمَا تُكَذِّبَانِ}$$

"Everyone that is therein will pass away; There remains but the countenance of your Lord of Might and Glory. Which is it, of the favors of your Lord, that you deny?" (*al-Rahmaan* 26-28). In *Sahih al-Bukhari* it is reported from Ibn Abbas that the Prophet used to say,

$$\text{أَعُوذُ بِعِزَّتِكَ الَّذِي لَا إِلَهَ إِلَّا أَنْتَ الَّذِي لَا يَمُوتُ وَالْجِنُّ وَالْإِنْسُ يَمُوتُونَ}$$

"I seek refuge, by your Glory, the One, whom there is no other god but You, the One who does not die, and the jinn and mankind do die."

Concerning the length of their lives, we do not know much except what Allah has said concerning the accursed Satan who has been given respite and life until the Day of Judgment. Allah says,

$$\text{قَالَ أَنْظِرْنِي إِلَى يَوْمِ يُبْعَثُونَ ۝ قَالَ إِنَّكَ مِنَ الْمُنْظَرِينَ}$$

"He said: Reprieve me till the day when they are raised (from the dead). He said: Lo! you are of those reprieved" (*Al-Asaaf* 14-15).

Concerning other jinn or devils, we do not know their lifespans. But we do know that their lifespans are longer than that of the humans.

Further evidence that they do die is the report that Khaalid ibn Waleed killed the devil of al-Uza (a tree that the Arabs used to worship). And a Companion killed a jinn that took the shape of a serpent, as shall be discussed later.

## The residence of the jinn and their places and the times that they can be found

The jinn live upon the same earth as humans do. Most of them can be found among the ruins and dilapidated areas, as well as the places where there are many impure things, such as, bathrooms, hashish dens, the places of the camels, cemeteries. For that reason, as Ibn Taimiya said, those people who are close to Satan usually inhibit such areas. There are hadith that say that one should not pray in bathrooms due to the impurities present and because it is the abode of Satan, or in cemeteries as this leads to polytheism and it is also a home for the devils.

Many of them are in the places which may be sources of evil, such as the marketplaces. The Prophet (peace be upon him) gave the following advice to one of his Companions,

$$\text{لَا تَكُونَنَّ إِنِ اسْتَطَعْتَ أَوَّلَ مَنْ يَدْخُلُ السُّوقَ وَلَا آخِرَ مَنْ يَخْرُجُ مِنْهَا فَإِنَّهَا مَعْرَكَةُ الشَّيْطَانِ وَبِهَا يَنْصِبُ رَايَتَهُ}$$

"If you can, do not be the first one to enter the marketplace. And do not be the last to leave it. For they are the places of Satan and therein he raises his banner." This hadith was recorded in *Sahih Muslim*.

The devils live in the same houses in which people live. One can stop them from entering or repel them from such houses by mentioning Allah upon entering those houses, by remembering or mentioning Allah (Ar., *dhikr*), reciting the Quran, in particular, *surah al-Baqara* and "the verse of the Throne" (verse 255 of that *surah*). The Prophet (peace be upon him) stated that the devils spread out and roam about increasingly when the dark first comes, and, therefore, he has advised Muslims to bring in their children during that period of time. This is stated in a hadith that was recorded by both Al-Bukhari and Muslim.

And the devils run away from the call to prayer and cannot stand listening to it. And in the month of Ramadhaan they are chained.

## The places where the devils sit or gather

The devils love to sit between the shade and the sunlight. For this reason the Prophet (peace be upon him) forbade the Muslims to sit in such places. This hadith was recorded in the books of *Sunan* and other works and it is *sahih*.

## The animals of the jinn

In the hadith of Ibn Masud, recorded in *Sahih Muslim*, the jinn asked the Prophet about their provisions. He told them, "Every bone on which the name of Allah is recited is your provision. The time it will fall in your hand it would be covered with flesh. And the dung of (the camels) is fodder for your animals." Thus the Prophet (peace be upon him) has informed us that they possess animals and that the fodder for their animals is the dung of the animals of mankind.

## Specific animals that the devils accompany

The devils accompany some animals, such as camels. The Prophet (peace be upon him) said,

إن الإبل خلقت من الشياطين وإن وراء بعير شيطانا

"Verily the camel has been created from devils. And behind every camel is a devil."[1] For this reason, the Prophet (peace be upon him) has prohibited us from praying in the pastures of the camels. It is recorded in *Musnad Ahmad* and *Sunan Abu Dawud* that the Prophet (peace be upon him) said,

لا تصلوا في مبارك الإبل فإنها من الشياطين وصلوا في مرابض الغنم فإنها بركة

"Do not pray in the pastures of the camels, for they are from the devils. But pray in the fields of the sheep, for they are blessed."[2] Ibn Majah recorded in his *Sunan*, with a *sahih* chain,

لا تُصَلُّوا فِي أَعْطَانِ الْإِبِلِ فَإِنَّهَا خُلِقَتْ مِنَ الشَّيَاطِينِ

"Do not pray in the resting places of the camels [that they go to after being] watered, for they have been created from the devils." These

---

[1] This was recorded by Saeed ibn Mansoor in his *Sunan* with a *mursal hasan* chain. See *Sahih al-Jaami*, vol. 2, p. 25.
[2] This translator could not find all of this as one statement as in the text. Instead, the Prophet (peace be upon him), as recorded in the referred to works, was asked about praying in the camel pastures and in the fields of sheep and he responded to each question separately. Allah knows best.—JZ

hadith refute the claims of those who state that the reason it is forbidden to pray in the places of the camels is that their urine and dung are impure. Actually, the urine and the dung of any animal that is permissible to eat is not considered impure.

## The ugliness of Satan

Satan has a very ugly appearance. This is something well-accepted by the mind. Allah compares the branches of the tree of Zuqqum in Hell to the heads of the devils. Allah says,

$$ إِنَّهَا شَجَرَةٌ تَخْرُجُ فِي أَصْلِ الْجَحِيمِ ۝ طَلْعُهَا كَأَنَّهُ رُءُوسُ الشَّيَاطِينِ $$

"Is it better as a welcome, or the tree of Zaqqum? Lo! We have appointed it a torment for wrong-doers. Lo! It is a tree that springs in the heart of hell. Its crop is as it were the heads of the devils" (al-Saaffaat 62-65).

Christians of the Middle Ages used to picture Satan as a black man with a pointed beard, raised eyebrows, a mouth that emits flames, horns and hoofs and a tail.[1]

## Satan has two horns

In *Sahih Muslim*, it is recorded from Ibn Umar that the Prophet (peace be upon him) said,

$$ لَا تَحَرَّوْا بِصَلَاتِكُمْ طُلُوعَ الشَّمْسِ وَلَا غُرُوبَهَا فَإِنَّهَا تَطْلُعُ بِقَرْنَيْ شَيْطَانٍ $$

---
[1] See *Dairat al-Maarif al-Haditha*, p. 357.

"Do not seek to pray when the sun is rising or when it is setting, verily it rises [and sets] between the two horns of a devil." In *al-Bukhari* and *Muslim*, it is also recorded that the Prophet (peace be upon him) said,

إذا طلع حاجب الشمس فدعوا الصلاة حتى تغيب ولا تحيّنوا بصلاتكم طلوع الشمس ولا غروبها فإنها تطلع بين قرني شيطان

"If the sun is setting then leave the prayer until it disappears. And do not wait for your prayer until the sun is rising, nor while it is setting. For verily it sets and rises between the two horns of Satan."[1] These hadith are referring to the polytheists of the Arabs who used to worship the sun and would prostrate to it when it would set or rise, for that reason Satan would establish himself in that direction so that their worship could be directed towards him.

The Prophet (peace be upon him) has forbidden us to pray during that time. Actually, the correct opinion is that prayer during that time is permissible if there is some reason for it, such as the prayer upon entering the mosque. It is not allowed, though, if there is no reason for it, such as simply a supererogatory prayer.[2]

The meaning of the Prophet's words is that one should not intentionally set that time for prayer.

And from among the other narrations that mention the horn of Satan is the following hadith that is recorded in *Sahih al-Bukhari*: Ibn Umar related that he saw the Prophet (peace be upon him) pointing to the east and state,

إِنَّ الْفِتْنَةَ هَا هُنَا إِنَّ الْفِتْنَةَ هَا هُنَا مِنْ حَيْثُ يَطْلُعُ قَرْنُ الشَّيْطَانِ

---

[1] With that exact wording, the hadith does not seem to be in either *al-Bukhari* or *Muslim*. However, it is close to a hadith in *al-Bukhari* and a hadith with a similar meaning may also be found in *Muslim*.—JZ
[2] This is a matter in which there is some difference of opinion on this question. The author is simply stating the opinion he prefers.—JZ

"Verily, the trial will come from here, the calamity will come from here, where the horn of Satan rises." The latter statement is referring to the East.

## Their ability and strength

Allah has given the jinn power and ability that He has not given humans. Allah has informed us of some of their ability, including great speed and movement.

One of the *afreet* of Satanic Jinn promised Solomon that he would be able to bring the throne of Sheba to Jerusalem in a period of time that was so short that a man would not be able to stand from his place of sitting. But one who had knowledge of the Book said, "I will bring it before your gaze returns to you." Allah has described this incident in the Quran with the following verses,

$$\text{قَالَ عِفْرِيتٌ مِّنَ ٱلْجِنِّ أَنَا۠ ءَاتِيكَ بِهِۦ قَبْلَ أَن تَقُومَ مِن مَّقَامِكَ ۖ وَإِنِّى عَلَيْهِ لَقَوِىٌّ أَمِينٌ ۝ قَالَ ٱلَّذِى عِندَهُۥ عِلْمٌ مِّنَ ٱلْكِتَٰبِ أَنَا۠ ءَاتِيكَ بِهِۦ قَبْلَ أَن يَرْتَدَّ إِلَيْكَ طَرْفُكَ ۚ فَلَمَّا رَءَاهُ مُسْتَقِرًّا عِندَهُۥ قَالَ هَٰذَا مِن فَضْلِ رَبِّى}$$

"A stalwart of the Jinn said: I will bring it to you before you can rise from your place. Lo! I verily am strong and trusty for such work. One with whom was knowledge of the scripture said: I will bring it to you before your gaze returns to you. And when he saw it set in his presence, and he said, 'This is from the bounties of my Lord.'" (al-Naml 39-40).

## They preceded mankind in matters related to space

The jinn used to go to the lowest heaven to eavesdrop on the inhabitants of the heavens in order to find out what event would occur in the future. When the Prophet was sent with his message the number of "guards" in the heavens were increased. Allah says in the Quran,

$$وَأَنَّا لَمَسْنَا ٱلسَّمَآءَ فَوَجَدْنَٰهَا مُلِئَتْ حَرَسًا شَدِيدًا وَشُهُبًا ۝ وَأَنَّا كُنَّا نَقْعُدُ مِنْهَا مَقَٰعِدَ لِلسَّمْعِ ۖ فَمَن يَسْتَمِعِ ٱلْءَانَ يَجِدْ لَهُۥ شِهَابًا رَّصَدًا$$

"And (the Jinn who had listened to the Quran said): We had sought the heaven but had found it filled with strong warders and meteors. And we used to sit on places (high) therein to listen. But he who listens now finds a flame in wait for him" (al-Jinn 8-9).

The Prophet (peace be upon him) himself described how the jinn tried to steal the messages in the heaven. Abu Huraira reported that the Prophet (peace be upon him) informed him, "When Allah decrees a matter in heaven, the angels move their wings in submission to His word which is like a chain on a smooth stone. When their hearts are delivered from fear they say, 'What did your Lord say?' and receive the reply, 'That which He said is the truth and He is the Most High and the Most Great.' Then those who listen by stealth hear it (i.e., the jinn), and they are like this, some above others (and Sufyan, a narrator, illustrated this point by turning his hand over and separating the fingers). Then one who hears the word passes it on to the one below him, and so forth until one of them passes it to the tongue of a soothsayer or diviner. Often a flame catches him before he is able to pass it on. He then mixes with it one hundred lies. People then ask, 'Isn't it true that he not made such a statement on a specific date,' and he is believed because of that one word which was heard from the heavens." (Recorded by al-Bukhari in his *Sahih*.)

## Superstitions during the period of ignorance

Knowledge of the reason why they were being pelted with meteors put an end to superstitious belief that the people of ignorance used to pass on. Ibn Abbas narrated from one of the companions of the

Prophet (peace be upon him), from among the Ansar, who said that they were with the Prophet one night and they witnessed a shooting star. The Prophet asked them, "What did you say during the days of ignorance concerning a shooting star like that?" They said, "Allah and His Messenger know best. We used to say that on that night an important person was born or an important person had died." The Prophet said, "It does not do so because of the death or birth of anyone. But when Allah decides an affair, the inhabitants who carry the Throne sing His praise, and so do the ones of the next heaven and so forth until the lowest heaven. Then those are close to those who carry the Throne say to those who carry the Throne, 'What did your Lord say?' And they are then informed about what Allah has decreed. And they pass this news to the next heaven and so forth until it reaches the lowest heaven. Then the jinn listen in and pass on the word to their servants. When the angels notice them they attack them with meteors. If all that they [the jinn] would relate is only that which they actually had heard, they would be truthful; but, instead, they mix it with lies and make additions to it." (This hadith was recorded in *Sahih Muslim*.)

## Their knowledge in building and other crafts

Allah has informed us that the jinn which were subjected to the control of the Prophet Solomon performed many feats which were evidence of their physical ability, intelligence and skill. Allah says in the Quran,

وَمِنَ ٱلْجِنِّ مَن يَعْمَلُ بَيْنَ يَدَيْهِ بِإِذْنِ رَبِّهِۦ وَمَن يَزِغْ مِنْهُمْ عَنْ أَمْرِنَا نُذِقْهُ مِنْ عَذَابِ ٱلسَّعِيرِ ۝ يَعْمَلُونَ لَهُۥ مَا يَشَآءُ مِن مَّحَارِيبَ وَتَمَٰثِيلَ وَجِفَانٍ كَٱلْجَوَابِ وَقُدُورٍ رَّاسِيَٰتٍ

"And (We gave him) certain of the jinn who worked before him by permission of his Lord. And such of them as deviated from Our command, them We caused to taste the punishment of flaming fire. They made for him what he willed: Synagogues and statues, basins like wells and boilers built into the ground" (*Saba* 12-13). And, perhaps, they also had the ability to communicate between locations and reach places in a way similar to radios and televisions. Ibn Taimiya stated that one of the *shaikh*s who had contact with the jinn told him that the jinn showed them something sparkling like water or glass. And they showed him therein whatever they wanted of news [apparently it was something like a crystal ball] The one reporting this to ibn Taimiya said, "They would bring the speech of the one who was seeking my help to me and I would respond and they would take my speech back to that person."[1]

Perhaps they were able to discover things, like the technology of radios and televisions, a long time ago.

## Their ability to take on other shapes

The jinn have the ability to take on the shapes of humans or animals. On the day of the Battle of Badr, Satan approached the polytheists in the form of a man called Suraaqa ibn Malik and he promised the polytheists aid and victory on that day. Concerning this event, Allah has revealed the following,

$$ وَإِذْ زَيَّنَ لَهُمُ ٱلشَّيْطَٰنُ أَعْمَٰلَهُمْ وَقَالَ لَا غَالِبَ لَكُمُ ٱلْيَوْمَ مِنَ ٱلنَّاسِ وَإِنِّى جَارٌ لَّكُمْ $$

"And when Satan made their deeds seem fair to them and said: No one of mankind can conquer you this day, for I am your protector." (*al-Anfaal* 48).

But when the armies met and Satan saw the angels descending from the sky, he fled. [The above verse continues:]

---

[1] *Majmu Fatawa*, vol. 11, p. 309.

$$\text{فَلَمَّا تَرَاءَتِ الْفِئَتَانِ نَكَصَ عَلَىٰ عَقِبَيْهِ وَقَالَ إِنِّي بَرِيءٌ مِّنكُمْ إِنِّي أَرَىٰ مَا لَا تَرَوْنَ إِنِّي أَخَافُ اللَّهَ وَاللَّهُ شَدِيدُ الْعِقَابِ}$$

"But when the armies came in sight of one another, he took flight, saying: Lo! I am innocent of you. Lo! I see that which you do not. Lo! I fear Allah. And Allah is severe in punishment" (*al-Anfaal* 48).

Abu Huraira has related the following incident that was recorded in *Sahih al-Bukhari* and other books. Abu Huraira said that the Prophet had put him in charge of guarding the zakat of Ramadhaan. He related, "Someone came to me and began to take portions of the food. I caught him and told him that I was going to take him to the Messenger of Allah. The man complained, 'I am in great need and I have children dependent on me.' Therefore I let him go. In the morning, the Prophet (peace be upon him) asked me, 'What happened to the one you caught last night, Abu Huraira?' I replied, 'Oh Messenger of Allah, he pleaded with me concerning his great need and his dependent children, so I felt pity for him and let him go.' The Prophet (peace be upon him) said, 'He lied to you and he will be back.' I knew that he would therefore return because the Prophet (peace be upon him) had said so. I waited for him. When he came, he again began to take loads of food. I caught him again and again told him that I was going to take him to the Messenger of Allah (peace be upon him). But when he pleaded, 'Let me go. I am in great need and have children dependent on me,' I again had mercy on him and let him go. In the morning, the Messenger of Allah (peace be upon him) again asked me, 'Oh Abu Huraira, what happened to your prisoner last night?' I replied, 'Oh Messenger of Allah, he complained to me of his great need and dependent children so I let him go again.' The Prophet (peace be upon him) said, 'He has lied to you and he will return.' I again waited for him and again he came and began to take loads of food. I caught him once again. I told him, 'This time I will definitely take you to the Messenger of Allah. This is the third time you have done such an act.' This time the man said to me, 'If you let me go I will teach you some words by which Allah will greatly benefit you! When you go to your bed recite the verse of the throne [*al-Baqara* 255], from, "Allah, there is no god but He, the Living, the Eternal," to the end of the verse. If you do so a guardian from Allah will come and protect you from the devils until the morning.' I decided to let him go. In the morning, the Messenger of Allah (peace be upon him) again asked me, 'What happened to your prisoner last night, Abu Huraira?' I answered, 'He claimed that he would teach me some words that would benefit me greatly.' The Prophet (peace be upon him) said, 'He has told the truth although he is a liar. Do you know who was that person you've been talking to for the last three nights?' I replied in the negative. The Prophet (peace be upon him) told me, 'That was a devil.'" In this hadith it is clear that devil jinn took the form of a human being.

They may also take the form of certain animals, for example, camels, donkeys, cows, dogs or cats. But, in particular, they take the form of a black dog. The Prophet (peace be upon him) has said that the black dog interrupts the prayer and he gave the reason for that that it is a devil. Ibn Taimiya said, "The black dog is the devil of the dogs. And the jinn often take its form. Similarly, they take the form of a black cat.[1] The color black has the greatest strength for the devils as opposed to other colors; in it is the power of the heat."

## The jinn of the houses

The jinn take the forms of snakes and appear in front of humans. It is for this reason that the Prophet (peace be upon him) has forbidden the killing of the snakes found in the houses, out of fear that they may be jinn that have embraced Islam. It is recorded in *Sahih Muslim* on the authority of Abu Saeed al-Khudri that the Prophet (peace be upon him) said,

---

[1] This translator is not aware of any evidence from the Quran or sunnah that shows that it is common or correct to say that devils take on the form of black cats. A statement of that nature needs to be supported from authentic evidences.—JZ

إن بالمدينة نفرا من الجن قد أسلموا فمن رأى شيئا من هذه العوامر
فليؤذنه ثلاثا فإن بدا له بعد فليقتله فإنه شيطان

"A group of jinn in Madina have embraced Islam. So he who sees anyone of them, should warn it three times. And if it appears after that it should be killed, for it must be a devil."

One of the Companions of the Prophet (peace be upon him) killed one of the snakes in the house and this led to his death. Muslim has recorded it in his *Sahih* that Abu al-Saib went to Abu Saeed's house and found him praying. Abu al-Saib was waiting for him to finish his prayer when he heard some rumbling in the bundles of wood which were lying in the corner of the house. He looked and he found it was a snake. He was about to kill it when Abu Saeed gestured to him to sit down. After the prayer, Abu Saeed pointed to a room and he said, "Do you see this room?" "Yes," answered al-Saib. Abu Saeed said, "There was once a man who was a newlywed and we went to participate with the Prophet (peace be upon him) in the Battle of the Trench. He used to ask the Prophet's permission to go to his wife and the Prophet cautioned him to take along his weapons for he feared [an attack from behind by] the tribe Quraidha. The man took his weapons and when he returned to his family he found his wife standing between the doors of the apartment. He was enraged from jealousy and took a stab at her with his spear. She told him to keep his spear away and to enter the house to see what had made her go outside. He entered and found a big snake on the bed. He struck it with his spear and pierced it. He was bent upon taking it outside, but the snake had enough strength to bite him. No one knows who died first from that incident, the snake or the man. The people made mention of this incident to the Messenger of Allah (peace be upon him), asking him to ask Allah to bring that man back to life. Instead, the Prophet (peace be upon him) said, "Ask forgiveness for our companion. In Madina there are jinn that embraced Islam. if any of you should see one of them [that is, a snake], he should give him warning for three days. If it appears after that, it should be killed because it is, therefore, a devil."

## Important notes

1. This regulation concerning the prohibition of killing such animals is with respect to snakes only and not with respect to all animals.

2. The regulation does not extend to every snake but only to those that are found in the house. Those that are found outside of the houses may be killed.

3. If one sees a snake in the house then he should warn it, in other words, order it to leave, by saying something similar to, "I adjure you by Allah to leave this house and take your evil away from us, if you do not do so we shall kill you." If you see it after three days, you should kill it.

4. The reason that it is to be killed only after three days is a precautionary step in order to ensure that one does not kill a jinn that had become Muslim. If he was such a jinn, he would leave the house. If he does not leave, then he deserves to be killed, as it is, in that case, a rebellious non-believing jinn that deserves to be killed due to the harm that it brings to the inhabitants of the house.

5. There is one type of snake that is found in the house which we have been given special permission to kill without first requesting it to leave. In *Sahih-al-Bukhari* it is recorded from Abu Lubaba that the Prophet (peace be upon him) said,

لا تَقْتُلُوا الْجِنَّانَ إِلاَّ كُلَّ أَبْتَرَ ذِي طُفْيَتَيْنِ فَإِنَّهُ يُسْقِطُ الْوَلَدَ وَيُذْهِبُ الْبَصَرَ فَاقْتُلُوهُ

"Do not kill the jinn, except every one with two streaks on the back, for they cause miscarriages and take away the eyesight. Therefore, kill them."

Does this ruling that snakes are jinn mean that every snake is a jinn or only some of them? The Prophet (peace be upon him) said,

$$\text{الحيّات مسخ الجن صورة كما مسخت القردة والخنازير من بني إسرائيل}$$

"Snakes are the forms of the transmutations of the shape of the jinn in the same way that the apes and swine were transmutations of the tribe of Israel."[1]

## Satan is able to flow in the descendants of Adam like blood flows through a vein.

In *Sahih al-Bukhari* and *Sahih Muslim* it is recorded that the Prophet (peace be upon him) said,

$$\text{إنَّ الشَّيْطَانَ يَجْرِي مِنَ الْإِنْسَانِ مَجْرَى الدَّم}$$

"Verily, Satan flows in the human like the flowing of the blood." It is also recorded in the two *Sahih*s that Safiyya bint Hayy, the wife of the Prophet, said, "The Messenger of Allah was making 'seclusion' (*itikaaf*) in the mosque and I brought him his loin cloth during the night. We talked and then I stood to leave. He also stood with me and walked with me. I was living in the house of Usama ibn Zaid. Two men from the Ansar passed by us. When the Prophet (peace be upon him) saw them he went quickly to them and said, 'It is only Safiyya bint Hayy.' They said, 'May Allah be glorified, Oh Messenger of Allah [we had no bad suspicion about you].' The Prophet (peace be upon him) told them,

---

[1] This hadith was recorded by at-Tabaraani and Abu ash-Shaikh in *Al-Udhma* with a *sahih* chain. See Muhammad Nasir al-Din al-Albani, *Silsilaat al-Ahadith al-Sahiha*, vol. 3, p. 103. [That is the reference given in the text in Arabic. In reality, it is vol. 4, p. 439. Furthermore, al-Albani makes the following important point on p. 440, "Know that this hadith does not mean that the snakes that are in existence today are from the transmuted jinn. Instead, what it means is that some jinn were transmuted into snakes, as what happened to those Jews who were transmuted into apes and swine. However, they did not procreate, as is stated in another authentic hadith, 'Verily, Allah did not make for any of the transmuted beings procreation or posterity.' In fact, apes and swine were in existence before that."—JZ]

$$إِنَّ الشَّيْطَانَ يَجْرِي مِنَ الْإِنْسَانِ مَجْرَى الدَّمِ وَإِنِّي خَشِيتُ أَنْ يُلْقِيَ فِي أَنْفُسِكُمَا شَيْئًا$$

'Satan flows in the human like the flowing of the blood. I feared that he would cast some evil allegation in your souls.'"

## Their weaknesses and inabilities

In some aspects, the jinn and devils are strong while in others they are weak. Allah says,

$$إِنَّ كَيْدَ الشَّيْطَانِ كَانَ ضَعِيفًا$$

"Verily, the plot of Satan is weak" (*al-Nisaa* 76). We shall mention some of those aspects that Allah and His Messenger (peace be upon him) have informed us about.

## They have no power over the pious worshippers of Allah

Allah did not give Satan the ability to compel mankind or force them to misguidance and disbelief. Allah says in the Quran,

$$إِنَّ عِبَادِي لَيْسَ لَكَ عَلَيْهِمْ سُلْطَانٌ وَكَفَىٰ بِرَبِّكَ وَكِيلًا$$

"Lo! My faithful bondsmen- over them you have no power, and your Lord suffices as their guardian" (*al-Israa* 65). And He also said,

$$وَمَا كَانَ لَهُ عَلَيْهِم مِّن سُلْطَانٍ إِلَّا لِنَعْلَمَ مَن يُؤْمِنُ بِٱلْآخِرَةِ مِمَّنْ هُوَ مِنْهَا فِى شَكٍّ$$

"And Satan indeed found his calculation true concerning them, for they follow him, all save a group of true believers. And he had no warrant whatsoever against them, save that We would know him who believes in the Hereafter from him who is in doubt thereof" (*Saba* 20-21). The meaning is that Satan has no means of mastery over them, either through proofs against them or through any power over them. And Satan, himself, recognizes that fact as one can see in the following verse,

$$قَالَ رَبِّ بِمَآ أَغْوَيْتَنِى لَأُزَيِّنَنَّ لَهُمْ فِى ٱلْأَرْضِ وَلَأُغْوِيَنَّهُمْ أَجْمَعِينَ ﴿٣٩﴾ إِلَّا عِبَادَكَ مِنْهُمُ ٱلْمُخْلَصِينَ$$

"He (Satan) said: My Lord! Because you have sent me astray, I verily shall adorn the path of error for them in the earth, and shall mislead them every one, save such of them as are your perfectly devoted slaves" (*al-Hijr* 39-40).

His mastery is over those humans and jinn who are pleased with his ideas and those who are pleased to follow and obey him. Allah has said,

$$إِنَّ عِبَادِى لَيْسَ لَكَ عَلَيْهِمْ سُلْطَانٌ إِلَّا مَنِ ٱتَّبَعَكَ مِنَ ٱلْغَاوِينَ$$

"Lo! As for My slaves, you have no power over any except such of the froward as follow you" (*al-Hijr* 42). On the Day of Resurrection, Satan will say to those who followed him in this world to misguidance and destruction,

$$\text{وَمَا كَانَ لِىَ عَلَيْكُم مِّن سُلْطَٰنٍ إِلَّآ أَن دَعَوْتُكُمْ فَٱسْتَجَبْتُمْ لِى}$$

"[Lo! Allah promised you a promise of truth; and I promised you, then failed you.] And I had no power over you save that I called unto you and you obeyed me. I cannot help you, nor can you help me" (*Ibraheem* 22). And another verse says,

$$\text{إِنَّمَا سُلْطَٰنُهُۥ عَلَى ٱلَّذِينَ يَتَوَلَّوْنَهُۥ وَٱلَّذِينَ هُم بِهِۦ مُشْرِكُونَ}$$

"His power is only over those who make him an ally, and those who ascribe partners to Allah" (*al-Nahl* 100).

His mastery over them is through seduction and misguidance. He agitates and stirs them and leads them to disbelief and polytheism. He harasses them until they enter into it. And he never leaves them alone. Allah says in the Quran,

$$\text{أَلَمْ تَرَ أَنَّآ أَرْسَلْنَا ٱلشَّيَٰطِينَ عَلَى ٱلْكَٰفِرِينَ تَؤُزُّهُمْ أَزًّا}$$

"Do you not see that We have set the devils on the disbelievers to confound them with confusion" (*Maryam* 83).

His power over them is not due to any proofs or arguments but is simply because the actions that he calls them to are in accordance with their own desires and wishes. They have harmed themselves. They allow their true enemy, Satan, to become their friend and master because they are in agreement with what he wants from them. When they stretch their hands to him, they become his prisoner as a type of punishment for their own acts. Allah did not give Satan power over any of his slaves until the slave himself opened the way for Satan by obeying him and associating him with Allah. Then Allah allows Satan to subjugate the slave and have power over him.

## He has power over the believers due to their sins

A hadith states, "Allah is with the judge as long as he does not commit any injustice. If he commits any injustice, Allah is free from him and keeps Satan with him."[1]

Abu al-Faraj ibn al-Jauzi has related a unique story from al-Hassan al-Basri. The story, depending on how authentic it is, shows the ability of a human in overpowering Satan if he is sincere to Allah in his religion and it shows how Satan can take advantage of the human when he strays. Al-Hasan al-Basri narrated that there was a tree that was worshipped instead of Allah. One man decided to chop down that tree. He was going to chop down the tree out of anger for the sake of Allah. On the way to the tree he met Iblees who was in the form of a man. Iblees asked him, "What do you plan on doing?" The man answered, "I am going to chop down that tree that is worshipped instead of Allah." Satan said, "If you do not worship it, why should it harm you if others do so?" The man replied, "I will chop it down." Satan then told him, "Would you like something better than that? Do not cut it and you will get two dinars every morning under your pillow." "From where will I get that?" the man asked. "I will give it to you," said Iblees. The man returned and the next morning he found two *dinars* under his pillow. The following morning he again found two *dinars* under his pillow. On the following morning he did not find anything. He got upset and went to chop down the tree. Satan again appeared to him in the shape of the same man. Satan asked him, "What do you want to do?" The man answered, "I plan on cutting down that tree that is worshipped instead of Allah!" Iblees said, "You have lied. There is no way you will be able to do it." The man left to chop it down. The earth swallowed him and choked him until it almost killed him. Iblees asked, "Do you know who I am? I am Satan. I met you for the first time when you were angry for the

---

[1] This was recorded by al-Haakim and al-Baihaqi with a *hasan* chain. See al-Albani, *Sahih al-Jaami*, vol. 2, p. 130.

sake of Allah and I had no power over you. I deceived you by two dinars and you stopped what you had intended to do [for the sake of Allah]. Now you have come because you are angry about the two dinars, and I have gotten mastery over you."[1]

Allah has also informed us in His Book about a person who was given the signs of Allah and was aware of them, but then he left all of that and Allah let Satan gain mastery over him. Satan then seduced him and misled him and he became a lesson for others and a story that has been passed on. Allah says in the Quran,

وَٱتْلُ عَلَيْهِمْ نَبَأَ ٱلَّذِىٓ ءَاتَيْنَٰهُ ءَايَٰتِنَا فَٱنسَلَخَ مِنْهَا فَأَتْبَعَهُ ٱلشَّيْطَٰنُ فَكَانَ مِنَ ٱلْغَاوِينَ ۝ وَلَوْ شِئْنَا لَرَفَعْنَٰهُ بِهَا وَلَٰكِنَّهُۥٓ أَخْلَدَ إِلَى ٱلْأَرْضِ وَٱتَّبَعَ هَوَىٰهُ فَمَثَلُهُۥ كَمَثَلِ ٱلْكَلْبِ إِن تَحْمِلْ عَلَيْهِ يَلْهَثْ أَوْ تَتْرُكْهُ يَلْهَث ذَّٰلِكَ مَثَلُ ٱلْقَوْمِ ٱلَّذِينَ كَذَّبُوا۟ بِـَٔايَٰتِنَا فَٱقْصُصِ ٱلْقَصَصَ لَعَلَّهُمْ يَتَفَكَّرُونَ

"Recite unto them the tale of him to whom We gave Our revelations, but he sloughed them off, so Satan overtook him and he became of those who were lead astray. And had We willed We would have raised him by their means, but he clung to the earth and followed his own lust. Therefore his likeness is as the likeness of a dog; if you attack him, he pants with his tongue out, and if you leave him alone he pants with his tongue out. Such is the likeness of the people who deny Our revelations.

---

[1] Ibn al-Jauzi, *Talbees Iblees*, p.43. [The author, al-Ashqar alluded to the fact that the authenticity of this story needs to be ascertained. Most likely, it is from the *Israaeeliyaat* or stories of the Jews and Christians. Al-Ashqar stated that the story demonstrates how a pious person can overcome Satan. Actually, the story does not demonstrate that since the person was originally going to chop down the tree for the sake of Allah but he was not able to overcome Satan's plot against him. Allah knows best.—JZ]

Narrate unto them the history (of the men of old), that haply they may take thought" (*al-Araaf* 175-76). It is clear that this parable applies to the one who knows the truth and refuses to accept it, like the Jews who knew that the Prophet Muhammad (peace be upon him) was a true messenger from the Lord but they disbelieved in him.

This is all of the story that Allah gives us. Some say that the verse refers to Balaam ibn Baoora who was a pious person and then he became a disbeliever. Some say it refers to Umayya ibn Abu as-Salit who worshipped Allah during the days of ignorance and who had met the Prophet but refused to believe in him out of envy. He had hoped that he would be the next messenger to be sent. We do not possess any authentic text that clearly identifies who the verse refers to. "To receive the signs of Allah and then to disbelieve in them" is a description of someone who is very similar to Satan. This is so because Satan became a disbeliever after he clearly knew and recognized the truth. This is one of the things that the Prophet (peace be upon him) feared most for his nation. Al-Hafez Abu Yala recorded from Hudhaifa bin al-Yaman that the Messenger of Allah (peace be upon him) said, "From the things that I fear for you is a man who recites the Quran until you see its splendor upon him. His cloak is Islam and he wears it until Allah wishes and then he throws it behind his back and attacks his neighbor with a sword and accuses him of polytheism." [Hudhaifa] said, "O Messenger of Allah, which should be killed, the one who is attacking or the one who is attacked." He (peace be upon him) said, "Nay, the one who is attacking."[1]

## Satan's fear and fleeing from some of the slaves of Allah

If a slave holds fast to Islam, has a sincere belief in his heart and stays within the bounds set by Allah, then Satan departs and flees from him. The Prophet (peace be upon him) said to Umar,

إن الشيطان ليفرق منك يا عمر

---

[1] Ibn Katheer said, "Its chain is good." *Tafseer ibn Katheer*, vol. 3, p. 252.

"Satan most certainly flees from you, O Umar."[1] He also said about Umar,

$$\text{إني لأنظر إلى شياطين الإنس والجن قد فروا من عمر}$$

"I certainly see the devils of jinn and mankind fleeing from Umar."[2]

But that situation was not solely for Umar. Whoever possesses a strong faith can overcome Satan, defeat him and belittle him. It states in a hadith,

$$\text{إن المؤمن لينضي شياطينه كما ينضي أحدكم بعيره في السفر}^3$$

"The believer emaciates his devil in the same way that one of you weakens his camel during traveling."[4] Ibn Katheer stated, after recording this hadith, "Seizing his devil means grabbing his forelock and overpowering him like what is done to a camel if he escapes and is captured."[5]

It is even the case that a Muslim may have such a strong effect on his "partner" or "companion" from among the jinn that the jinn becomes a Muslim. Muslim and Ahmad have recorded from the Prophet (peace be upon him),

---

[1] This was recorded by Ahmad, at-Tirmidhi and ibn Hibban with a *sahih* chain. See al-Albani, *Sahih al-Jaami*, vol. 2, p. 74.
[2] Recorded by al-Tirmidhi with a *sahih* chain. See *Sahih al-Jaami*, vol. 2, p. 329.
[3] The text of the hadith in the work by al-Ashqar has a number of mistakes to it. Above is the correct text taken from *Musnad Ahmad*.—JZ
[4] This was recorded by Ahmad. [Shuaib al-Arnaoot and Adil Murshid point out that the chain of this hadith is weak because it contains Abdullah ibn Lahiyah who was of weak memory. See Shuaib al-Arnaoot and Adil Murshid, *Musnad al-Imaam Ahmad* (Beirut: Muasassah al-Risaalah, 1997), vol. 14, p. 504. The chain also contains another weakness that they did not mention. This weakness is that the same ibn Lahiyah used to commit *tadlees* (wherein he would use a vague term that did not show how he received the hadith) and, in this narration, he used a vague term in the chain. Hence, one cannot be certain as to whom ibn Lahiyah actually heard this hadith from.—JZ
[5] Ibn Katheer, *Al-Bidaayah wa al-Nihaayah*, vol. 1, p. 73. [This interpretation by ibn Katheer is based on the incorrect wording of the hadith. Allah knows best.—JZ]

$$\text{مَا مِنْكُمْ مِنْ أَحَدٍ إِلَّا وَقَدْ وُكِّلَ بِهِ قَرِينُهُ مِنَ الْجِنِّ قَالُوا وَإِيَّاكَ يَا رَسُولَ اللَّهِ قَالَ وَإِيَّايَ إِلَّا أَنَّ اللَّهَ أَعَانَنِي عَلَيْهِ فَأَسْلَمَ فَلَا يَأْمُرُنِي إِلَّا بِخَيْرٍ}$$

"There is not one of you who does not have his partner from among the jinn." The people asked, "Even you, Oh Messenger of Allah?" He answered, "Even me, but Allah has helped me against him and, therefore, he only commands me to do good." Imam Ahmad has also recorded this hadith from Ibn Abbas with the wording, "But Allah has helped me against him and he embraced Islam." And Muslim recorded from Aisha, "But my Lord aided me against him until he submitted."

## The jinn were made subservient to Solomon

Allah made all the jinn and devils subservient to the Prophet Solomon (peace be upon him) and they all performed what he wished. He punished and imprisoned those who disobeyed. Allah says in the Quran,

$$\text{فَسَخَّرْنَا لَهُ الرِّيحَ تَجْرِي بِأَمْرِهِ رُخَاءً حَيْثُ أَصَابَ ۝ وَالشَّيَاطِينَ كُلَّ بَنَّاءٍ وَغَوَّاصٍ ۝ وَآخَرِينَ مُقَرَّنِينَ فِي الْأَصْفَادِ}$$

"So We made the wind subservient unto him, setting fair by His command whatever he intended. And the devils, every builder and diver (made We subservient), and others linked together in chains" (*Saad* 36-38). He also said,

$$\text{وَمِنَ ٱلْجِنِّ مَن يَعْمَلُ بَيْنَ يَدَيْهِ بِإِذْنِ رَبِّهِۦ ۖ وَمَن يَزِغْ مِنْهُمْ عَنْ أَمْرِنَا نُذِقْهُ مِنْ عَذَابِ ٱلسَّعِيرِ ۝ يَعْمَلُونَ لَهُۥ مَا يَشَآءُ مِن مَّحَـٰرِيبَ وَتَمَـٰثِيلَ وَجِفَانٍ كَٱلْجَوَابِ وَقُدُورٍ رَّاسِيَـٰتٍ}$$

"And unto Solomon (We gave) the wind, whereof the morning course was a month's journey and the evening course a month's journey, and We caused the fountain of copper to gush forth for him, and (We gave him) certain of the jinn who worked before him by permission of his Lord. And such of them as deviated from Our command, them We caused to taste the punishment of a flaming fire" (*Saba* 12).

This subjugation to Solomon was in response to a prayer that he made to Allah that is stated in the Quran,

$$\text{وَهَبْ لِى مُلْكًا لَّا يَنۢبَغِى لِأَحَدٍ مِّنۢ بَعْدِىٓ}$$

"He said: My Lord! Forgive me and bestow on me sovereignty such as shall not belong to any after me. Lo! You are the Bestower" (*Saad* 35). It was this supplication that prevented the Prophet Muhammad (peace be upon him) from keeping and showing the jinn that he had captured, who had put a burning branch in the Prophet's face and wanted to throw it at him. In *Sahih Muslim*, the following is related on the authority of Abu al-Darda: the Messenger of Allah (peace be upon him) stood (to pray) and he could be heard saying, "I seek refuge in Allah from you." After which he said, "I curse you with the curse of Allah." He stated that three times and then stretched out his arm, looking as if he was about to grab something. When he finished the prayer, he was asked, "Oh Messenger of Allah, during the prayer we heard you say something that we have not heard you say before in the prayer, and we saw you stretch out your arm." The Prophet (peace be upon him) told them, "The enemy of Allah, Iblees, came to me with a flame of fire to put it in my face, therefore I said three times, 'I curse you with Allah's curse.' Afterwards, I said three times, 'I seek refuge in Allah from you.' But he did not leave after any of these. Then I attempted to seize him. I swear by Allah, that had it not been for the supplication of my brother Solomon, he would have been fettered and made an object of sport for the children of Madina." And that type of incident occurred more than once.

Imam Muslim also recorded the following from Abu Huraira: The Messenger of Allah (peace be upon him) said,

إن عفريتا من الجن جعل يفتك علي البارحة ليقطع علي الصلاة وإن الله أمكنني منه فذعته فلقد هممت أن أربطه إلى جنب سارية من سواري المسجد حتى تصبحوا تنظرون إليه أجمعون أو كلكم ثم ذكرت قول أخي سليمان ( رب اغفر لي وهب لي ملكا لا ينبغي لأحد من بعدي ) فرده الله خاسئا

"An *afreet* [a type of devil] of the jinn escaped last night to interrupt my prayer, but Allah gave me power over him, therefore I seized him and I was planning on tying him to one of the pillars in the mosque, but then I remembered the supplication of my brother Solomon, 'My Lord! Forgive me and bestow on me sovereignty such as shall not belong to any after me.' So Allah returned him belittled and despised."

## The Jews lied about Solomon

The Jews and those who follow them in using jinn through the art of magic allege that Solomon used magic to gain mastery over the jinn. Many of the early scholars mention that when Solomon died, the devils recorded books of magic and disbelief and put them under his throne and they said, "Solomon used these books to subjugate the jinn."

This led others to say that if this art is not permissible why did Solomon perform it. Allah revealed the following,

$$\text{وَلَمَّا جَآءَهُمْ رَسُولٌ مِّنْ عِندِ ٱللَّهِ مُصَدِّقٌ لِّمَا مَعَهُمْ نَبَذَ فَرِيقٌ مِّنَ ٱلَّذِينَ أُوتُواْ ٱلْكِتَٰبَ كِتَٰبَ ٱللَّهِ وَرَآءَ ظُهُورِهِمْ كَأَنَّهُمْ لَا يَعْلَمُونَ}$$

"And when there comes unto them a messenger from Allah, confirming that which they possess, a party of those who have received the Scripture fling the Scripture of Allah behind their backs as if they knew not" (*al-Baqara* 101). Then He clarifies that they followed what was recited unto them by the devils during the life of Solomon, declaring Solomon innocent of magic and disbelief,

$$\text{وَٱتَّبَعُواْ مَا تَتْلُواْ ٱلشَّيَٰطِينُ عَلَىٰ مُلْكِ سُلَيْمَٰنَ وَمَا كَفَرَ سُلَيْمَٰنُ وَلَٰكِنَّ ٱلشَّيَٰطِينَ كَفَرُواْ}$$

"Solomon disbelieved not; but the devils disbelieved, teaching mankind magic and that which was revealed to the angels in Babel, Harut and Marut. Nor did they (the two angels) teach it to anyone till they had said: We are only a temptation, therefore disbelieve not (in the guidance of Allah)..." (*al-Baqara* 102).

## They are incapable of performing miracles

The jinn are not able to perform miracles like those of the Messengers that are meant as proof for the truth of their missions. Some of the disbelievers alleged that the Quran was from the workings of Satan, so Allah revealed,

$$﴿وَمَا تَنَزَّلَتْ بِهِ الشَّيَاطِينُ ۝ وَمَا يَنبَغِي لَهُمْ وَمَا يَسْتَطِيعُونَ ۝ إِنَّهُمْ عَنِ السَّمْعِ لَمَعْزُولُونَ﴾$$

"The devils did not bring it down. It is not proper for them [to bring it down], nor is it in their power. Lo! Verily they are banished from the hearing" (al-Shuaraa 210-212).

Allah challenges all of mankind and the jinn in the following verse,

$$﴿قُل لَّئِنِ اجْتَمَعَتِ الْإِنسُ وَالْجِنُّ عَلَىٰ أَن يَأْتُوا بِمِثْلِ هَـٰذَا الْقُرْآنِ لَا يَأْتُونَ بِمِثْلِهِ وَلَوْ كَانَ بَعْضُهُمْ لِبَعْضٍ ظَهِيرًا﴾$$

"Say: Verily, though mankind and jinn should assemble to produce the like of this Quran, they could not produce the like thereof though they were helpers one of another" (al-Israa 88).

## They are not able to appear like the Prophet (peace be upon him) in a vision or dream

The devils are incapable of appearing in the shape of the Prophet in a dream. At-Tirmidhi has recorded, with a *sahih* chain, that the Prophet (peace be upon him) said,

$$مَنْ رَآنِي فَإِنِّي أَنَا هُوَ فَإِنَّهُ لَيْسَ لِلشَّيْطَانِ أَنْ يَتَمَثَّلَ بِي$$

"Whoever sees me, then it is me, for the devils cannot appear like me."[1]
And in the two *Sahih*s the wording is,

---

[1] Al-Albani, *Sahih al-Jaami*, vol. 5, p. 245.

من رآني فقد رأي الحق فإن الشيطان لا يتزيا به

"Whoever sees me, then the vision is true for the devils cannot appear in my form."[1]

The apparent meaning of the hadith is that the devils are incapable of taking the true form of the Messenger of Allah (peace be upon him). But this does not prevent them from taking a form other than that of the Prophet (peace be upon him) and claiming that they are the Messenger of Allah (peace be upon him). Therefore it is not permissible to argue from this hadith that everyone who sees who he thinks is the Messenger of Allah (peace be upon him) in a dream has actually seen him, unless, of course, who he saw meets the description of the Prophet (peace be upon him) that is found in the books of hadith. Many people claim that they had seen the Prophet, yet they give a description of him that differs from what has been recorded in the trustworthy books.

## They are not able to go beyond the limit set for them in the skies

Allah says in the Quran,

يَٰمَعْشَرَ ٱلْجِنِّ وَٱلْإِنسِ إِنِ ٱسْتَطَعْتُمْ أَن تَنفُذُوا۟ مِنْ أَقْطَارِ ٱلسَّمَٰوَٰتِ وَٱلْأَرْضِ فَٱنفُذُوا۟ لَا تَنفُذُونَ إِلَّا بِسُلْطَٰنٍ ۝ فَبِأَىِّ ءَالَآءِ رَبِّكُمَا تُكَذِّبَانِ ۝ يُرْسَلُ عَلَيْكُمَا شُوَاظٌ مِّن نَّارٍ وَنُحَاسٌ فَلَا تَنتَصِرَانِ

"O company of jinn and men, if you have power to penetrate (all) regions of the heavens and the earth, then penetrate (them)! You will never penetrate them save with (Our) sanction. Which is it, of the favors of your Lord, do you deny? There will be sent, against you both, heat of

---

[1] This translator could not find this hadith with this exact wording in *al-Bukhari* or *Muslim*, but its meaning is found therein.—JZ

fire and flash of brass, and you will not escape" (*al-Rahmaan* 33-35). Despite their power and speed of movement, they are not able to go beyond such limits; if they try, they will be destroyed.

## They are not able to open the closed doors that have had the name of Allah mentioned over them

The Prophet (peace be upon him) stated,

وَأَجِيفُوا الْأَبْوَابَ وَاذْكُرُوا اسْمَ اللَّهِ عَلَيْهَا فَإِنَّ الشَّيْطَانَ لَا يَفْتَحُ بَابًا أُجِيفَ وَذُكِرَ اسْمُ اللَّهِ عَلَيْهِ

"Close the doors and mention Allah's name upon them, for Satan cannot open a door that has been closed up upon him [and has had the name of Allah mentioned over it]."[1] There is also the following hadith in the two *Sahih*s,

فَإِنَّ الشَّيْطَانَ لَا يَفْتَحُ بَابًا مُغْلَقًا وَأَوْكُوا قِرَبَكُمْ وَاذْكُرُوا اسْمَ اللَّهِ وَخَمِّرُوا آنِيَتَكُمْ وَاذْكُرُوا اسْمَ اللَّهِ وَلَوْ أَنْ تَعْرُضُوا عَلَيْهَا شَيْئًا وَأَطْفِئُوا مَصَابِيحَكُمْ

"Certainly, Satan does not open a shut door. Tie your buckets and mention Allah's name upon them, even if it is just putting something over it, and extinguish your lamps."[2]

In *Musnad Ahmad*, there is the following hadith,

أَغْلِقُوا أَبْوَابَكُمْ وَخَمِّرُوا آنِيَتَكُمْ وَأَطْفِئُوا سُرُجَكُمْ وَأَوْكُوا أَسْقِيَتَكُمْ فَإِنَّ الشَّيْطَانَ لَا يَفْتَحُ بَابًا مُغْلَقًا وَلَا يَكْشِفُ غِطَاءً وَلَا يَحُلُّ وِكَاءً

---

[1] This was recorded by Abu Dawud, Ahmad, ibn Hibban and al-Haakim with a *sahih* chain. See al-Albani, *Sahih al-Jaami*, vol. 1, p. 229.
[2] *Sahih al-Jaami*, vol. 1, p. 270.

"Close your doors and cover your vessels and tie up your waterskins and put out your lamps, for Satan does not open a closed door, nor does he take off a cover, nor does he untie the waterskins."

# 2
# RESPONSIBILITY FOR THEIR ACTIONS

## The Ultimate Purpose of Their Creation

The jinn were created for the same purpose that mankind was created,

$$وَمَا خَلَقْتُ الْجِنَّ وَالْإِنسَ إِلَّا لِيَعْبُدُونِ$$

"I created the jinn and humankind only that they worship Me" (*al-Dhaariyaat* 56). Therefore, jinn are responsible for their actions and have been ordered to perform some acts and to abstain from performing others. Concerning he who is obedient, Allah will be pleased with him and he will enter paradise. For whosoever disobeys and rebels, he is given the hell-fire. Many statements of the Quran and hadith indicate this fact.

On the Day of judgment, Allah will address both the jinn and mankind with the following words,

$$يَٰمَعْشَرَ الْجِنِّ وَالْإِنسِ أَلَمْ يَأْتِكُمْ رُسُلٌ مِّنكُمْ يَقُصُّونَ عَلَيْكُمْ ءَايَٰتِى وَيُنذِرُونَكُمْ لِقَآءَ يَوْمِكُمْ هَٰذَا ۚ قَالُوا۟ شَهِدْنَا عَلَىٰٓ أَنفُسِنَا ۖ وَغَرَّتْهُمُ الْحَيَوٰةُ الدُّنْيَا وَشَهِدُوا۟ عَلَىٰٓ أَنفُسِهِمْ أَنَّهُمْ كَانُوا۟ كَٰفِرِينَ$$

"O you assembly of jinn and humankind! Came there not unto you messengers of your own who recounted unto you My tokens and warned you of this Day? They will say: We testify against ourselves. And the life of this world beguiled them. And they testify against themselves that they were disbelievers" (*al-Anaam* 130). This verse proves that the command of Allah reached the jinn and that they had received messengers who warned them and conveyed the message to them.

The proofs that they will be punished in the fire are many:

$$قَالَ ٱدْخُلُوا۟ فِىٓ أُمَمٍ قَدْ خَلَتْ مِن قَبْلِكُم مِّنَ ٱلْجِنِّ وَٱلْإِنسِ فِى ٱلنَّارِ$$

"He says: Enter into the Fire among nations of the jinn and humankind who passed away before you" (*al-Araaf* 37);

$$وَلَقَدْ ذَرَأْنَا لِجَهَنَّمَ كَثِيرًا مِّنَ ٱلْجِنِّ وَٱلْإِنسِ$$

"Already have We urged unto hell many of the jinn and mankind, having hearts wherewith they understand not..." (*al-Araaf* 179);

$$لَأَمْلَأَنَّ جَهَنَّمَ مِنَ ٱلْجِنَّةِ وَٱلنَّاسِ أَجْمَعِينَ$$

"But the word from Me concerning evildoers took effect: that I will fill hell with the jinn and mankind together" (*al-Sajda* 13).

And the proofs that the believing jinn will enter paradise include,

$$وَلِمَنْ خَافَ مَقَامَ رَبِّهِۦ جَنَّتَانِ ۝ فَبِأَىِّ ءَالَآءِ رَبِّكُمَا تُكَذِّبَانِ$$

"But for him who fears the standing before his Lord there are two gardens. Which is it, of the favours of your Lord, that you deny?" (*al-Rahmaan* 46-47) This verse, as is clear from the previous verses and, in fact, the whole surah, is addressed to both jinn and mankind. The chapter talks about Allah's blessings to the jinn, of their entering paradise. If they were not to gain that bounty, how could it be mentioned as a blessing for them? Ibn Mufleh said in his book *al-Furu'*,

> The jinn are responsible for their actions according to the consensus. Their unbelievers will enter the fire, and this is agreed upon. Their believers will enter paradise according to Malik and ash-Shafi. In their opinion, they will not be turned to dust, like animals, and the reward for their believers is being saved from being in the hell-fire. And this opinion differs from that of Abu Hanifa, al-Laith ibn Saad and others. Apparently the first opinion is correct. They will be in the paradise with the humans in accordance with their measure of reward. This differs from those who say they will not eat or drink therein; this was said by Mujaahid. And this also differs from the opinion, held by Umar ibn Abdul Aziz, that says that they will be on the outskirts of paradise. Ibn Hamad said in his book, "The jinn are like humans with respect to responsibility for deeds and worship."[1]

## They are responsible according to their own specific standard

Ibn Taimiya said,

> The jinn are commanded to do the fundamental acts and the secondary acts according to their own ability. They are not exactly like humans in definition and nature. What they have been ordered to do or prohibited from is not, in its nature, exactly the same as what humans have been ordered to do or what they have been prohibited from. But they have in common with humans responsibility for doing what they have been ordered to, and to abstain from

---

[1] Quoted in *Lawaami al-Anwaar*, vol. 2, pp. 222-223.

what they have been forbidden. On this point, I know of no dispute among the Muslims.[1]

## A Misconception and its Reply

Some people have raised an objection or doubt, stating, "You accept the fact that the jinn have been created from fire. Then you say that the unbelievers from them will be punished in the hell-fire. And the one who tries to steal any news [from the heavens] will have a meteor flung at him. How will the fire harm them when they have been created from it?" The response is that in origin they are created from fire. But after their creation they were not exactly like fire. They became a creation different from fire. This point can be made clear with reference to humans who were created from soil. After their creation they certainly became different from soil. If one strikes another human with a large portion of soil one could badly harm the other or possibly kill the other. If a human is buried in soil, he will suffocate and die. Therefore, although he is from the earth or soil, the soil can certainly harm him. The same is the case with respect to jinn and fire.

## There is no relationship between the jinn and Allah, the Glorious

The jinn, as was just stated, are just one of the creations of Allah and, like all the other creations of Allah, are subservient to Him. They were created only to worship and obey Him and they are responsible for fulfilling His commands. All of that information puts an end to the superstitions that developed as a result of misconceptions concerning their true nature and lack of knowledge. The Jews and polytheistic Arabs believed that Allah took wives from the jinn and the result of their relationship were the angels. In the Quran, Allah refers to this false notion and states that it is false. He says,

---

[1] Ibn Taimiya, *Majmoo Fatawa*, vol. 4, p. 233.

$$\text{وَجَعَلُوا۟ بَيْنَهُۥ وَبَيْنَ ٱلْجِنَّةِ نَسَبًا ۚ وَلَقَدْ عَلِمَتِ ٱلْجِنَّةُ إِنَّهُمْ لَمُحْضَرُونَ}$$

$$\text{سُبْحَٰنَ ٱللَّهِ عَمَّا يَصِفُونَ ﴿١٠٩﴾ إِلَّا عِبَادَ ٱللَّهِ ٱلْمُخْلَصِينَ ﴿١٥٨﴾}$$

"And they imagine kinship between Him and the jinn, whereas the jinn know well that they will be brought before (Him). Glorified be Allah from that which they attribute (unto Him)" (*al-Saaffaat* 158-159). In his commentary to this verse, Ibn Katheer writes,

> Mujahid said, "The polytheists said, 'The angels are the daughters of Allah, exalted be He above what they say.' Abu Bakr said to them, 'Who are their mothers?' They answered, 'The daughters of the best of the jinn.'" Ibn Zaid and Qatada both made statements similar to that of Mujahid... Al-Aufi narrated on the authority of ibn Abbas, 'The enemies of Allah alleged that He- The Most Honorable and Most High- and Iblees were brothers. And Allah is much greater than this grave allegation.'"

## How does Allah's revelation reach them?

Since they are responsible for their actions, there is no doubt that the revelation of Allah must reach them and establish "the proof" against them. But how does this occur? Do they have messengers from among themselves like humans do or are the same human messengers also sent to them?

Allah says in the Quran,

$$\text{يَٰمَعْشَرَ ٱلْجِنِّ وَٱلْإِنسِ أَلَمْ يَأْتِكُمْ رُسُلٌ مِّنكُمْ}$$

"O you assembly of jinn and mankind, came there not unto you messengers of your own who recounted unto you of My tokens..."

(*al-Anaam* 130). This verse shows that Allah sent messengers to them. But this verse does not make it clear who these messengers were; were they jinn or man? The Arabic word used in the verse, *minkum* [translated by Pickthall as "of your own"], could imply either that the messengers were of the same species as the jinn or it could imply that the one human messenger was sent to both of them together. Consequently, there is a difference of opinion concerning which is meant. Basically, there are two opinions on this point. The first opinion is that the jinn received messengers of their own kind. This was the opinion of al-Dhuhhaak. Ibn al-Jauzi said that this is the most obvious meaning of the verse. Ibn Hazm said that no human messenger was also a messenger to the jinn before the Prophet Muhammad (peace be upon him).

The second opinion is that all of the messengers that were sent to the jinn were humans. Al-Suyooti stated in *Luqat al-Marjaan* that the majority of the early and later scholars stated that the jinn never had a messenger or prophet from their kind; this opinion was related from ibn Abbas, Mujahid, al-Kalbi and Abu Ubaid.[1]

What makes the latter opinion seem stronger is the statement of the jinn upon hearing the Quran,

$$إِنَّا سَمِعْنَا كِتَابًا أُنزِلَ مِنْ بَعْدِ مُوسَىٰ$$

"They [the jinn] said, 'O our people, lo, we have heard a scripture which has been revealed after Moses...'" (*al-Ahqaaf* 30). But this verse is still not a clear proof for this particular question.

The debated question does not require any action on the part of the Muslims, nor is there any clear text concerning it; therefore, there is no need to discuss this question in any greater detail.

---

[1] Quoted in *Lawaami al-Anwaar*, vol. 2, pp. 223-4.

## The message of Muhammad (peace be upon him) is for both jinn and humans

The Prophet Muhammad (peace be upon him) was sent to both jinn and humans. Ibn Taimiya stated, "There is agreement on this principle among the Companions and those that followed their way and the leaders of the Muslims and the rest of the different groups of Muslims, the *ahl al-sunnah wa al-jamaa* and others. May Allah be pleased with all of them."[1]

What suggests this is the challenge of the Quran to both the jinn and humans to compose a work similar to the Quran. Allah says in the Quran,

$$\text{قُل لَّئِنِ ٱجْتَمَعَتِ ٱلْإِنسُ وَٱلْجِنُّ عَلَىٰٓ أَن يَأْتُوا۟ بِمِثْلِ هَٰذَا ٱلْقُرْءَانِ لَا يَأْتُونَ بِمِثْلِهِۦ وَلَوْ كَانَ بَعْضُهُمْ لِبَعْضٍ ظَهِيرًا}$$

"Say: Verily, though mankind and jinn should assemble to produce the like of this Quran, they could not produce the like thereof though they would be helpers, one of another" (*al-Israa* 88).

Some of the jinn quickly became believers when they heard the Quran recited. The Quran states,

$$\text{قُلْ أُوحِيَ إِلَيَّ أَنَّهُ ٱسْتَمَعَ نَفَرٌ مِّنَ ٱلْجِنِّ فَقَالُوٓا۟ إِنَّا سَمِعْنَا قُرْءَانًا عَجَبًا ۝ يَهْدِىٓ إِلَى ٱلرُّشْدِ فَـَٔامَنَّا بِهِۦ ۖ وَلَن نُّشْرِكَ بِرَبِّنَآ أَحَدًا}$$

---

[1] Ibn Taimiya, *Majmoo al-Fatawa*, vol. 19, p. 9.

"Say: It is revealed unto me that a company of the jinn listened, and they said, 'Lo, it is a marvelous Quran, which guides unto righteousness, so we believe in it and we ascribe no partner unto our Lord'" (*al-Jinn* 1-2).

Those who listened to the Quran and believed in it are the same ones who are mentioned in the following verse from *surah al-Ahqaaf*,

$$\text{وَإِذْ صَرَفْنَآ إِلَيْكَ نَفَرًا مِّنَ ٱلْجِنِّ يَسْتَمِعُونَ ٱلْقُرْءَانَ فَلَمَّا حَضَرُوهُ قَالُوٓاْ أَنصِتُواْۖ فَلَمَّا قُضِىَ وَلَّوْاْ إِلَىٰ قَوْمِهِم مُّنذِرِينَ ۝ قَالُواْ يَٰقَوْمَنَآ إِنَّا سَمِعْنَا كِتَٰبًا أُنزِلَ مِنۢ بَعْدِ مُوسَىٰ مُصَدِّقًا لِّمَا بَيْنَ يَدَيْهِ يَهْدِىٓ إِلَى ٱلْحَقِّ وَإِلَىٰ طَرِيقٍ مُّسْتَقِيمٍ ۝ يَٰقَوْمَنَآ أَجِيبُواْ دَاعِىَ ٱللَّهِ وَءَامِنُواْ بِهِۦ يَغْفِرْ لَكُم مِّن ذُنُوبِكُمْ وَيُجِرْكُم مِّنْ عَذَابٍ أَلِيمٍ ۝}$$

$$\text{وَمَن لَّا يُجِبْ دَاعِىَ ٱللَّهِ فَلَيْسَ بِمُعْجِزٍ فِى ٱلْأَرْضِ وَلَيْسَ لَهُۥ مِن دُونِهِۦٓ أَوْلِيَآءُۚ أُوْلَٰٓئِكَ فِى ضَلَٰلٍ مُّبِينٍ}$$

"And when We inclined toward you (Muhammad) certain of the jinn, who wished to hear the Quran and, when they were in its presence, said, 'Give ear.' And when it was finished, turned back to their people, warning [them]. They said, 'O our people, lo, we have heard a scripture which has been revealed after Moses, confirming that which was before it, guiding unto the truth and a right road. O our people, respond to Allah's summoner and believe in Him. He will forgive you some of your sins and guard you from a painful doom. And whosoever does not respond to Allah's summoner, he can nowise escape in the earth, and you can find no protecting friends instead of Him. Such are in error manifest" (*al-Ahqaaf* 29-32). They heard the Quran, they believed in it and returned to their people to call them towards the oneness of Allah and faith and they gave them good tidings as well as a warning.

The story of their listening to the Prophet (peace be upon him) has been recorded by al-Bukhari and Muslim on the authority of ibn Abbas. Ibn Abbas reported that the Messenger of Allah (peace be upon him) departed with some of his companions, intending to go to the bazaar at Ukaz. At that time, there had been obstruction between the devils and the news from the heavens. And flames were being hurled at the jinn. Therefore, the jinn went back to their people and were asked about what had happened. They answered, "Some barriers have been put between us and the news from the heavens." They said, "This could only happen due to some important event. So go to the eastern parts of the earth and its western parts to find out what has happened to cause these barriers between us and the news from the heavens." They did so. A group of them proceeded to Tihama which is a palm grove close to the fair of Ukaz. At that time, the Prophet (peace be upon him) was leading his Companions in the dawn prayer. When the jinn heard the recitation of the Quran, they said, "Listen to it." Then they said, "This is what has caused the barriers between us and the news of the heavens." They returned to their people and said, "O our people, we have heard a marvelous Quran that guides us to the straight path and we believe in it." Then Allah revealed to His Prophet Muhammad (peace be upon him),

قُلْ أُوحِيَ إِلَيَّ أَنَّهُ اسْتَمَعَ نَفَرٌ مِنَ الْجِنِّ

"Say: It is revealed to me that a company of the jinn listened..." (*al-Jinn* 1). Allah revealed to the Prophet (peace be on him) what the jinn had stated

## The delegation from the jinn

The incident mentioned above was the first time that the jinn became aware of the message of the Prophet (peace be upon him). They listened to the Quran without the Prophet (peace be upon him) being aware of their presence. A group of them believed in it and went back to their people to spread the message.

After that incident, a delegation of the jinn met with the Prophet (peace be upon him) to gain some knowledge from him. The Prophet (peace be upon him) gave them an appointment and met with them and taught them what Allah prescribed for them and he read the Quran to them and informed them of the news of the heavens. This latter incident occurred in Makkah before the Prophet's migration to Madina.

Muslim, in his *Sahih*, and Ahmad, in his *Musnad*, recorded from Alqama that he had asked Abdullah ibn Masud if anyone had accompanied the Prophet (peace be upon him) on the night that the Prophet (peace be upon him) met with the jinn. Ibn Masud said, "No, none of us did. But we were in the company of the Messenger of Allah (peace be upon him) that night in Makkah and we missed him. We searched for him in the valleys and the hills and said, 'He has either been taken away [by the jinn] or has been secretly killed.' He said, 'We spent the worst night which people could ever spend. When it was dawn we saw him coming from the direction of Hiraa. We said, 'Messenger of Allah, we missed you and searched for you but we could not find you and we spent the worst night which people could ever spend.' He [the Prophet] said, 'There came to me someone inviting me on behalf of the jinn and I went along with him and recited to them the Quran.' He said, 'He then went along with us and showed us their traces and traces of their embers.' They [the jinn] asked him about their food and he said, 'Every bone on which the name of Allah is recited is your provision. The time it will fall in your hands, it would be covered with flesh. And the dung of the camels is fodder for your animals.'" And in al-Tabari's narration from ibn Masud, "I stayed one night reciting to the jinn at a place called *al-Hujoon* [in Makkah]."

From among the verses that he recited to them was *surah al-Rahmaan*. In another hadith, the Prophet (peace be upon him) said, "I read it [*surah al-Rahmaan*] to the jinn on the night of the jinn and they had a better response to it than you did. When I came to, 'Which of the favors of your Lord do you deny?' they responded with, 'There is none of your bounties, o Lord, that we deny. And for you is the praise.'"[1]

That was not the only time that the Prophet (peace be upon him) recited to the jinn but such meetings were repeated a number of times afterwards. In his commentary to *surah al-Ahqaaf*, ibn Katheer records various hadith in which the Prophet (peace be upon him) met with the jinn. In some of these hadith, it states that ibn Masud was very close to the Prophet (peace be upon him) during such a night.

In a hadith recorded in *Sahih al-Bukhari*, there is the description of some jinn from a place called Naseeb in Yemen visiting the Prophet (peace be upon him). Al-Bukhari recorded from Abu Huraira that the Prophet (peace be upon him) said,

أَتَانِي وَفْدُ جِنٍّ نَصِيبِيينَ وَنِعْمَ الْجِنُّ فَسَأَلُونِي الزَّادَ فَدَعَوْتُ اللَّهَ لَهُمْ أَنْ لَا يَمُرُّوا بِعَظْمٍ وَلَا بِرَوْثَةٍ إِلَّا وَجَدُوا عَلَيْهَا طَعَامًا

"A delegation of the jinn of Naseeb [a part of Yemen] came to me— and how nice these jinn are— and asked me for provisions. I supplicated to Allah for them that they would never pass by a bone or dung of an animal except that they would find food upon it."

## The jinn preaching to the humans

In some of the authentic hadith there are reports that some jinn played a role in guiding some humans. In *Sahih al-Bukhari*, it is recorded that Umar ibn al-Khattab asked a man who used to be a diviner during the days of ignorance about the most amazing thing that his female jinn had ever informed him of. The ex-diviner told Umar, "One day she came to me in a state of fright. She said, 'Have you not seen the despair of the jinn and their defeat [i.e., from listening to the news in the heavens] and, therefore, they now only follow the camel riders.'" Umar said, "Such is the truth." I was sleeping near some idols and there came a

---

[1] This was recorded by al-Bazzaar, al-Haakim and ibn Jarir with a *sahih* chain. See al-Albani, *Sahih al-Jaami*, vol. 1, p. 30.

man with a calf and he sacrificed it for the idol. It let out a scream the like of which I have never heard. It said, 'O Julaih, o you arrogant sinner, you have a matter of success in front of you. A man of fair speech is saying, 'None has the right to be worshipped save You (o Allah).' The people fled from the sight (due to fear). Then the same cry came again. I then went away and a few days later, the people were saying, 'A prophet has appeared...'"

After recording this hadith in his commentary to *surah al-Ahqaaf*, Ibn Katheer wrote, "This is the text of al-Bukhari. Al-Baihaqi has recorded something similar to it from ibn Wahb." Then he stated, "Apparently this narration follows the mistaken notion that it was Umar himself who heard the scream at the time of the sacrifice. This is made explicit in weak narrations from Umar. All of the other narrations point to the diviner as being the one who reported what he had seen and heard. Allah knows best." Then he adds, "That man who was the diviner was Sawaad ibn Qaarib."

## Their order to do good deeds and being witnesses for Muslims

The hadith from the Prophet (peace be upon him) in which he states that his partner from among the jinn submitted and ordered him only to do good deeds will be mentioned later.

Abu Saeed al-Khudri said to Abu Sasa al-Ansari, "I see that you like sheep and wilderness. Therefore, whenever you are with your sheep or in the wilderness, make the call to prayer and raise your voice while doing so. Whoever hears the call to prayer, whether he be human, jinn or any other being, will be a witness for it on the Day of Resurrection." Abu Saeed added, "I heard that from the Messenger of Allah." [Recorded by al-Bukhari.] He stated that the jinn who heard the call to prayer will be witnesses for him on the Day of Resurrection.

## They are at different levels of good and evil

The jinn are of different varieties; some of them are fully devoted to doing good and righteousness; others are less so. Some of them are heedless; others are outright disbelievers and they are by far the majority. Allah says, concerning those who listened to the Quran,

$$وَأَنَّا مِنَّا الصَّالِحُونَ وَمِنَّا دُونَ ذَٰلِكَ ۖ كُنَّا طَرَائِقَ قِدَدًا$$

"And among us there are righteous folk and among us there are some that are far from that. We are sects having differences" (*al-Jinn* 11). In other words, some of them are completely pious, some are less so and so on. They are of different ways and thoughts like the human beings.

Allah also states about them, quoting them,

$$وَأَنَّا مِنَّا الْمُسْلِمُونَ وَمِنَّا الْقَاسِطُونَ ۖ فَمَنْ أَسْلَمَ فَأُولَٰئِكَ تَحَرَّوْا رَشَدًا ۝ وَأَمَّا الْقَاسِطُونَ فَكَانُوا لِجَهَنَّمَ حَطَبًا$$

"And there are among us some who have surrendered to Allah and there are among us some who are unjust. And whoso has surrendered to Allah, such have taken the right path purposefully. And as for those who are unjust, they are firewood for hell" (*al-Jinn* 14-15). In other words, some of them are Muslims and some have wronged their own souls by being unbelievers. Whoever submitted has set himself upon the path of guidance by his actions and whosoever among them wronged their own souls will be fuel for the hell-fire.

# The nature of Satan

Allah gave the jinn the ability to become believers or disbelievers. Thereby, Satan used to worship Allah along with the angels before he became an ingrate. When he became such, he became pleased with evil and sought it even though it would be the cause of his punishment. He was pleased by the performance of evil and encouraged others to perform evil deeds.

$$\text{قَالَ فَبِعِزَّتِكَ لَأُغْوِيَنَّهُمْ أَجْمَعِينَ ۝ إِلَّا عِبَادَكَ مِنْهُمُ الْمُخْلَصِينَ}$$

"He [Satan] said, 'Then, by Your might, I will surely beguile them, everyone, save your single-minded slaves among them" (*Saad* 82-83).

The same is the case with a human. If his soul becomes evil, he desires what harms him and becomes gratified by such actions; in fact, he becomes passionately in love with such things to the extent that he ruins his mind, religion, character, body and wealth. It is sufficient to consider, as examples, those who drink alcohol or smoke cigarettes. These things kill the one who consumes them. They are sufficient to cause the person's death yet the person is not able to leave them save through hardship.

## Can a devil embrace Islam?

It is apparent from the hadith[1] that it is possible for a devil to embrace Islam as the devil of the Prophet (peace be upon him) did so. Some scholars, though, reject this statement and state that a devil cannot become a believer. The commentator of *al-Aqeeda al-Tahaawiya* is of the latter opinion. The people of this school argue that the word *aslam* [mentioned in the hadith concerning the submission of the Prophet's devil] means that the devil submitted to the laws of Islam [without any belief or faith]. Some scholars say that the correct narration of the hadith is the Prophet (peace be on him) saying, "I am safe from him." The commentator on *al-Tahaawiya* is of the opinion that the narration putting the word *aslam* in the nominative case is a mistake; but

---

[1] The hadith that states that the Messenger of Allah (peace be on him) was helped by Allah over his devil and that his devil submitted and only ordered him to good shall be presented later.

al-Nawawi, in his commentary to *Sahih Muslim*, states, "They are two well-confirmed narrations." He states that al-Khattaabi thinks that the stronger narration is with the *dhamma* (that is, with the word in its nominative form).

From among those who say that a devil can embrace Islam is ibn Hibban. Commenting on the hadith referred to above, he stated, "In this report there is evidence that the devil of the Prophet (peace be upon him) embraced Islam and he did not incite the Prophet (peace be upon him) to do anything but good deeds. Otherwise, the Messenger of Allah (peace be on him) was safe from him even if the devil were a disbeliever."

There is some doubt concerning the opinion of the commentator on *al-Aqeeda al-Tahaawiya* that a devil can only be an unbeliever. If he means that the word devil is only used for the disbelievers of the jinn, then his opinion is correct. But if he means a devil can never change and convert to Islam, then his opinion is far from correct and the hadith is an evidence against him.[1]

---

[1] From a *Shariah* point of view, it does not seem sound that the disbelieving jinn are responsible for their actions and, at the same time, they are not able to embrace Islam. They are only to be punished if the message reaches them and they reject the message. This, in itself, implies that they have the freedom to be believers or disbelievers. Hence, they certainly can become Muslims if they so will.—JZ

# 3
# THE ENMITY BETWEEN SATAN AND MANKIND

## The reason behind the enmity, its history, and its severity

The enmity between humans and Satan is rooted in an incident that took place a long time ago. One must go back to the day that Allah formed Adam, before He breathed His spirit into him. Satan went around him and said, "[Adam,] if you are given mastery over me, I will surely disobey you. And if I am given mastery over you, I will destroy you."

It is recorded in *Sahih Muslim* on the authority of Anas that the Prophet (peace be upon him) said,

لَمَّا صَوَّرَ اللَّهُ آدَمَ فِي الْجَنَّةِ تَرَكَهُ مَا شَاءَ اللَّهُ أَنْ يَتْرُكَهُ فَجَعَلَ إِبْلِيسُ يُطِيفُ بِهِ يَنْظُرُ مَا هُوَ فَلَمَّا رَآهُ أَجْوَفَ عَرَفَ أَنَّهُ خُلِقَ خَلْقًا لَا يَتَمَالَكُ

"When Allah fashioned Adam in Paradise, He left him as long as He wished to leave him. Then Iblees roamed around him to see what he actually was and when Iblees found him to be hollow from within, he recognized that the new creature had been created with a disposition such that it would not have control over itself."

When Allah breathed into Adam his spirit, he ordered the angels to prostrate to Adam. Iblees used to worship Allah with the angels so the order was also addressed to him. But Iblees considered himself too great and, out of pride, he refused to prostrate to Adam. He cried, "I am better than him. You created me from fire and you created him from clay."

Then when Adam opened his eyes he found a great and generous gesture: the angels bowing down to him. But he also found a great enemy waiting for him that would try to lead him and his descendants to destruction and misguidance.

Satan was cast out of paradise due to his pride but he took a promise from Allah to be left alive until the day of judgment.

قَالَ أَنظِرْنِىٓ إِلَىٰ يَوْمِ يُبْعَثُونَ ۝ قَالَ إِنَّكَ مِنَ ٱلْمُنظَرِينَ

"He said: Reprieve me till the day when they are raised (from the dead). He said: Lo! You are of those who are reprieved" (*al-Araaf* 14-15). Then the accursed one made a promise and vow to himself that he would mislead the offspring of Adam and plot against them.

قَالَ فَبِمَآ أَغْوَيْتَنِى لَأَقْعُدَنَّ لَهُمْ صِرَٰطَكَ ٱلْمُسْتَقِيمَ ۝ ثُمَّ لَآتِيَنَّهُم مِّنۢ بَيْنِ أَيْدِيهِمْ وَمِنْ خَلْفِهِمْ وَعَنْ أَيْمَٰنِهِمْ وَعَن شَمَآئِلِهِمْ ۖ وَلَا تَجِدُ أَكْثَرَهُمْ شَٰكِرِينَ

"He said: Now, because you have sent me astray, verily I shall lurk in ambush for them on your Right Path. Then I shall come upon them from before them and from behind them and from their right and from their left, and you will not find most of them beholden (to You)" (*al-Araaf* 15-16). This latter statement of his shows how great will be his struggle to mislead the offspring of Adam. He will take every path he can against them, on their right, left, in front of them and behind them. He will attack them from every direction. Al-Zamakhshari said in his commentary to this verse, "He will come to them from all four directions as the enemy usually does, such as his 'sneaking whispers' to them. He will entice them in every way that he can. As in the [Quranic] statement, 'And excite any of them whom you can with your voice, and urge your horse and foot against them, and be a partner in their wealth and children, and promise them. Satan promises them only to deceive' (al-Israa 64)."

## Allah's warning to us concerning Satan

The Quran warns us at length about Satan since he is such a great test for humanity. Allah warns humans about Satan's misguidance and his desire to mislead people. Allah says,

$$يَـٰبَنِىٓ ءَادَمَ لَا يَفْتِنَنَّكُمُ ٱلشَّيْطَـٰنُ$$

"O Children of Adam! Let not Satan seduce you..." (al-Araaf 27). And,

$$إِنَّ ٱلشَّيْطَـٰنَ لَكُمْ عَدُوٌّ فَٱتَّخِذُوهُ عَدُوًّا$$

"Lo! The devil is an enemy for you, so treat him as an enemy" (Faatir 6). Again,

$$وَمَن يَتَّخِذِ ٱلشَّيْطَـٰنَ وَلِيًّا مِّن دُونِ ٱللَّهِ فَقَدْ خَسِرَ خُسْرَانًا مُّبِينًا$$

"Whoever chooses Satan for an ally instead of Allah is verily a loser and his loss is manifest" (al-Nisaa 119).

The enmity from Satan will not change or vanish. This is because Satan sees the father of the humans, Adam, as the cause for his being expelled from paradise and the reason behind Allah's curse upon Satan. There is no doubt that he will seek revenge from Adam and his offspring.

$$قَالَ أَرَأَيْتَكَ هَٰذَا الَّذِي كَرَّمْتَ عَلَيَّ لَئِنْ أَخَّرْتَنِ إِلَىٰ يَوْمِ الْقِيَامَةِ لَأَحْتَنِكَنَّ ذُرِّيَّتَهُ إِلَّا قَلِيلًا$$

"He said: Do You see this (creation) that you have honored above me? If you give me grace until the Day of Resurrection I will verily seize his seed, save but a few" ( *al-Israa* 62).

The scholars who deal in matters related to behavior and conduct often discuss the shortcomings and weaknesses of humans' souls but they do not put enough stress on this fierce enemy, although Allah warns us against him at many different places in the Quran. And He orders us to seek refuge from him while Allah does not order us to seek refuge from our souls anywhere. Only in the opening to an oratory did the Prophet (peace be upon him) state about the evil in the souls, "And we seek refuge in Allah from the evil in our souls and the evil of our deeds."

## The goals or the aims of Satan

### Long-term Goal

Satan has one long term goal. This is his ultimate ambition. This goal is to see humans thrown into the hellfire and prevented from entering paradise.

$$إِنَّمَا يَدْعُوا حِزْبَهُ لِيَكُونُوا مِنْ أَصْحَابِ السَّعِيرِ$$

"He only summons his faction to be owners of the flaming Fire" (*Faatir* 6).

# Short-term Goals

The above is Satan's long-term goal. But he has many short-term goals including:

## 1. To get the slave involved in disbelief and idolatry[1]

This is done by calling people to worship beings or idols other than Allah. Satan calls the people to disbelief in Allah and to disobey His commands.

كَمَثَلِ ٱلشَّيْطَٰنِ إِذْ قَالَ لِلْإِنسَٰنِ ٱكْفُرْ فَلَمَّا كَفَرَ قَالَ إِنِّى بَرِىٓءٌ مِّنكَ

"Or the likeness of Satan when he tells man to disbelieve, but when he disbelieves, he says, 'Verily, I am innocent of you'" (*al-Hashr* 16).

Imam Muslim records in his *Sahih* on the authority of Iyaadh ibn Hamaar that the Prophet (peace be upon him) addressed them saying,

أَلَا إِنَّ رَبِّي أَمَرَنِي أَنْ أُعَلِّمَكُمْ مَا جَهِلْتُمْ مِمَّا عَلَّمَنِي يَوْمِي هَذَا كُلُّ مَالٍ نَحَلْتُهُ عَبْدًا حَلَالٌ وَإِنِّي خَلَقْتُ عِبَادِي حُنَفَاءَ كُلَّهُمْ وَإِنَّهُمْ أَتَتْهُمْ الشَّيَاطِينُ فَاجْتَالَتْهُمْ عَنْ دِينِهِمْ وَحَرَّمَتْ عَلَيْهِمْ مَا أَحْلَلْتُ لَهُمْ وَأَمَرَتْهُمْ أَنْ يُشْرِكُوا بِي مَا لَمْ أُنْزِلْ بِهِ سُلْطَانًا

---

[1] In reality, the consequences of this goal are the same as that of the previous goal if a person should die in a state of unbelief.—JZ

"O people, Allah has commanded me to teach you that which you do not know which He has taught me today. (It is that) any bounty which I have conferred upon them is lawful for them. I have created my servants with a natural inclination toward My worship but the Devils turn them away from the right religion and he makes the things that are unlawful to be lawful and he orders them to make partners with Me although they have no authority to do so."

## 2. If he is not able to lead them to disbelief, he leads them to sins[1]

If he is not able to lead the slave to idolatry or disbelief, Satan does not despair. He then becomes pleased with things that are less than that, such as sins and disobedience to Allah. He also plants enmity and hatred in their ranks. Al-Tirmidhi and Ibn Majah have recorded in their *Sunan*s, with a *hasan* chain, that the Messenger of Allah (peace be upon him) said,

أَلَا إِنَّ الشَّيْطَانَ قَدْ أَيِسَ أَنْ يُعْبَدَ فِي بَلَدِكُمْ هَذَا أَبَدًا وَلَكِنْ سَيَكُونُ لَهُ طَاعَةٌ فِي بَعْضِ مَا تَحْتَقِرُونَ مِنْ أَعْمَالِكُمْ فَيَرْضَى بِهَا

"Verily, Satan has despaired that he should ever be worshipped again in this land of yours. But he will be obeyed in some of your actions that you consider small. And he will be pleased by that." And it is recorded in *Sahih al-Bukhari* and elsewhere,

---

[1] The second goal that the author should have stated is, "If Satan cannot involve the person in unbelief, he leads him to innovations and heresies." Sufyaan al-Thauri stated, "Heresy is more beloved to Satan than sins." This is because heresies involve disobedience towards Allah as well as the firm belief that the person is doing something good. This is a very dangerous combination as it then becomes very difficult to take the person away from that innovation. For more on this point, see Jamaal al-Din Zarabozo, "Innovations and Islam I: The Meaning of *Bida*," *al-Basheer* (Vol. 1, No. 4, November 1987), pp. 19-20.—JZ

$$\text{إِنَّ الشَّيْطَانَ قَدْ أَيِسَ أَنْ يَعْبُدَهُ الْمُصَلُّونَ فِي جَزِيرَةِ الْعَرَبِ وَلَكِنْ فِي التَّحْرِيشِ بَيْنَهُمْ}$$

"Verily Satan despairs that he should ever be worshipped by the performers of prayer in the Arabian peninsula. But he will instigate between them."[1] In other words, he will cause hatred and enmity to occur in their midst and he will incite them against each other. This is as Allah says in the Quran,

$$\text{إِنَّمَا يُرِيدُ الشَّيْطَٰنُ أَن يُوقِعَ بَيْنَكُمُ ٱلْعَدَٰوَةَ وَٱلْبَغْضَآءَ فِى ٱلْخَمْرِ وَٱلْمَيْسِرِ}$$

"Satan seeks only to cast among you enmity and hatred by means of strong drink and games of chance..." (al-Maaidah 91). Satan enjoins every evil,

$$\text{إِنَّمَا يَأْمُرُكُم بِٱلسُّوٓءِ وَٱلْفَحْشَآءِ وَأَن تَقُولُوا۟ عَلَى ٱللَّهِ مَا لَا تَعْلَمُونَ}$$

"He enjoins upon you only the evil and the foul, and that you should say concerning Allah that which you know not" (al-Baqara 169).

In sum, any action that is loved by Allah is hated by Satan and every act of disobedience that is hated by the Merciful is loved by Satan.

## 3. Blocking the slave from obeying Allah

It is not sufficient for him to call people to disbelief, idolatry and evil deeds. He also tries to block the way to any good deed. There is no path of goodness that man may follow except that he sits there, lurking

---

[1] Al-Ashqar stated that this hadith is from *Sahih al-Bukhari*. However, it seems that it is from *Sahih Muslim* and other sources but is not to be found in *Sahih al-Bukhari*. Allah knows best.—JZ

and waiting to turn mankind away. It is stated in a hadith, "Satan sits in all the paths of the children of Adam. He sits in the path to Islam and says, 'Will you embrace Islam and leave the religion of your father and grandfathers?' The man disobeys him and embraces Islam. Then he sits in the path to migration (*hijra*) and says, 'Will you migrate and leave your native land? The emigrant is like one on an arduous journey.' The man disobeys him and migrates. Then Satan sits in the path to jihad and says, 'The struggle is with your life and wealth. If you fight you will be killed and your wives will marry others and your wealth will be distributed.' He disobeys him and makes jihad. Whoever does that has the right upon Allah to enter paradise. And who is killed has a right upon Allah to enter paradise. And whoever drowns has the right upon Allah to enter paradise. And whoever has his neck broken by his animal has the right upon Allah to enter paradise."[1]

The above hadith is confirmed by Allah's saying in the Quran concerning Satan,

قَالَ فَبِمَآ أَغْوَيْتَنِى لَأَقْعُدَنَّ لَهُمْ صِرَٰطَكَ ٱلْمُسْتَقِيمَ ۝ ثُمَّ لَآتِيَنَّهُم مِّنۢ بَيْنِ أَيْدِيهِمْ وَمِنْ خَلْفِهِمْ وَعَنْ أَيْمَٰنِهِمْ وَعَن شَمَآئِلِهِمْ ۖ وَلَا تَجِدُ أَكْثَرَهُمْ شَٰكِرِينَ

"He said: Now, because You have sent me astray, verily I shall lurk in ambush for them on Your Right Path. Then I shall come upon them from before them and from behind them and from their right hands and from their left hands, and You will not find most of them beholden (to You)" (*al-Araaf* 16-17).

The statement, "I shall sit for them on Your Path," could either mean, "I shall cling to Your Path [to misguide them]," "I shall keep them from Your Path," or "I shall make them deviate from it."

---

[1] This was recorded by Ahmad, al-Nasaai and Ibn Hibbaan with a *sahih* chain. See al-Albani, *Sahih al-Jaami*, vol. 2, p. 72.

The early scholars have explained this right path in different ways but all of their explanations, though, are quite similar and consistent. Ibn Abbas said that it is the clear religion. Ibn Masood said it is the book of Allah. Jaabir called it Islam while Mujaahid said it is "the truth."

Satan does not leave any path to good except that he sits there to turn people away from it.

## 4. Ruining the Acts of Obedience to Allah

If Satan is not able to block the way to acts of obedience, then he will do his best to ruin the act of obedience or worship by making it such that the person will not receive reward for the action. A companion came to the Prophet (peace be on him) and said, "Verily Satan comes between me and my prayer and my recitation of the Quran and confuses me." The Prophet (peace be upon him) said,

ذَاكَ شَيْطَانٌ يُقَالُ لَهُ خَنْزَبٌ فَإِذَا أَحْسَسْتَهُ فَتَعَوَّذْ بِاللَّهِ مِنْهُ وَاتْفِلْ عَلَى يَسَارِكَ ثَلاثًا

"That is a devil called *khinzab*. If you feel that occurring to you, seek refuge in Allah from him and spit (or blow[1]) on your left side three times." The companion said he did so and Allah took that devil away from him. (This was recorded by Muslim in his *Sahih*.)

When the Muslim begins his prayer, Satan comes to him and whispers to him and makes his mind busy with the affairs of this life rather than obedience to Allah. In *Sahih Muslim* it is recorded that the Prophet (peace be on him) said,

---

[1] The action is not actually that of spitting but it is actually something between blowing and spitting, where one simply "spits" out a large portion of air.—JZ

إِنَّ الشَّيْطَانَ إِذَا سَمِعَ النِّدَاءَ بِالصَّلَاةِ أَحَالَ لَهُ ضُرَاطٌ حَتَّى لَا يَسْمَعَ صَوْتَهُ فَإِذَا سَكَتَ رَجَعَ فَوَسْوَسَ فَإِذَا سَمِعَ الْإِقَامَةَ ذَهَبَ حَتَّى لَا يَسْمَعَ صَوْتَهُ فَإِذَا سَكَتَ رَجَعَ فَوَسْوَسَ

"Definitely when Satan hears the call to prayer, he turns his back and flees, noisily breaking wind in order not to hear the call. After the call is over he returns to whisper to those who are about to pray. When the second call (*al-iqaama*) is made, he again flees and noisily breaks wind in order not to hear the call. Again, when the call is over, he returns to (the people praying) and whispers to them (to distract them from the prayer)." And in another narration,

إِذَا قَضَى التَّثْوِيبَ أَقْبَلَ حَتَّى يَخْطِرَ بَيْنَ الْمَرْءِ وَنَفْسِهِ يَقُولُ اذْكُرْ كَذَا اذْكُرْ كَذَا لِمَا لَمْ يَكُنْ يَذْكُرُ حَتَّى يَظَلَّ الرَّجُلُ لَا يَدْرِي كَمْ صَلَّى

"When the call is finished, he turns back and comes between the person and his soul, saying to him, 'Remember this and remember that,' which the man did not think of before [the prayer] until he does not know how much he has prayed." (Recorded by al-Bukhari and Muslim.)

## Every disobedience to the Merciful is obedience to Satan

Allah says in the Quran,

إِن يَدْعُونَ مِن دُونِهِ إِلَّا إِنَٰثًا وَإِن يَدْعُونَ إِلَّا شَيْطَٰنًا مَّرِيدًا ۝ لَّعَنَهُ ٱللَّهُ وَقَالَ لَأَتَّخِذَنَّ مِنْ عِبَادِكَ نَصِيبًا مَّفْرُوضًا

"They invoke in His stead only females; they pray to none other than Satan, a rebel whom Allah cursed, and he said; Surely I will take of Your bondsmen an appointed portion" (*al-Nisaa* 117-118). Therefore, everything that is worshipped instead of Allah, be it statues, idols, the sun, the moon, one's desires, another human, some ideology or whatever, is actually the worship of Satan. This is true whether the person is pleased with that fact or denies it, because it was Satan that ordered and sought that action. For example, the worshippers of the angels are actually worshipping Satan. Allah says in the Quran,

وَيَوْمَ يَحْشُرُهُمْ جَمِيعًا ثُمَّ يَقُولُ لِلْمَلَٰٓئِكَةِ أَهَٰٓؤُلَاءِ إِيَّاكُمْ كَانُوا۟ يَعْبُدُونَ ۞ قَالُوا۟ سُبْحَٰنَكَ أَنتَ وَلِيُّنَا مِن دُونِهِم ۖ بَلْ كَانُوا۟ يَعْبُدُونَ ٱلْجِنَّ ۖ أَكْثَرُهُم بِهِم مُّؤْمِنُونَ

"And on the day when He will gather them all together, He will say unto the angels: Did these worship you? They will say: Be You glorified. You are our Protector from them! Nay, but they worshipped the jinn, most of them were believers in them" (*Saba* 40-41). So the angels never asked the people to worship them, but it was the jinn that ordered them to do so in order to have them worship the devils who appeared to them and led them. Similarly, every idol has devils [encouraging others to it].

## Conclusion

What one can conclude is that Satan orders and encourages every evil and strives his best for evil; he tries to forbid every good and, in fact, he fears every good deed. He wants the person to do the former and to leave the latter. Allah says,

ٱلشَّيْطَٰنُ يَعِدُكُمُ ٱلْفَقْرَ وَيَأْمُرُكُم بِٱلْفَحْشَآءِ ۖ وَٱللَّهُ يَعِدُكُم مَّغْفِرَةً مِّنْهُ وَفَضْلًا

"The devil promises you destitution and enjoins upon you lewdness. But Allah promises you forgiveness from Himself with bounty" (*al-Baqara* 268). Satan makes humans fear poverty. He says to them, "If you spend your wealth in the way of Allah you will become poor." And he orders humans to acts of lewdness. He leads humans to every evil and lewd act, from being miserly to adultery and so on.

## 5. Psychologically and physically harming humans

In the same way that it is the goal of Satan to mislead mankind by disbelief and sins, it is also his goal to physically and psychologically harm the Muslim. The following are some of what is known concerning such attacks:

### a. Attacking the Prophet

Later we shall present a hadith in which Satan attacked the Prophet (peace be upon him) by trying to throw a flame of fire into his face.

### b. The dreams from Satan

Satan has the ability to bring dreams to the human while he is sleeping to molest and distress the person in order to worry and harm him.

The Prophet (peace be upon him) has stated that dreams in sleep are of three types: from the Most Merciful, of anguish from Satan, and from the person himself.[1] In *Sahih al-Bukhari*, it is recorded that the Prophet (peace be upon him) said.

إِذَا رَأَى أَحَدُكُمُ الرُّؤْيَا يُحِبُّهَا فَإِنَّهَا مِنَ اللَّهِ فَلْيَحْمَدِ اللَّهَ عَلَيْهَا وَلْيُحَدِّثْ بِهَا وَإِذَا رَأَى غَيْرَ ذَلِكَ مِمَّا يَكْرَهُ فَإِنَّمَا هِيَ مِنَ الشَّيْطَانِ فَلْيَسْتَعِذْ مِنْ شَرِّهَا وَلَا يَذْكُرْهَا لِأَحَدٍ فَإِنَّهَا لَنْ تَضُرَّهُ

---

[1] See al-Albani, *Sahih al-Jaami*, vol. 3, pp. 184-185.

"If one of you sees a dream that he likes, it is from Allah. He should praise Allah for it and he should relate it to others. If he sees what he dislikes, it is from Satan. He should seek refuge in Allah from it and not mention it to anyone. Thereby, it will not harm him."

### c. Burning down houses

Satan may use animals that he spurs on for this purpose. Abu Dawud has recorded in his *Sunan* and ibn Hibbaan in his *Sahih*, with a *sahih* chain, that the Prophet (peace be upon him) said,

إِذَا نِمْتُمْ فَأَطْفِئُوا سُرُجَكُمْ فَإِنَّ الشَّيْطَانَ يَدُلُّ مِثْلَ هَذِهِ عَلَى هَذَا فَتُحْرِقَكُمْ

"When you sleep at night, extinguish your lamps for Satan guides one like this (mouse) to one like this (lamp) and they burn your place down."

### d. Satan fights and plays with the human at the time of death

The Prophet (peace be upon him) used to seek refuge in Allah from that. He used to say,

اللَّهُمَّ إِنِّي أَعُوذُ بِكَ مِنَ التَّرَدِّي وَالْهَدْمِ وَالْغَرَقِ وَالْحَرِيقِ وَأَعُوذُ بِكَ أَنْ يَتَخَبَّطَنِي الشَّيْطَانُ عِنْدَ الْمَوْتِ وَأَعُوذُ بِكَ أَنْ أَمُوتَ فِي سَبِيلِكَ مُدْبِرًا وَأَعُوذُ بِكَ أَنْ أَمُوتَ لَدِيغًا

"Oh Allah, I seek refuge in You from death through falling. I seek refuge in You from my house falling on me. I seek refuge in You from falling into a ditch, drowning, burning and decrepitude. I seek refuge in You from the devil harming me at the time of my death.[1] I seek refuge in

---

[1] Al-Khataabi has explained the meaning of this phrase in various ways, including: the Satan tries to get power over the servant at the time of his death, or he keeps him away from repenting before death, or he makes him despair of Allah's mercy or he makes him very sad at leaving this world. All of these aspects may be implied in this supplication of the Prophet (peace be upon him). On the other hand, ibn al-Atheer said that its meaning is that Satan fights and sports with the person at his death. Allah knows best. See al-Suyooti or al-Sindi's commentary on the margin of Ahmad al-Nasaai, *Sunan al-Nasaai* (Beirut: Ihyaa al-Turaath al-Arabi, n.d.), vol. 8, pp. 282-283; Ibn al-Atheer, *al-Nihaayah fi Ghareeb al-Hadith* (under the heading خبط).—JZ

You from dying while fleeing from the enemy. I seek refuge in You from dying from a poisonous sting."[1]

### e. Harming the child at the time of its birth

The Prophet (peace be upon him) said,

$$\text{كُلُّ بَنِي آدَمَ يَمَسُّهُ الشَّيْطَانُ يَوْمَ وَلَدَتْهُ أُمُّهُ إِلَّا مَرْيَمَ وَابْنَهَا}$$

"Every child of Adam is touched by Satan on the day that his mother gives birth to him except Mary and her son." (Recorded by Muslim.[2]) And in *Sahih al-Bukhari* it is recorded that,

$$\text{كُلُّ بَنِي آدَمَ يَطْعُنُ الشَّيْطَانُ فِي جَنْبَيْهِ بِإِصْبَعِهِ حِينَ يُولَدُ غَيْرَ عِيسَى ابْنِ مَرْيَمَ ذَهَبَ يَطْعُنُ فَطَعَنَ فِي الْحِجَابِ}$$

"When any human is born, Satan touches him at both sides of the body with his two fingers, except in the case of Jesus, the son of Mary. Satan tried to do so but failed and touched the placenta instead." In another hadith in *Sahih al-Bukhari*, the following is stated,

$$\text{مَا مِنْ بَنِي آدَمَ مَوْلُودٌ إِلَّا يَمَسُّهُ الشَّيْطَانُ حِينَ يُولَدُ فَيَسْتَهِلُّ صَارِخًا مِنْ مَسِّ الشَّيْطَانِ غَيْرَ مَرْيَمَ وَابْنِهَا}$$

"There is no one born among the offspring of Adam except that Satan touches it. The child cries loudly at birth, therefore, from the touch of Satan, except Mary and her child." The reason that Mary and her child were exempted from such an action was the supplication that the mother of Mary made,

---

[1] Recorded by an-Nasaai and al-Haakim with a *sahih* chain. See al-Albani, *Sahih al-Jaami*, vol. 1, p. 405.
[2] Al-Albani, *Sahih al-Jaami*, vol. 4, p. 171.

$$\text{وَإِنِّى أُعِيذُهَا بِكَ وَذُرِّيَّتَهَا مِنَ ٱلشَّيْطَٰنِ ٱلرَّجِيمِ}$$

"[My Lord, I have vowed to You that which is in my belly as a consecrated (offspring)...] and lo! I crave Your protection for her and for her offspring from Satan the outcast" (*ali-Imraan* 36). Since she was sincere in her request, Allah answered that supplication and protected Mary and her son from Satan.

Ammaar ibn Yaasir was also protected by Allah from Satan. In *Sahih al-Bukhari* it is recorded that Abu ad-Darda said, "Is there among you the one that was protected from Satan according to what the Prophet said." Al-Mughira said, "The one who was protected from Satan according to the tongue of His Prophet means Ammar."

### f. Plague is from the jinn

The Prophet (peace be upon him) stated, "The end of this nation would come through calumnies and plague. These are the pierces from the enemy of the humans of the jinn. And whoever dies due to this infliction has attained martyrdom."[1] In *al-Mustadrak* of al-Haakim it is recorded that the Prophet (peace be upon him) said, "Plague is the piercing of your enemies from among the jinn. And for you it is martyrdom." Perhaps what occurred to the Prophet Job (peace be on him) was from the jinn, as it states in the Quran,

$$\text{وَٱذْكُرْ عَبْدَنَآ أَيُّوبَ إِذْ نَادَىٰ رَبَّهُۥٓ أَنِّى مَسَّنِىَ ٱلشَّيْطَٰنُ بِنُصْبٍ وَعَذَابٍ}$$

"And make mention of Our bondsman Job, when he cried unto his Lord (saying): Lo! the devil does afflict (lit., touch) me with distress and torment" (*Saad* 41).

---

[1] This was recorded by Ahmad and at-Tabaraani with a *sahih* chain. See al-Albani, *Sahih al-Jaami*, vol. 4, p. 90.

### g. Various other diseases

The Prophet (peace be upon him) said, concerning the prolonged flow of blood that occurs to some women,

$$إِنَّمَا هَذِهِ رَكْضَةٌ مِنْ رَكَضَاتِ الشَّيْطَانِ$$

"It is but a kick from the kicks of Satan."[1]

### h. They share in the food, drink and lodging of the humans

One of the ways by which Satan harms humans is by sharing in their food, drink and lodging. This occurs if the human contradicts the guidance of Allah or if he is unmindful of Him. If he sticks to the guidance of Allah or is constant in His remembrance, Satan would not have any path to his wealth or housing. It is not allowed for Satan to take any food unless it is "offered" to him by someone who has neglected to mention the name of Allah over it. If it has had the name of Allah mentioned over it, it is forbidden for Satan. In *Sahih Muslim*, it is related from Hudhaifa that they were attending a meal with the Prophet (peace be upon him) and they did not touch the meal until the Prophet (peace be upon him) did so. A girl came quickly as if chased and was about to grab some food when the Prophet (peace be upon him) caught her hand. Then a bedouin came and did similarly. Then the Prophet (peace be upon him) said,

$$إِنَّ الشَّيْطَانَ لَيَسْتَحِلُّ الطَّعَامَ الَّذِي لَمْ يُذْكَرِ اسْمُ اللهِ عَلَيْهِ وَإِنَّهُ جَاءَ بِهَذَا الْأَعْرَابِيِّ يَسْتَحِلُّ بِهِ فَأَخَذْتُ بِيَدِهِ وَجَاءَ بِهَذِهِ الْجَارِيَةِ يَسْتَحِلُّ بِهَا فَأَخَذْتُ بِيَدِهَا فَوَالَّذِي نَفْسِي بِيَدِهِ إِنَّ يَدَهُ لَفِي يَدِي مَعَ أَيْدِيهِمَا$$

"Satan is permitted that food which has not had the name of Allah pronounced over it. He brought this girl in order for the food to be lawful for him. And he brought this bedouin in order for the food to be

---

[1] Recorded by Abu Dawud, al-Nasaai, at-Tirmidhi and Ibn Majah with a *hasan* chain. See al-Albani, *Sahih al-Jaami*, vol. 3, p. 196.

lawful for him. So I caught their hands. By the One in whose Hand is my soul, his [Satan's] hand is in my hand along with theirs."

The Prophet (peace be upon him) ordered us to protect our wealth from Satan by closing doors, covering vessels and mentioning the name of Allah upon them. That will protect them from Satan. The Prophet (peace be upon him) said,

أَغْلِقُوا الْأَبْوَابَ وَاذْكُرُوا اسْمَ اللَّهِ فَإِنَّ الشَّيْطَانَ لَا يَفْتَحُ بَابًا مُغْلَقًا وَأَوْكُوا قِرَبَكُمْ وَاذْكُرُوا اسْمَ اللَّهِ وَخَمِّرُوا آنِيَتَكُمْ وَاذْكُرُوا اسْمَ اللَّهِ وَلَوْ أَنْ تَعْرُضُوا عَلَيْهَا شَيْئًا وَأَطْفِئُوا مَصَابِيحَكُمْ

"Close the doors and make mention of Allah. For Satan does not open a closed door. And tighten the mouths of the waterskins and mention the name of Allah. Cover your utensils and mention the name of Allah even though you may only put something over them. And extinguish your lamps." (Recorded by Muslim.)

Also Satan drinks and eats with the human if he should drink or eat with his left hand. The same is the case if he drinks standing. In *Musnad Ahmad* it is recorded on the authority of Aisha that the Prophet said,

مَنْ أَكَلَ بِشِمَالِهِ أَكَلَ مَعَهُ الشَّيْطَانُ وَمَنْ شَرِبَ بِشِمَالِهِ شَرِبَ مَعَهُ الشَّيْطَانُ

"Whoever eats with his left hand, Satan eats with him. Whoever drinks with his left hand, Satan drinks with him."[1]

---

[1] This hadith was recorded by Ahmad and al-Tabaraani in *al-Ausat*. Ahmad's chain is weak due to the presence of Rishdeen ibn Saad, who was a pious person but a weak narrator. Furthermore, the chain also contains Moosa ibn Sarjis whose condition as a n is not known and he was not classified as trustworthy by any scholar. Al-Tabaraani's chain contains ibn Lahiyah and the hadith is narrated by him with a vague term, thus not expressing how he received the hadith. Furthermore, the chain also contains Ahmad ibn Rishdeen who was considered, according to al-Darweesh, a liar. Therefore, the hadith must be considered a weak hadith. Allah knows best. See

Also in the *Musnad* it is recorded on the authority of Abu Huraira that the Prophet (peace be upon him) saw a man drinking while standing and said to him, "*Qih*[1]." The man said, "Why do you say so?" The Prophet (peace be upon him) said,

$$\text{أَيَسُرُّكَ أَنْ يَشْرَبَ مَعَكَ الْهِرُّ قَالَ لَا قَالَ فَإِنَّهُ قَدْ شَرِبَ مَعَكَ مَنْ هُوَ شَرٌّ مِنْهُ الشَّيْطَانُ}$$

"Would you be pleased if a cat drank with you?" The man said, "No." The Prophet (peace be upon him) said, "Verily there is someone worse than that drinking with you, and that is Satan."[2]

Satan is repelled from one's place of residence when the person does not neglect to mention the name of Allah upon entering his home. The Prophet (peace be upon him) pointed that out to us. He said,

$$\text{إِذَا دَخَلَ الرَّجُلُ بَيْتَهُ فَذَكَرَ اللَّهَ عِنْدَ دُخُولِهِ وَعِنْدَ طَعَامِهِ قَالَ الشَّيْطَانُ لَا مَبِيتَ لَكُمْ وَلَا عَشَاءَ وَإِذَا دَخَلَ فَلَمْ يَذْكُرِ اللَّهَ عِنْدَ دُخُولِهِ قَالَ الشَّيْطَانُ أَدْرَكْتُمُ الْمَبِيتَ وَإِذَا لَمْ يَذْكُرِ اللَّهَ عِنْدَ طَعَامِهِ قَالَ أَدْرَكْتُمُ الْمَبِيتَ وَالْعَشَاءَ}$$

"If a man enters his house and mentions the name of Allah upon entering and upon eating, Satan says, 'There is no lodging or food for us here.' If he enters without mentioning the name of Allah, Satan says, 'I have

---

Ahmad ibn Hanbal, *Musnad Ahmad*, vol. 6, p. 77; Sulaimaan al-Tabaraani, *al-Mujam al-Ausat* (Riyadh: Maktabah al-Maarif, 1985), vol. 1, pp. 203-204; Abdullah al-Darweesh, *Bughyat al-Raaid fi Tahqeeq Majma al-Zawaaid wa Manba al-Fawaaid* (Beirut: Dar al-Fikr, 199 ), vol. 5, p. 24; Bashaar Maroof and Shuaib al-Arnaoot, *Tahreer Taqreeb al-Tahdheeb* (Beirut: Muasassah al-Risaalah, 1997), vol. 1, pp. 401-402 and vol. 3, p. 430.—JZ

[1] An expression showing disapproval.—JZ

[2] This chain contains Abu Ziyaad al-Tahaan. Only Shubah is known to have narrated from him. Based on that, some scholars, such as ibn Maeen and ibn Abu Haatim, seem to accept him. Al-Dhahabi, however, says that he is not known and that seems to be the correct view. Al-Arnaoot and Murshid conclude that the hadith is *ghareeb*, which, in general, signifies that it is weak. See al-Arnaoot and Murshid, vol. 13, p. 381.—JZ

found lodging for you.' And if he does not mention Allah upon eating, Satan says, 'I have found lodging and food for you'" [Recorded by Muslim.]

### i. The touch of Satan upon the humans [possession by jinn]

Ibn Taimiya said,

> The jinn entering the body of the humans is confirmed by the agreement of the leaders of the people of the sunna and the community (*ahl al-sunna wa al-jamaa*). Allah says in the Quran, "Those who swallow usury cannot rise up save as he arises whom the devil has prostrated by his touch" (*al-Baqara* 275). And in the *Sahih* it is recorded on the authority of the Prophet (peace be upon him), "Satan flows in the children of Adam like the flowing of the blood."[1]

Abdullah, the son of Imam Ahmad ibn Hanbal said, "I said to my father, 'Some people say that the jinn does not enter the body of the possessed.' He said, 'Oh my son, they are lying. It is that which speaks by his tongue.'" Ibn Taimiya said,

> What he [Ahmad] said is well-known. The possessed person speaks a language that he himself does not understand. And his body may be struck with a ferocious beating, such that it would leave a great mark on a camel. The possessed person does not perceive the strike nor does he perceive the words that he is speaking. The possessed may lift others heavier than him. He may pull out the carpet he is sitting upon... and other such things that have been witnessed and reported by reliable sources. He speaks with the tongue of the human and he moves with that body but he is a specie other than a human.

And ibn Taimiya also wrote, "None of the leaders of the Muslims reject the notion that the jinn enters into the body of the possessed and others. Those who reject it and claim that the Islamic law states it to be false are

---

[1] Ibn Taimiya, *Majmoo al-Fatawa*, vol. 24, p. 276.

stating a lie concerning Islamic law, as there is no proof therein that denies its occurrence."

Ibn Taimiya also mentioned that some of those who deny that the jinn enter the body of the possessed include Mutazilahs such as al-Jubbai and Abu Bakr al-Raazi.[1]

We shall return to this point and discuss it in more detail in the fifth chapter.

## The Leader of the Battle

Iblees is the one who lays out the strategy of the battle against humans and is the leader. From his seat, he sends his troops and armies to different places for different purposes. He meets with his troops and reviews what they have accomplished. He praises those who created a great deal of mischief and misguidance among the people. Imam Muslim records in his *Sahih* on the authority of Jabir that the Prophet (peace be upon him) said,

إِنَّ إِبْلِيسَ يَضَعُ عَرْشَهُ عَلَى الْمَاءِ ثُمَّ يَبْعَثُ سَرَايَاهُ فَأَدْنَاهُمْ مِنْهُ مَنْزِلَةً أَعْظَمُهُمْ فِتْنَةً يَجِيءُ أَحَدُهُمْ فَيَقُولُ فَعَلْتُ كَذَا وَكَذَا فَيَقُولُ مَا صَنَعْتَ شَيْئًا قَالَ ثُمَّ يَجِيءُ أَحَدُهُمْ فَيَقُولُ مَا تَرَكْتُهُ حَتَّى فَرَّقْتُ بَيْنَهُ وَبَيْنَ امْرَأَتِهِ قَالَ فَيُدْنِيهِ مِنْهُ وَيَقُولُ نِعْمَ أَنْتَ

"Iblees sets his throne on the water. From there, he sends out his troops to tempt mankind. The one whom he regards as closest to him is the one who causes the greatest temptation. One of them returns to him and says, 'I stayed with so and so and did not leave him until he did such and such,' and he is told, 'You have done nothing.' Then one comes and reports, 'I did not leave him until he separated from his wife.' Iblees then brings him near to him and says, 'How fine you are.'"

---

[1] Ibn Taimiya, *Majmoo al-Fatawa*, vol. 19, p. 12.

In *Musnad Ahmad* it is recorded that the Prophet (peace be upon him) said to ibn Sa-id (concerning whom he had a suspicion that he was the anti-Christ), "What do you see?" He replied, "I see a throne upon the sea and around it are serpents." The Prophet (peace be upon him) said, "He has told the truth. That is the throne of Iblees."[1]

Satan is very well versed in the ways of misguidance. He has well-conceived plans and works of deception. And he will continue to live and will not cease in this adventure as long as humans are alive, until the day of Judgment. The Quran says,

قَالَ أَنظِرْنِى إِلَىٰ يَوْمِ يُبْعَثُونَ ۝ قَالَ إِنَّكَ مِنَ ٱلْمُنظَرِينَ

"He [Satan] said: My Lord reprieve me till the Day when they are raised. He [Allah] said: Then lo! you are of those reprieved" (*al-Araaf* 14-15). He made a vow to urge until evil as many of mankind as he can. He does not give up nor does he get bored. There is a hadith that states,

إن الشيطان قال وعزتك يا رب لا أبرح أغوي عبادك ما دامت أرواحهم في أجسادهم قال الرب وعزتي وجلالي لا أزال أغفر لهم ما استغفروني

"Verily, Satan has said, 'By your Honor and Grandeur [O Allah], my enticements will not depart from your slaves as long as their souls are in their bodies.' And the Lord said, 'By My Honor and My Grandeur, I will not cease forgiving those who ask for my forgiveness.'"[2]

## The Soldiers

He has two types of soldiers: one from among jinn and one from among humans.

---

[1] Muslim has also recorded something similar to that.—JZ
[2] Recorded by Ahmad and al-Haakim with a *hasan* chain. See al-Albani, *Sahih al-Jaami*, vol. 2, p. 72.

## His soldiers from the jinn

Satan has supporters and soldiers from among the jinn. We have already mentioned the hadith that states that he sends his troops out from his throne. And it says in the Quran,

$$\text{وَٱسْتَفْزِزْ مَنِ ٱسْتَطَعْتَ مِنْهُم بِصَوْتِكَ وَأَجْلِبْ عَلَيْهِم بِخَيْلِكَ وَرَجِلِكَ}$$

"And excite any of them whom you can with your voice, and urge your horse and foot against them..." (*al-Israa* 64). He has soldiers that attack while riding and on foot. He sends them against Allah's slaves to incite them to evil,

$$\text{أَلَمْ تَرَ أَنَّا أَرْسَلْنَا ٱلشَّيَٰطِينَ عَلَى ٱلْكَٰفِرِينَ تَؤُزُّهُمْ أَزًّا}$$

"Do you not see that we have set the devils on the disbelievers to confound them with confusion?" (*Maryam* 83).

## Every human has a "partner"

Every human has a devil with him that never leaves him. Muslim recorded that Aisha narrated that one night the Prophet (peace be upon him) left her room and she felt jealous. When he returned he saw her upset. He said to her, "Oh Aisha, what has happened to you? Are you jealous?" She responded, "How could it be that a woman like myself would not be jealous with respect to a man like yourself?" He told her, "It was your devil that came to you." She asked, "Oh Messenger of Allah, is there a devil with me?" He said, "Yes." She asked, "Is there a devil attached to everyone?" He said, "Yes." She again asked, "Oh Messenger of Allah, even with you?" He answered, "Yes, but my Lord has aided me against him and, therefore, I am absolutely safe from his actions."

It is also recorded in *Sahih Muslim* and *Musnad Ahmad* that the Prophet (peace be on him) said,

$$\text{مَا مِنْكُمْ مِنْ أَحَدٍ إِلَّا وَقَدْ وُكِّلَ بِهِ قَرِينُهُ مِنَ الْجِنِّ قَالُوا وَإِيَّاكَ يَا رَسُولَ اللَّهِ قَالَ وَإِيَّايَ إِلَّا أَنَّ اللَّهَ أَعَانَنِي عَلَيْهِ فَأَسْلَمَ فَلَا يَأْمُرُنِي إِلَّا بِخَيْرٍ}$$

"There is none among you except that he has a partner entrusted to him from among the jinn." The companions asked, "You too, Oh Messenger of Allah?" He responded, "Yes, but Allah aids me against him so I am safe from him and he only orders me to do good."

In the Quran it states,

$$\text{وَمَن يَعْشُ عَن ذِكْرِ الرَّحْمَٰنِ نُقَيِّضْ لَهُ شَيْطَانًا فَهُوَ لَهُ قَرِينٌ}$$

"And he whose sight is dim to the remembrance of the Beneficent, We assign unto him a devil who becomes his comrade" (*al-Zukhruf* 36). And in another verse,

$$\text{وَقَيَّضْنَا لَهُمْ قُرَنَاءَ فَزَيَّنُوا لَهُم مَّا بَيْنَ أَيْدِيهِمْ وَمَا خَلْفَهُمْ}$$

"And We assigned them comrades, who made their present and their past fair seeming unto them" (*Fusilat* 25).

## His patrons from among the humans

Satan is man's first enemy who rushes to take him to his eternal destruction. Although that is the case, most humans take him as their friend and ally. They follow in his footsteps. They are pleased with his thoughts. It shows how senseless the human, who has been bestowed a mind, is that he takes his most devoted enemy as his loyal ally. Allah says,

$$\text{أَفَتَتَّخِذُونَهُ وَذُرِّيَّتَهُ أَوْلِيَاءَ مِن دُونِي وَهُمْ لَكُمْ عَدُوٌّ بِئْسَ لِلظَّالِمِينَ بَدَلًا}$$

"Will you choose him and his seed for your protecting friends instead of Me, when they are an enemy unto you? Calamitous is the exchange of evildoers" (*al-Kahf* 50).

The one who takes him as an ally will suffer a great loss due to that choice. Allah says,

$$\text{وَمَن يَتَّخِذِ الشَّيْطَانَ وَلِيًّا مِّن دُونِ اللَّهِ فَقَدْ خَسِرَ خُسْرَانًا مُّبِينًا}$$

"Whosoever chooses Satan for an ally instead of Allah is verily a loser and his loss is manifest" (*al-Nisaa* 119). They lose because Satan misguides and ruins their souls; he prohibits them from the bounty of guidance; and he throws at them misguidance and doubts. Allah says,

$$\text{وَالَّذِينَ كَفَرُوا أَوْلِيَاؤُهُمُ الطَّاغُوتُ يُخْرِجُونَهُم مِّنَ النُّورِ إِلَى الظُّلُمَاتِ أُولَٰئِكَ أَصْحَابُ النَّارِ هُمْ فِيهَا خَالِدُونَ}$$

"As for those who disbelieve, their patrons are false deities. They bring them out of light into darkness. Such are the rightful owners of the Fire. They will abide therein" (*al-Baqara* 257). And they will lose because he will lead them to the fire on the Day of Resurrection.

$$\text{إِنَّمَا يَدْعُواْ حِزْبَهُۥ لِيَكُونُواْ مِنْ أَصْحَٰبِ ٱلسَّعِيرِ}$$

"He only summons his faction to be owners of the Flaming Fire" (*Faatir* 6). Those patrons of Satan are used by him as his troops in order to carry out his plans and to meet his goals.

## He deceives and disappoints his patrons

Many humans follow and support Satan. He is deceiving them and leading them to what will end in their ultimate destruction and ruin. He will, in the end, abandon them and forsake them. He even laughs at them. Furthermore, he will point them out and even expose them. He orders them to steal, kill, commit adultery, and so on, and then he discloses their acts to others and disgraces them. He did that to the unbelievers at the battle of Badr when he came to them in the shape of Suraaqa ibn Maalik. He had promised them succor and victory by saying, "No one of mankind can conquer you today for I am your protector" (*al-Anfaal* 48). When he saw the angels coming to aid the believers, Satan fled the battlefield and he left the unbelievers to be defeated. Hassaan ibn Thabit said (in words of poetry), "He guided them by deception and then he left them. The evil person is the one who follows him out of deception." He did the same thing to the monk who killed the woman and her child. It was Satan who ordered him to commit fornication with her and then to kill her. Then Satan pointed him out to her family and disclosed what he had done. Then he ordered the man to prostrate to him. When he did so, he fled from him and left him. We shall present that story later.

On the day of Resurrection, he will say to his patrons after he and all of them have entered the fire,

$$إِنِّى كَفَرْتُ بِمَآ أَشْرَكْتُمُونِ مِن قَبْلُ$$

"[And Satan says, when the matter has been decided, 'Lo! Allah promised you a promise of truth; and I promised you, then failed you. And I had no power over you save that I called unto you and you obeyed me. So blame me not, but blame yourselves. I cannot help you, nor can you help me.] Lo! I disbelieved in that which you before ascribed to me'" (*Ibrahim* 22). First, he encouraged them to every evil and then he claimed complete innocence of them.

We shall present the story later of the channeler who claimed to know the world of the spirits. Satan left him after he became very famous. Finally, he was left lost and disgraced, not knowing what to do.

## Satan uses his patrons as troops to serve him and to help him in his battle against the believers

Humans are of two groups: allies and servants of Allah, the Most Merciful, and allies of Satan. The patrons of Satan are all of the unbelievers, regardless of what group they belong to or what affiliation they may profess. Allah says,

$$إِنَّا جَعَلْنَا ٱلشَّيَٰطِينَ أَوْلِيَآءَ لِلَّذِينَ لَا يُؤْمِنُونَ$$

"Lo! We have made the devils protecting friends for those who believe not" (*al-Araaf* 27).

Satan gets power over them to mislead the believers by way of doubts and skepticism. Allah says,

$$وَإِنَّ ٱلشَّيَٰطِينَ لَيُوحُونَ إِلَىٰٓ أَوْلِيَآئِهِمْ لِيُجَٰدِلُوكُمْ$$

"Lo! The devils do inspire their followers to dispute with you" (*al-Anaam* 121). The doubts and misconceptions that the Orientalists, missionaries, Jews, atheists and others spread are of this nature.

He urges them to psychologically injure the believers. Allah says,

$$إِنَّمَا ٱلنَّجْوَىٰ مِنَ ٱلشَّيْطَٰنِ لِيَحْزُنَ ٱلَّذِينَ ءَامَنُواْ$$

"Lo! Secret talks and conspiracy are only of Satan, that he may vex those who believe" (*al-Mujaadala* 10). He incited the polytheists to speak secretly among themselves whenever the Muslims were close by so the Muslims would think that they were conspiring against them.

He also urges the unbelievers to fight against the believers. Allah says,

$$ٱلَّذِينَ ءَامَنُواْ يُقَٰتِلُونَ فِى سَبِيلِ ٱللَّهِ وَٱلَّذِينَ كَفَرُواْ يُقَٰتِلُونَ فِى سَبِيلِ ٱلطَّٰغُوتِ فَقَٰتِلُوٓاْ أَوْلِيَآءَ ٱلشَّيْطَٰنِ إِنَّ كَيْدَ ٱلشَّيْطَٰنِ كَانَ ضَعِيفًا$$

"Those who believe do battle for the cause of Allah; and those who disbelieve do battle for the cause of idols. So fight the friends of Satan. Lo! Satan's strategy is ever weak" (*al-Nisaa* 76).

And he always tries to put the fear of his patrons into the believers.

$$إِنَّمَا ذَٰلِكُمُ ٱلشَّيْطَٰنُ يُخَوِّفُ أَوْلِيَآءَهُۥ فَلَا تَخَافُوهُمْ وَخَافُونِ إِن كُنتُم مُّؤْمِنِينَ$$

"It is only Satan who would make (men) fear his allies. Fear them not; fear Me, if you are truly believers" (*ali-Imraan* 175). And his patrons and supporters are large in number,

$$وَلَقَدْ صَدَّقَ عَلَيْهِمْ إِبْلِيسُ ظَنَّهُ فَٱتَّبَعُوهُ إِلَّا فَرِيقًا مِّنَ ٱلْمُؤْمِنِينَ$$

"And Satan indeed found his calculation true concerning them [humans], for they follow him, all save a group of true believers" (*Saba* 20).

## The ways of Satan in leading humans astray

Satan does not come to the human and say, "Leave this good deed and do this evil deed in order to make your life in this world and the next a miserable one." If he behaved in that manner no one would follow him. Instead, he uses many ways to deceive the slaves of Allah, including:

### (1) Making evil look good

This is the way that Satan used and still uses to mislead mankind. He makes the false appear in the form of truth. And he makes what is true appear like falsehood. He will always try to make humans like falsehood and dislike truth until the human is pushed to doing evil deeds and turning away from the truth. As Satan himself to the Lord,

$$قَالَ رَبِّ بِمَا أَغْوَيْتَنِي لَأُزَيِّنَنَّ لَهُمْ فِي ٱلْأَرْضِ وَلَأُغْوِيَنَّهُمْ أَجْمَعِينَ ۝ إِلَّا عِبَادَكَ مِنْهُمُ ٱلْمُخْلَصِينَ$$

"He said: My Lord! Because you have sent me astray, I verily shall adorn the path of error for them in the earth, and shall mislead every one of them, save such of them as are Your perfectly devoted slaves" (*al-Hijr* 39-40).

On this point, ibn al-Qayyim wrote[1],

> From his stratagem is that he always bewitches the mind until he can deceive the person. No one is safe from his bewitching except whomsoever Allah wills. He makes good looking to him what harms him the most, until he imagines that it is the most beneficial act for himself. And he makes him flee from the most beneficial act until he thinks it is something harmful to him. Certainly, there is no god but Allah. How many humans have been tested by such sorcery. How many hearts have been kept from Islam, faith and goodness [by such sorcery]. And how many support and present falsehood in the best form and hate truth and present it in the worst form [because of his deception]. And how much falseness is adored and shown in a desirous manner to the alert. And how much falseness is spread even among the wise. He is the one who bewitches the mind until it follows different desires and various evil opinions. He makes them follow every path of misguidance. He leads them to actions, one after another, that cause their destruction. He makes appealing to them the worship of idols, the breaking of familial relations, the killing of daughters, marrying one's mother and so on. And he promises them the victory of paradise with their infidelity, wickedness and acts of disobedience. He presents to them polytheism in the most honorable fashion. And he presents rejection of Allah's attributes, of His transcendence and of His speech in the guise of anti-anthropomorphism of Allah. He presents abandoning ordering good and eradicating evil in the guise of having

---

[1] *Ighaatha al-Luhfaan*, vol. 1, p. 130.

mercy for others, behaving with others in a good manner, and applying the verse, "O believers, you are in charge of your own souls" (*al-Maaidah* 105). And he presents turning away from what has come from the Messenger in the guise of blindly following the Imams (*taqleed*) and the sufficiency of following one who is more knowledgeable. And he presents hypocrisy and compromising with respect to Allah's religion in the guise of being flexible and mixing admirably with the people.

In that way, the cursed Iblees plotted against Adam as he made the eating from the tree look like a good and beneficial act for Adam although Allah had prohibited that for him. Satan continually told Adam that it was the tree of eternity and that if he ate from it he would be able to live forever in paradise or become like one of the angels. He continued this deception until Adam finally ate from it and was, therefore, expelled from paradise.

We can look at the allies of Satan today to see how they use this same method to mislead the slaves of Allah. For example, the socialists and communists are calling people to their ideologies and claiming that their ideologies will put an end to confusion, perturbation, waste, hunger and so on. Similar they call women to come out of their houses, dressed but naked, in the name of freedom. And they call people to illicit movies and plays that insult honor and dignity and involve people in forbidden things, all in the name of art. It is this poisonous way of thinking that leads people to put their money in the banks and to take the interest from such money in the name of progress and profit. These people call being religious "backwardness", "old fashioned" and "being behind". And they call Muslim preachers crazy and agents of the East and West.

All of that is part of this strategy of Satan since the time of Adam. He makes the falsehood look beautiful and correct and distorts the truth to the point that people hate it.

تَٱللَّهِ لَقَدْ أَرْسَلْنَآ إِلَىٰٓ أُمَمٍ مِّن قَبْلِكَ فَزَيَّنَ لَهُمُ ٱلشَّيْطَٰنُ أَعْمَٰلَهُمْ

"By Allah, We verily sent messengers unto the nations before you, but the devil made their deeds fair-seeming unto them" (*al-Nahl* 63).

This is a very serious threat to mankind. If a human sees falsehood as true and right, he then strives with all of his might to enforce that "truth" even though it may only lead to his destruction.

$$\text{قُلْ هَلْ نُنَبِّئُكُم بِٱلْأَخْسَرِينَ أَعْمَٰلًا ۝ ٱلَّذِينَ ضَلَّ سَعْيُهُمْ فِى ٱلْحَيَوٰةِ ٱلدُّنْيَا وَهُمْ يَحْسَبُونَ أَنَّهُمْ يُحْسِنُونَ صُنْعًا}$$

"Say: Shall We inform you who will be the greatest losers by their works? Those whose effort goes astray in the life of the world, and yet they reckon that they do good work" (*al-Kahf* 103-104).

Such people do their best to prevent the others from the religion of Allah and they fight against the servants of Allah. They actually believe that they are following the truth and are rightly guided!

$$\text{وَإِنَّهُمْ لَيَصُدُّونَهُمْ عَنِ ٱلسَّبِيلِ وَيَحْسَبُونَ أَنَّهُم مُّهْتَدُونَ}$$

"And Lo! They surely turn them from the way of Allah, and yet they deem that they are rightly guided" (*al-Zukhruf* 37).

This deception is the reason that the unbelievers concern themselves only with this life and turn away from working for the hereafter. Allah says,

$$\text{۞ وَقَيَّضْنَا لَهُمْ قُرَنَآءَ فَزَيَّنُوا۟ لَهُم مَّا بَيْنَ أَيْدِيهِمْ وَمَا خَلْفَهُمْ}$$

"And We assigned them comrades (in the world), who made their present and their past fair-seeming unto them" (*Fusilat* 25). The comrades are the devils. They make what is in front of them of this world very alluring so they are overcome by it. And they call them to deny the life of the hereafter. Satan makes that seem so pleasing and correct to them that they reject the notions of resurrection, accountability, paradise and hell.

## Giving pleasing names to forbidden things

Among the deceptions of Satan is that he names the evil actions with names that are very pleasing to the human to entice him to take part in them. In this way, he dupes the human and makes a forgery of the reality of the situation. For example, Satan called the tree that was forbidden to Adam, "the tree of everlasting life" in order to make it appealing to Adam:

فَوَسْوَسَ إِلَيْهِ ٱلشَّيْطَٰنُ قَالَ يَٰٓـَٔادَمُ هَلْ أَدُلُّكَ عَلَىٰ شَجَرَةِ ٱلْخُلْدِ وَمُلْكٍ لَّا يَبْلَىٰ

"[But Satan whispered to him, saying,[1]] 'Oh Adam, shall I show you the tree of immortality and power that wastes not away?'" (*Taha* 120).

Ibn al-Qayyim stated, "From Satan, his followers inherited this trait of using names that are loved by the soul for forbidden objects. For example, wine is called 'the mother of glee,' interest is called a 'business transaction,' and taxes and tolls are called 'the right of the government.'"

Today interest is referred to as profit; dancing, music and plays are called art.

## (2) Going to extremes

Ibn al-Qayyim beautifully elaborated this point when he wrote,

Allah never orders anything except that Satan takes two contradictory stances towards it: either shortcoming and

---

[1] These words form part of the verse but al-Ashqar excluded them from the original work.—JZ

negligence or overzealousness and exaggeration. It does not matter [to him] by which of these two mistakes he becomes victorious over the slave. He comes to the heart of the slave and examines it. If he finds in it listlessness and looking for loopholes, he deals with him from that vantage. He impedes him and makes him sit. He strikes him with laziness, listlessness and lethargy. He opens for him the door to reinterpretations (*taweel*), hopes and so forth until the slave may not fulfill anything of what he is commanded.

If he finds in the slave's heart alertness, seriousness, desire to work and potential, Satan despairs from attacking him through the above means. Instead, he orders him to strive even harder. He convinces him that what he is doing is not sufficient for him. His ambition is to be greater than that. He must work more than the other workers. He should not sleep when they sleep. He should not break his fast when they break their fasts. He should not rest when they rest. If one of them washes his hands and face three times, he should was them seven times. If one makes *wudhu* for prayer, he must make *ghusl*. [He orders him to] similar other acts of exaggeration and extremism. He makes him go to extremes and beyond the limits. He makes him stray from the straight path in the same way that he makes the first person [described above] fall short of the straight path and not approach it. Satan's intention for both is to keep them from the straight path: the first by making him not come close or near to it and the second by making him pass it and go beyond it. Many of creation are misled by these two strategies. There is no escape from them except deep knowledge, faith and the strength to fight Satan and stay along the middle path.[1]

---

[1] ibn al-Qayyim, *al-Waabil al-Sayib*, p. 19.

## (3) Satan hinders the slave from acting by means of procrastination and laziness

Concerning this point, Satan has many ways and means. It is recorded in *Sahih al-Bukhari* that the Prophet (peace be upon him) said,

يَعْقِدُ الشَّيْطَانُ عَلَى قَافِيَةِ رَأْسِ أَحَدِكُمْ إِذَا هُوَ نَامَ ثَلَاثَ عُقَدٍ يَضْرِبُ كُلَّ عُقْدَةٍ عَلَيْكَ لَيْلٌ طَوِيلٌ فَارْقُدْ فَإِنِ اسْتَيْقَظَ فَذَكَرَ اللَّهَ انْحَلَّتْ عُقْدَةٌ فَإِنْ تَوَضَّأَ انْحَلَّتْ عُقْدَةٌ فَإِنْ صَلَّى انْحَلَّتْ عُقْدَةٌ فَأَصْبَحَ نَشِيطًا طَيِّبَ النَّفْسِ وَإِلَّا أَصْبَحَ خَبِيثَ النَّفْسِ كَسْلَانَ

"During your sleep, Satan ties three knots at the back of your necks. He breathes the following into them, 'The night is long so keep on sleeping.' If the person wakes and praises Allah, then one of the knots is unfastened. And if he performs ablution, the second knot is unfastened. When he prays, all of the knots are unfastened. After that he will be energetic and happy in the morning. Otherwise he would get up listless and grouchy."

It is also recorded in *Sahih al-Bukhari* and *Sahih Muslim* that he said,

إِذَا اسْتَيْقَظَ أَحَدُكُمْ مِنْ مَنَامِهِ فَلْيَسْتَنْثِرْ ثَلَاثَ مَرَّاتٍ فَإِنَّ الشَّيْطَانَ يَبِيتُ عَلَى خَيَاشِيمِهِ

"When one of you rises from your sleep he should make ablution. He should rinse his nose three times. For Satan stays in the upper part of one's nose during the night."

Al-Bukhari also records that the Prophet (peace be upon him) was asked about a man who sleeps until the morning comes, that is, after the time of the dawn prayer. He said,

$$\text{ذَاكَ رَجُلٌ بَالَ الشَّيْطَانُ فِي أُذُنَيْهِ}$$

"That is a man whom Satan has urinated into his two ears."

What we have mentioned is from among the ways that Satan hinders the human from doing some actions. He also whispers into the human a love for laziness, postponing or procrastinating actions and thinking about what a long period of time one has for such and such action or work. Ibn al-Jauzi has written on this topic, stating,

> How many of the Jews or Christians have considered in their hearts love for Islam. But Iblees always hinders them. He says to them, "Do not be hasty. Look closer into the matter." And they postpone their conversion until they die as unbelievers. In the same way the one who is disobedient to Allah postpones his repentance. He sets his sights on his desires and he hopes he will repent later. But, as the poet said, "Do not rush to perform the sins you desire and think about the period of repentance beforehand." How many are determined to do something and then they postpone it. Perhaps a scholar is determined to return to his study. Satan says, "Rest for a while." Or a servant is alerted to the prayer at night and he says to him, "You have plenty of time." He will not stop making people love laziness and postponing of actions and he makes the person rely on hopes and dreams.

It is necessary for the energetic person to take matters into his own hand and act upon his energy. The energetic finds the time to do things and does not procrastinate and he turns away from just dreaming. The one who has a real fear of Allah does not feel safe of punishment.. The soul never stops in its dispute about evil and facing the good. But it always expects that it will have plenty of time to complete the good. One of the early scholars said, "Beware of procrastinating. It is the greatest of the soldiers of Satan." The serious, non-procrastinating person and the one who rests on his hopes and puts off working are like two who are passing through a city while journeying. The serious, energetic one buys his provisions early and waits for his traveling out of the city. The procrastinator says, "I will wait, as perhaps we will stay here a month," and continues to put off buying his provisions and preparing for his departure, until the last minute wherein he becomes rushed and mistake prone. This is how people are in this world. Some of them are prepared and alert. When the angel of death comes, he is not sorrowful. Others are deceived by thinking they can procrastinate and they will despair when the time to move on comes. It is part of one's nature to love laziness and dreams but then Iblees comes and builds upon that. This makes it difficult to struggle against him in that matter. But the one who is alert knows that he is in the middle of a battle. He knows that his enemy does not rest. And if it seems that he is resting, it is actually just part of his strategy...[1]

## (4) Promises and hopes

Satan makes false promises to humans and gives them sweet dreams in order to mislead them. Allah says,

$$يَعِدُهُمْ وَيُمَنِّيهِمْ وَمَا يَعِدُهُمُ ٱلشَّيْطَٰنُ إِلَّا غُرُورًا$$

"He promises them and stirs up desires in them, and Satan promises them only to beguile" (*al-Nisaa* 120).

In their battle against the believers, he promised the disbelievers aid, honor and victory. Then he fled from them and left them by themselves.

---

[1] Ibn al-Jauzi, *Talbees Iblees*, p. 458.

$$\text{وَإِذْ زَيَّنَ لَهُمُ ٱلشَّيْطَٰنُ أَعْمَٰلَهُمْ وَقَالَ لَا غَالِبَ لَكُمُ ٱلْيَوْمَ مِنَ ٱلنَّاسِ وَإِنِّى جَارٌ لَّكُمْ ۖ فَلَمَّا تَرَآءَتِ ٱلْفِئَتَانِ نَكَصَ عَلَىٰ عَقِبَيْهِ وَقَالَ إِنِّى بَرِىٓءٌ مِّنكُمْ}$$

"And when Satan made their deeds seem fair to them and said: No one of mankind can conquer you this day, for I am your protector. But when the armies came in sight of one another, he took flight, saying, 'Lo! I am innocent of you.'" (al-Anfaal 48).

He also promises the wealthy among the unbelievers more wealth and possessions in the life after this one. One of them said,

$$\text{وَمَآ أَظُنُّ ٱلسَّاعَةَ قَآئِمَةً وَلَئِن رُّدِدتُّ إِلَىٰ رَبِّى لَأَجِدَنَّ خَيْرًا مِّنْهَا مُنقَلَبًا}$$

"I think not that the Hour will ever come, and if indeed I am brought back unto my Lord I surely shall find better than this as a resort" (al-Kahf 36). Allah destroyed his garden in this life and he realized that he had been deceived.

The human becomes busy with sweet dreams concerning which there is no possibility of fulfillment in this life. Therefore, he does not take part in the beneficial and fruitful deeds. Instead, he becomes pleased with dreaming and hoping, and he does nothing.

## (5) Satan appears as a sincere advisor to humans

Satan calls man to disobedience of Allah and he alleges that he is giving him sincere advice and he only desires the best for him. He swore to Adam that he was only giving him sincere advice:

$$\text{وَقَاسَمَهُمَآ إِنِّى لَكُمَا لَمِنَ ٱلنَّٰصِحِينَ}$$

"And he swore unto them (saying): Lo! I am a sincere adviser unto you" (*al-Araaf* 21).

Wahb ibn Munabbih has related the following lengthy story from the people of the book.[1] We present it here to show the way of Satan in his attempt to mislead mankind. The story warns humans about Satan's "sincere advice". One must oppose the thing that Satan is calling to.

Wahb said,

> There was a pious worshipper of the tribe of Israel. He was the most pious person of his time. During his time, there were three brothers who had a sister. She was a virgin. And they had no sister other than her. They were all about to leave the town to go to war. They did not know with whom to leave their sister and who they could trust to look after her. They all agreed to leave her with that pious person. They all trusted him. They went to him and asked if they could leave her with him. She would be in the building next to him until they return from the fighting. He refused their request and sought refuge in Allah from them and their sister. They persisted until he finally acquiesced. He said, "Put her in the house next to my place of worship." So they put her in that house and they left, leaving her there. She remained living next to that pious person for some time. He would put food for her in front of his building of worship. Then he would lock the door and return to his place of worship. He would then tell her to come out of her house and take the food. Then Satan approached him softly. He encouraged him to treat her kindly. He told him that it was not good to make the woman come out of her house during the day as

---

[1] This story, and others similar to it, are from the *Israaeeliyaat* or stories which have their source in the books or tales of the Jews and Christians. We do not say it is true nor do we say it is false, but it is allowed to narrate them as the Prophet (peace be upon him) said, "Narrate stories about the Tribe of Israel and there is no harm in that."

someone may come upon her. If he took the food directly to her door that would mean a greater reward for him.

He continued for some time to go to her door and place the food at the front of her door without speaking to her. Then Iblees came again and encouraged him to do good and get more reward. He said, "If you took her the food and placed it in the house for her, you would get a greater reward." He continued to encourage him. So he started to take the food into her house. He continued like that for some time.

Then Iblees came again and again encouraged him to do good. He said, "If you talk to her for a while she will be put to ease by your conversation as she is in a state of fear and she is all alone." He then started talking to her from atop his place of worship.

Then Iblees came again. He said, "If you were to come down and talk to her while she sits at her door and talks to you, that would be even more comforting for her." He continued to encourage him until he came down and sat at his door and would talk to her. The girl would come out of her building and sit at her door and they would talk for a while.

Then Iblees came again and encouraged him to get great rewards for treating her well. He said, "If you were to go from the door of your place of worship and sit close to her door, that would be even more comforting for her." He continued exhorting him until he did so. He continued that act for a while. Then Iblees came again. This time he said, "If you enter her house and talk to her, and not make her show her face in public it would be even better for you." He continued exhorting him until he entered her house and spent the whole day talking to her. Then when night fell, he returned to his place of worship.

Then Iblees came to him after that and continued to make her more appealing to him. Until the worshipper got upon her and kissed her. And Iblees continued to make her look nice in his eyes and desire her until he finally had sex with her. She got pregnant and gave birth to a boy. Then Iblees came and told the worshipper, "Do you not realize what the brothers of the girl will do to you when they see she has given birth to your son? You will not be safe if your matter becomes clear. You should go to the boy and kill it and bury it, that way you can conceal your affair and they will not do anything to you for what you did to her." Then he said to him, "Do you think she will conceal from her brothers what you did to her and your killing of her son. Take her, kill her and bury her with her son." He continued spurring him on until he killed her and threw her in the ditch with her son. Then he put a large rock over them and leveled it. Then he returned to his place of worship and worshipped therein. He stayed in that state for as long as Allah willed until the brothers came back from the fighting. They came to him and asked him about their sister. He mourned her loss and started to cry. He said, "She was the best of women and that is her grave." The brothers came to the grave and cried over their sister and asked Allah to have mercy on her. They stayed at her grave for a few days and then went to their families. When the night overtook them and they went to their beds, Satan came to them in their sleep in the form of a traveler. He started with the eldest and asked him about their sister. The brother told him what the pious man had stated and how they were shown her grave. Satan told him that the pious man had lied. He said, "He did not tell you the truth about your sister. He got her pregnant and she had his son and then he killed and buried her out of fear of you. Then he threw them in a ditch he dug behind the door of the house she was staying in, to the right of the entrance. Go and enter the house in which she stayed and on the right of the entrance you will find everything I told you about." Then he went to the middle brother and did the same. Then he went to the youngest brother and did the same. When they woke, they were all surprised at what they had seen. When they met each other, they all said, "I saw an amazing thing last night," and they informed each other of what they had seen.

The eldest said, "That dream has nothing to it so just ignore it." The youngest said, "I will not leave it until I go and look at that place." They all went until they reached the door of the place where there sister stayed. They opened the door and looked for the place that was described to them in their dreams. They found their sister and her son buried in a ditch, as they were told. They asked the worshipper about it and he confirmed what Iblees had told them. They then took him and were about to crucify him. When they had him on the wooden cross, Satan said to him, "You know that I am your companion who tempted you by the woman until you got her pregnant and you killed her and her son. If you obey me today and deny Allah, who formed and shaped you, I will rescue you from your predicament." The worshipper then belied Allah. When he belied Allah, Satan left from being between him and the others and they were able to crucify him.[1]

Many scholars related this story in their commentary to the following verse,

---

[1] Qoted in ibn al-Jauzi, *Talbees Iblees*, p. 39.

$$\text{كَمَثَلِ ٱلشَّيْطَانِ إِذْ قَالَ لِلْإِنسَانِ ٱكْفُرْ فَلَمَّا كَفَرَ قَالَ إِنِّي بَرِيٓءٌ مِّنكَ}$$

"Or the likeness of Satan when he tells man to disbelieve, then, when he disbelieves, says to him, 'Lo! I am innocent of you. Lo! I fear Allah, the Lord of the Worlds'" (*al-Hashr* 16). They mention that this verse refers to this worshipper and to others similar to him. Allah knows best.

## (6) He uses a step-by-step approach to misguide mankind

From the previous story we can note one of the methods that Satan uses to mislead mankind. He takes the human step by step, not all at one time, to misguidance. He neither over does it nor does he bore the person. Every time the person is pleased by a step, he takes the human to a greater act of disobedience. This continues until he can take him to the greatest sin and the person's destruction. This is Allah's pattern with respect to His slaves. If they deviate from Allah's path, He allows Satan to gain control over them.

$$\text{فَلَمَّا زَاغُوٓا۟ أَزَاغَ ٱللَّهُ قُلُوبَهُمْ}$$

"So when they went astray, Allah sent their hearts astray" (*al-Saff* 5).

## (7) The slave of Allah is made to forget what is good and best for him

Satan whispered to Adam until he forgot what Allah had commanded him.

$$\text{وَلَقَدْ عَهِدْنَا إِلَىٰ ءَادَمَ مِن قَبْلُ فَنَسِىَ وَلَمْ نَجِدْ لَهُ عَزْمًا}$$

"And verily We made a covenant of old with Adam, but he forgot, and We found no constancy in him" (*Taha* 115). And the companion of Moses said to him,

$$\text{فَإِنِّى نَسِيتُ ٱلْحُوتَ وَمَا أَنسَىٰنِيهُ إِلَّا ٱلشَّيْطَٰنُ أَنْ أَذْكُرَهُ}$$

"I forgot the fish— and none but Satan caused me to forget to mention it" (*al-Kahf* 63).

Allah prohibited His messenger and his Companions from sitting in any meeting in which mockery was being made of the signs of Allah but Satan makes humans forget what their Lord wants from them and they sit with those people who mock the religion.

$$\text{وَإِذَا رَأَيْتَ ٱلَّذِينَ يَخُوضُونَ فِىٓ ءَايَٰتِنَا فَأَعْرِضْ عَنْهُمْ حَتَّىٰ يَخُوضُوا۟ فِى حَدِيثٍ غَيْرِهِۦ وَإِمَّا يُنسِيَنَّكَ ٱلشَّيْطَٰنُ فَلَا تَقْعُدْ بَعْدَ ٱلذِّكْرَىٰ مَعَ ٱلْقَوْمِ ٱلظَّٰلِمِينَ}$$

"And when you see those who meddle with Our revelations, withdraw from them until they meddle with another topic. And if Satan causes you to forget, sit not, after the remembrance, with the congregation of wrongdoers" (*al-Anaam* 68).

When the Prophet Joseph was in the prison he told his companion, whom Joseph knew would be released from prison, to mention his case to the ruler. But Satan made the other forget and, therefore, Joseph stayed in the prison for a number of years.

$$\text{وَقَالَ لِلَّذِى ظَنَّ أَنَّهُ نَاجٍ مِنْهُمَا اذْكُرْنِى عِندَ رَبِّكَ فَأَنسَىٰهُ ٱلشَّيْطَٰنُ ذِكْرَ رَبِّهِۦ فَلَبِثَ فِى ٱلسِّجْنِ بِضْعَ سِنِينَ}$$

"And he said unto him of the two who he knew would be released: Mention me in the presence of your lord. But Satan caused him to forget to mention it to his lord, so he (Joseph) stayed in prison for some years" (*Yusuf* 42).

If Satan gains complete control over the human, he will make the human forget Allah completely.

$$\text{ٱسْتَحْوَذَ عَلَيْهِمُ ٱلشَّيْطَٰنُ فَأَنسَىٰهُمْ ذِكْرَ ٱللَّهِ أُوْلَٰٓئِكَ حِزْبُ ٱلشَّيْطَٰنِ أَلَآ إِنَّ حِزْبَ ٱلشَّيْطَٰنِ هُمُ ٱلْخَٰسِرُونَ}$$

"Satan has engrossed them and so he has caused them to forget the remembrance of Allah. They are the devil's party. Lo! is it not the devil's party who will be the losers?" (*al-Mujaadala* 19). This verse is referring to the hypocrites, as is clear from the verses that precede it. The way to remember is by the remembrance of Allah which repels Satan:

$$\text{وَٱذْكُر رَّبَّكَ إِذَا نَسِيتَ}$$

"And remember your Lord when you forget" (*al-Kahf* 24).

## (8) Making the believers fear his supporters

Included among his means is causing the believers to fear his supporters and soldiers. The believer finds himself not fighting against them, not ordering them to do good and not ordering them to abstain from evil [due to some fear that he possesses of them]. This is one of his greatest plots against faith. Allah has told us about that in His statement,

$$\text{إِنَّمَا ذَٰلِكُمُ ٱلشَّيْطَٰنُ يُخَوِّفُ أَوْلِيَآءَهُۥ فَلَا تَخَافُوهُمْ وَخَافُونِ إِن كُنتُم مُّؤْمِنِينَ}$$

"It is the devil who would make (men) fear his allies. Fear them not; fear Me, if you are truly believers" (*ali-Imraan* 175). In other words, he is feared by way of his patrons. Qataada said, "Their status is raised in the hearts of men. For that reason Allah said do not fear them but fear Me if you are truly believers. Whenever the faith of anyone is increased, the fear of the allies of Satan is removed from his heart. Whenever the faith of a person decreases, his fear of Satan's supporters increases."

## (9) He gets to the person through what the person loves or desires

On this topic, ibn al-Qayyim wrote,

Satan flows in humans like blood to the point that he meets with the human's soul and mixes with it. He asks it what it loves and what affects it. When he gets that knowledge, he uses it against the person. He gets to him through those means. Similarly, he informs his brothers and devotees. Among humans, when they desire their evil from each other, they get to each other through what they love and desire. For the one who enters through this door, it is a gate through which he will never be dissatisfied. If someone attempts to get to him through other means, the door will be closed to him. And he will be on a path that is closed in front of him.[1]

From this way Satan was able to approach Adam and Eve in paradise. As Allah says,

$$وَقَالَ مَا نَهَىٰكُمَا رَبُّكُمَا عَنْ هَـٰذِهِ ٱلشَّجَرَةِ إِلَّا أَن تَكُونَا مَلَكَيْنِ أَوْ تَكُونَا مِنَ ٱلْخَـٰلِدِينَ$$

"He said: Your Lord forbade you from this tree only lest you should become angels or become of the immortals" (*al-Araaf* 20). Ibn al-Qayyim stated, "The enemy of Allah examined the two parents [Adam and Eve]. He sensed from them that they were inclined to and pleased with staying forever in the world of bounties. He knew that this would be the only way he could get to them. He swore by Allah to them that he was a sincere well-wisher for them. And he told them, 'Your Lord forbade you from this tree only lest you should become angels or become of the immortals' (*al-Araaf* 20)."

## (10) Casting doubts in the person's mind

Part of the plan of Satan to mislead mankind is to shake their faith by confusing humans with doubts and suspicions. The Prophet (peace be upon him) warned us about some of those doubts. In *Sahih al-Bukhari* and *Sahih Muslim* it is recorded on the authority of Abu Huraira that the Prophet (peace be upon him) said,

$$مَنْ خَلَقَ كَذَا مَنْ خَلَقَ كَذَا حَتَّى يَقُولَ مَنْ خَلَقَ رَبَّكَ فَإِذَا بَلَغَهُ فَلْيَسْتَعِذْ بِاللَّهِ وَلْيَنْتَهِ$$

---

[1] Ibn al-Qayyim, *Ighaatha al-Luhfaan*, vol. 1, p. 132.

"Satan comes to you and says, 'Who created such and such?' repeatedly, until he asks, 'Who created your Lord?' So when he inspires such a thought, one should seek refuge in Allah and turn away from such thoughts."

Even the Companions of the Prophet were not safe from such thoughts occurring to them. Some of them went to the Prophet (peace be upon him) to complain about the notions that kept creeping into their minds. In *Sahih Muslim* it is recorded on the authority of Abu Huraira that some people came to the Prophet and said, "We find in our mind great things that we cannot dare talk about!" He asked them, "Does it really occur to you?" They said, "Yes." And the Prophet (peace be upon him) said, "This is the clear faith." He meant by that latter statement that to reject and dislike such thoughts and whispers from Satan and to consider such thoughts a grave matter is part of the clear and true faith.

We can see how hard this was on the Companions of the Prophet (peace be upon him). Abu Dawud records in his *Sunan* on the authority of ibn Abbas that a man came to the Prophet (peace be upon him) and said, "My soul says something to me concerning which I would rather be turned to ashes rather than convey it to others." The Prophet (peace be upon him) said,

الحمد لله الذي رد أمره إلى الوسوسة

"All praise is due to Allah who rejects the orders of the whisperer."[1] Allah has informed us about such occurrences, in general, with His statement,

---

[1] Recorded by Abu Dawud. According to a-Albani, it is *sahih*. See Muhammad Nasir al-Din al-Albani, *Sahih Sunan Abi Dawud* (Riyadh: Maktab al-Tarbiyyah al-Arabi li-Duwal al-Khaleej, 1989), vol. 3, pp. 962-963.—JZ

وَمَا أَرْسَلْنَا مِن قَبْلِكَ مِن رَّسُولٍ وَلَا نَبِيٍّ إِلَّا إِذَا تَمَنَّىٰ أَلْقَى ٱلشَّيْطَٰنُ فِىٓ أُمْنِيَّتِهِۦ فَيَنسَخُ ٱللَّهُ مَا يُلْقِى ٱلشَّيْطَٰنُ ثُمَّ يُحْكِمُ ٱللَّهُ ءَايَٰتِهِۦ ۗ وَٱللَّهُ عَلِيمٌ حَكِيمٌ ۝ لِّيَجْعَلَ مَا يُلْقِى ٱلشَّيْطَٰنُ فِتْنَةً لِّلَّذِينَ فِى قُلُوبِهِم مَّرَضٌ وَٱلْقَاسِيَةِ قُلُوبُهُمْ ۗ وَإِنَّ ٱلظَّٰلِمِينَ لَفِى شِقَاقٍۭ بَعِيدٍ ۝ وَلِيَعْلَمَ ٱلَّذِينَ أُوتُوا۟ ٱلْعِلْمَ أَنَّهُ ٱلْحَقُّ مِن رَّبِّكَ فَيُؤْمِنُوا۟ بِهِۦ فَتُخْبِتَ لَهُۥ قُلُوبُهُمْ ۗ وَإِنَّ ٱللَّهَ لَهَادِ ٱلَّذِينَ ءَامَنُوٓا۟ إِلَىٰ صِرَٰطٍ مُّسْتَقِيمٍ

"Never sent We a messenger or a Prophet before you but when he recited (the message), Satan attempted to throw some falsehood into it. But Allah abolishes that which Satan proposes. Allah is Knower, Wise. That He may make that which Satan proposes a temptation for those in whose hearts is a disease, and those whose hearts are hardened— Lo! the evildoers are in open schism. And that those who have been given knowledge may know that it is the truth from your Lord, so that they may believe therein and their hearts may submit humbly unto Him. Lo! Allah verily is guiding those who believe unto a right path" (*al-Hajj* 52-54).

What is meant in the above verse is the thought within one's own soul. This means that Satan tried to use a stratagem of whispering to the Prophet some thoughts, for example, if you ask Allah for more war bounties it would be sufficient for the Muslims, or asking Allah for all the people to embrace Islam and so on. But Allah wiped out whatever Satan tried to whisper to the Prophet (peace be upon him) and He alerted him to the truth and only the truth. Those who say that the meaning of the verse is that Satan entered some things into the Quran have strayed far from the correct position. The Messenger of Allah (peace be upon him) has been protected by Allah from making any sin or mistake in propagating and teaching the message.

Shaqeeq, a well-known scholar, was clarifying the doubts that Satan creates in the soul of the person. He said, "No morning occurs except that it finds Satan setting an ambush for me in four places: in front of me, behind me, on my left and on my right. He says, 'Do not fear for Allah is the Forgiving, the Merciful!' So I read to him, 'And lo! verily I am Forgiving toward him who repents and believes and does good, and afterward walks aright' (*Taha* 82). Those behind me try to frustrate me by making me think that I will not sustain those whom I leave behind. I read to them, 'And there is not a beast in the earth but the sustenance thereof depends on Allah' (*Hood* 6). And from the right they approach me in the form of women and I read, 'And lo! the sequel is for those who keep their duty to Allah' (*al-Araaf* 128). And from the left they approach me in the form of desires. I read to those, 'And a gulf is set between them and that which they desire' (*Saba* 54)."

## (11-14) Alcohol, games of chance, idols and divining arrows

Allah says in the Quran,

$$\text{إِنَّمَا ٱلْخَمْرُ وَٱلْمَيْسِرُ وَٱلْأَنصَابُ وَٱلْأَزْلَٰمُ رِجْسٌ مِّنْ عَمَلِ ٱلشَّيْطَٰنِ فَٱجْتَنِبُوهُ لَعَلَّكُمْ تُفْلِحُونَ ۞ إِنَّمَا يُرِيدُ ٱلشَّيْطَٰنُ أَن يُوقِعَ بَيْنَكُمُ ٱلْعَدَاوَةَ وَٱلْبَغْضَاءَ فِى ٱلْخَمْرِ وَٱلْمَيْسِرِ وَيَصُدَّكُمْ عَن ذِكْرِ ٱللَّهِ وَعَنِ ٱلصَّلَوٰةِ ۖ فَهَلْ أَنتُم مُّنتَهُونَ}$$

"O you who believe, strong drink and games of chance and idols and divining arrows are only an infamy of Satan's handiwork. Leave it aside in order that you may succeed. Satan seeks only to cast among you enmity and hatred by means of strong drink and games of chance, and to turn you from the remembrance of Allah and from (His) worship" (*al-Maaida* 90-91). "Strong drink" is anything that intoxicates. "Games of chance" refers to gambling. "Idols" are anything that are worshipped besides Allah, such as stones, trees, statues, graves, and so on. "Divining arrows" were objects used to determine what course of action should be followed. They could be spears, arrows, pebbles or whatever. On one of the arrows they would have written, "My Lord orders this to be done," while another may say, "My Lord orders that you do not do such an action." If someone wanted to marry or travel, he would reach and grab one of the arrows. If it said to do the act, he would do it; otherwise, he would leave the act.

Satan persuades humans to do these four evil acts because they are types of misguidance in themselves. They intermingle with and become part and parcel of the person's character and lead to evil results. They all leave an evil effect on the person. For example, alcohol makes the person lose his senses. When he loses his senses, he does forbidden acts and he leaves the obedience to Allah and he harms other Muslims. Ibn Katheer, in his commentary to the Quran, quotes the following statement from Uthman ibn Affan, "Stay away from alcohol as it is the mother of all evils. There was a man in previous times who separated from his people in order to worship Allah. A coveting woman was after him. She sent her slave girl to him to ask him to come and be a witness. When he came, every time he entered a room, the door was locked behind him. Until he came to a room in which there was a woman with a small boy and a casket of wine. She said, 'By Allah, I did not call you here to bear witness but I called you here to have intercourse with me, or to kill this boy or to drink this alcohol.' He took a glass and drank it. Afterwards, he said, 'Give me more.' And he did not finish until he had intercourse with her and had killed the boy. Verily that (alcohol) and faith can never combine in a person except that one of them will soon leave the person." (Al-Baihaqi recorded it and ibn Katheer said its chain is *sahih*.)

Muslim[1] and the authors of the *Sunan* works record that one of the Ansaar made a dinner for some of the Companions. He gave them some alcohol to drink [since] it was before its prohibition. When they got drunk, they began to boast. They then fought. Saad ibn Abu Waqqas was injured in the fighting. He was stuck with a camel's jawbone and scarred for the rest of his life. And one of the Companions stood to lead the others in prayer while he was drunk, before the prohibition of alcohol, and he read, "Say: O unbelievers, I worship that which you worship" [instead of "I worship not that which you worship"]. Therefore, Allah revealed, "Oh you who believe, draw not near to prayer when you are drunken, until you know that which you utter" ( *al-Nisaa* 43).

We have seen elderly respectable people being turned into such crazy fools by alcohol that the young and old alike have to laugh at their behavior.

Gambling is also a serious disease like alcohol. If one gets involved in it, it becomes very difficult to free one's self from it. It is a way of wasting time and wealth, it harbors feelings of hatred and pushes the person to forbidden acts.

Satan encourages the building of altars, statues and tombs in order for them to be later taken as objects of worship other than Allah. The worship of statues and idols has been widespread in the past and is currently still widespread. Devils always accompany such statues. Sometimes, they address the worshippers. They sometimes show them things that make the worshippers more convinced [of the correctness of their worship]. The worshippers come to them with their needs. They pray to them during times of hardship. They seek their aid during wars. They present offerings and sacrifices to them. They dance and chant around them. They have festivals and holidays at their sites. Many

---

[1] Al-Ashqar mentions that the following hadith is to be found in *Sahih Muslim* but this translator has never found it in any of the published editions of *Sahih Muslim* nor has he seen any other authority ascribe it to *Sahih Muslim*. The above hadith was recorded by al-Tirmidhi; and Abu Dawud has something very similar to it. According to al-Albani, it is *sahih*. See Muhammad Nasir al-Din al-Albani, *Sahih Sunan al-Tirmidhi* (Riyadh: Maktab al-Tarbiyyah al-Arabi li-Duwal al-Khaleej, 1988), vol. 3, p. 39. Allah knows best.—JZ

people are misled by such acts, as is clear in the prayer of Ibrahim to his Lord,

$$وَٱجْنُبْنِي وَبَنِيَّ أَن نَّعْبُدَ ٱلْأَصْنَامَ ۝ رَبِّ إِنَّهُنَّ أَضْلَلْنَ كَثِيرًا مِّنَ ٱلنَّاسِ$$

"[My Lord,] keep me and my sons from serving idols. My Lord, lo, they have led many of mankind astray" (*Ibraheem* 35-36). The worship of graves is still widespread among Muslims. They pray to those buried there, circumambulate their graves and make sacrifices to them. A new innovation has occurred today— that must make Satan laugh at humans— and this is what is called the "Tomb of the Unknown Soldier". They say it represents the soldier who was killed. They honor it with presents, flowers and respect. Every time a leader visits the country, he visits the tomb and gives it an offering. All of that is a kind of worship of idols that is of the deeds of Satan.

## Divining Arrows

The events of the future are kept hidden and are something that only Allah knows. For this reason the Prophet (peace be upon him) has instructed Muslims to pray *salat al-istikhaarah* and to pray to Allah for Him to guide them in the right manner for any traveling, marriage or any deed he plans to do in the future. We pray that Allah will guide us to the best action.

Attempting to know the future by such means as divining arrows is futile because arrows and spears do not know wherein lies good. Consulting them is a sign of a lack of intelligence. Similar to that is the one who takes a bird as an omen when he is about to embark on a trip. When he leaves his house and he sees the bird fly to the right, it is a good omen. If it flies to the left, it is taken as a bad omen. All of that is misguidance and delusion.

## (15) Magic

From the things that Satan uses to mislead mankind is magic. The devils teach this knowledge that contains no benefit but only harm. This knowledge can be used to separate a man from his wife. This is one of the most favored deeds to Satan, as was described earlier in a hadith.

Allah says,

$$\text{وَمَا كَفَرَ سُلَيْمَٰنُ وَلَٰكِنَّ ٱلشَّيَٰطِينَ كَفَرُوا۟ يُعَلِّمُونَ ٱلنَّاسَ ٱلسِّحْرَ وَمَآ أُنزِلَ عَلَى ٱلْمَلَكَيْنِ بِبَابِلَ هَٰرُوتَ وَمَٰرُوتَ وَمَا يُعَلِّمَانِ مِنْ أَحَدٍ حَتَّىٰ يَقُولَآ إِنَّمَا نَحْنُ فِتْنَةٌ فَلَا تَكْفُرْ فَيَتَعَلَّمُونَ مِنْهُمَا مَا يُفَرِّقُونَ بِهِۦ بَيْنَ ٱلْمَرْءِ وَزَوْجِهِۦ وَمَا هُم بِضَآرِّينَ بِهِۦ مِنْ أَحَدٍ إِلَّا بِإِذْنِ ٱللَّهِ وَيَتَعَلَّمُونَ مَا يَضُرُّهُمْ وَلَا يَنفَعُهُمْ وَلَقَدْ عَلِمُوا۟ لَمَنِ ٱشْتَرَىٰهُ مَا لَهُۥ فِى ٱلْأَخِرَةِ مِنْ خَلَٰقٍ وَلَبِئْسَ مَا شَرَوْا۟ بِهِۦٓ أَنفُسَهُمْ لَوْ كَانُوا۟ يَعْلَمُونَ}$$

"And they follow that which the devils falsely related against the kingdom of Solomon. Solomon disbelieved not; but the devils disbelieved, teaching mankind magic and that which was revealed to the two angels in Babel, Harut and Marut. Nor did they (the two angels) teach it to anyone till they had said: We are only a temptation, therefore disbelieve not (in the guidance of Allah). And from these two (angels) people learn that by which they cause division between man and wife; but they injure thereby none save by Allah's leave. And they learn that which harms them and profits them not. And surely they do know that he who traffics therein will have no portion in the Hereafter; and surely evil is the price for which they sell their souls, if they but knew" (*al-Baqara* 102).

## Is magic real?

There is a difference of opinion among the scholars on this point. Some say it is only a deception and is not real.

$$\text{قَالَ بَلْ أَلْقُوا۟ فَإِذَا حِبَالُهُمْ وَعِصِيُّهُمْ يُخَيَّلُ إِلَيْهِ مِن سِحْرِهِمْ أَنَّهَا تَسْعَىٰ}$$

"[Moses] said, 'No, you throw.' Then lo! their cords and their staves, by their magic, appeared to him as though they ran" (*Taha* 66). While others say it is real as the verse from *al-Baqara* above shows. In fact, magic is of two kinds: (a) a kind of illusion which is basically where "the hand is quicker than the eye," and (b) the true magic that can do actual harm and, for example, causes a man to separate from his wife.

## The spell of the Jew on the Prophet (peace be upon him)

Aisha narrated that magic was worked on the Prophet (peace be upon him) by a Jew from the tribe of Zuraiq. His name was Labeed ibn Al-Asam. The Prophet (peace be upon him) began to imagine that he did something while, in reality, he did not. One day he supplicated to Allah over and over and said, "I feel that Allah has shown me the cure to my problem. Two persons came to me in a dream and sat, one by my head and one by my feet. One asked, 'What is the problem with this man?' The other one answered, 'He is bewitched.' The other man asked then, 'Who has bewitched him?' The other answered, 'Labeed ibn al-Asam.' The man again asked, 'What did he use?' The other said, 'A comb with hair gathered on it and the outer skin of the pollen of a male date-palm.' The other man then asked, 'Where is it?' The other answered, "It is in a well of Dhi-Arwan.'" So the Prophet (peace be upon him) went to that well and returned and said to Aisha, "Its water was like yellow henna and its date-palms were like the heads of devils." She asked, "Did you take out those things that caused the spell?" He said, "No, because I have been cured by Allah and I feared that such an action would cause evil among the people. I only ordered the well to be filled." (This hadith was recorded by al-Bukhari and Muslim.)

This magic had no affect on him as a Prophet and Messenger as the affects of magic cannot go beyond his body and affect the heart or mind. But it was like all the other diseases that the Prophet (peace be upon him) was inflicted with and protected from. As for the Quran, sunnah or Islamic law in general, they are guarded from any distortion by Allah. Allah says,

إِنَّا نَحْنُ نَزَّلْنَا ٱلذِّكْرَ وَإِنَّا لَهُۥ لَحَٰفِظُونَ

"Lo! We, even We, reveal the Reminder, and lo! We are its Guardian" (*al-Hijr* 9).

## (16) Human weaknesses

Humans have many points of weakness. They are, in fact, types of diseases. Satan penetrates deeply into the weaknesses of the souls of humans. They are openings for Satan to affect humans. These weaknesses include, among many others, weakness, despair, discouragement, desperation, recklessness, being full of oneself, vanity, pride, disdain, anger, evil temperament, doubts, confusion, fear, haste, miserliness, greediness, ignorance, love of this live and wealth, heedlessness, oppression, arrogance, suspiciousness, miserliness, haughtiness and so on.

Islam asks the person to make his soul healthy and free of such diseases. This calls for struggle and patience. It calls for patience in the face of hardships on the road to Allah. Following the "lower desires" and what the soul which orders evil inclines to is a very easy path. The path to Allah is like that of one who is climbing to the top of a mountain. The path of the one who follows desires is like the path of the one descending a mountain. It is for this reason that many people respond to the call of Satan because they find his path very easy and the call of Allah difficult.

We shall relate some of what the early scholars have said about Satan and his use of these different weaknesses.

Al-Mutamar ibn Sulaiman related that his father said, "It has been mentioned to me that the whispering Satan appears in the heart of the human when he anguishes or rejoices. If one mentions Allah, then Satan will withdraw."[1] Wahb ibn Munabih reported that a monk once asked Satan, "What characteristic in man is the most helpful for you against him?" Satan said, "His irascibility. If a slave is irascible, then we can turn him around like a young child spins a ball around."[2] Ibn al-Jauzi records that ibn Umar related that the Prophet Noah asked Satan about what characteristic he uses to destroy people. He said, "Envy and covetousness." This is similar to what Satan did to the brothers of Joseph when he planted in them jealousy of their brother. Joseph said,

$$\text{وَقَدْ أَحْسَنَ بِي إِذْ أَخْرَجَنِي مِنَ ٱلسِّجْنِ وَجَآءَ بِكُم مِّنَ ٱلْبَدْوِ مِنۢ بَعْدِ أَن نَّزَغَ ٱلشَّيْطَٰنُ بَيْنِي وَبَيْنَ إِخْوَتِيٓ}$$

"He [Allah] was indeed good to me when He took me out of the prison and has brought you (i.e., his father) to me from the desert after Satan had made strife between me and my brothers" (*Yusuf* 100).

---

[1] *Tafseer ibn Katheer*, vol. 7, p. 423.
[2] *Talbees Iblees*, p. 42.

## (17) Women and the love of this world

The Prophet (peace be upon him) has informed us that he has not left men a greater trial than that of women. For this reason he ordered the women to cover all of their bodies save the face and palms, and men have been ordered to lower their gaze. He also prohibited men to be in privacy with women he is not related to. He said that if two such people were alone, then Satan made the third of them. An-Nasai records in his *Sunan*, with a *sahih* chain,

$$\text{الْمَرْأَةُ عَوْرَةُ فَإِذَا خَرَجَتِ اسْتَشْرَفَهَا الشَّيْطَانُ}$$

"The woman is to be concealed and when she goes out, Satan makes her look beautiful to the men who look at her."[1]

In these days we have witnessed this calamity as the majority of women are going out of their houses in exactly the manner that the Prophet (peace be upon him) had described to us: they will be dressed but naked at the same time. Companies in the East and West have been established to show men and women undressed and in lewd acts in motion pictures and other forms of media in order to attract people to such acts.

As for the love of this world, it is the root of every sin. The spilling of blood, wasting of wealth, exploitation, cutting off of the ties of relationship only occur because people covet this world and compete for its pleasures and limited, depleting resources.

## (18) Singing and music

Singing and music are two tools of Satan that are used to ruin the heart of the human and to destroy his soul. Ibn al-Qayyim has

---

[1] Al-Ashqar stated that this hadith was recorded by al-Nasaai. However, that does not seem to be correct. Instead, it was recorded by al-Tirmidhi. According to al-Albani, the hadith is *sahih*. See Muhammad Nasir al-Din al-Albani, *Sahih al-Jaami al-Sagheer* (Beirut: al-Maktab al-Islami, 1986), vol. 2, p. 1134. Note that the above translation is based on one of the interpretations of that hadith.—JZ

written that from the machinations of the enemy of Allah and snares that he uses on those who are lacking in knowledge, intelligence and religion and by which he traps the hearts of the ignorant and foolish is by listening to clapping, whistling and singing to forbidden instruments that take the hearts away from the Quran and make them addicted to sins and lewdness. This is the "Quran" (reciting) of Satan and it keeps one from the Quran of the Merciful. It is the chant of the homosexuals and adulterers. Satan is able to deceive the wrongful souls by it. He makes it look good to them by way of deception. He inspires them with false thoughts to consider it something good. They accept his guidance and, therefore, neglect and avoid the Quran.[1]

One of the strangest phenomena is people using music and singing as a type of worship or a way of getting closer to Allah while at the same time they leave the recital of the Merciful for the recital of Satan.

Ibn al-Qayyim listed the following as terms used for such music: useless amusement, nonsense, futility, false speech, the invocation of adultery, the recital of Satan, the planting of hypocrisy in the heart, the sound of the foolish, the sound of the evil-doer, the sound of Satan and the psalms of Satan.[2]

In that work by ibn al-Qayyim he clearly shows the evil of music and he proves its forbidden status in Islamic law; the interested reader should consult it.

## (19) Making Muslims lackadaisical in fulfilling what they have been ordered to do

If a Muslim always adheres to the teachings of Islam, Satan will have no way to misguide or toy with him. But if he becomes negligent or lazy in some of his acts, then Satan has a chance with him. Allah says,

---

[1] *Ighaatha al-Luhfaan*, vol. 1, p. 242.
[2] *Ighaatha*, vol. 1, p. 256.

$$\text{يَا أَيُّهَا الَّذِينَ آمَنُوا ادْخُلُوا فِي السِّلْمِ كَافَّةً وَلَا تَتَّبِعُوا خُطُوَاتِ الشَّيْطَانِ إِنَّهُ لَكُمْ عَدُوٌّ مُبِينٌ}$$

"O you who believe, come, all of you, into submission (unto Him); and follow not the footsteps of Satan. Lo! He is an open enemy for you" (al-Baqara 207). This means to enter into Islam completely in every affair. This will free the person from Satan. An example of this is to stand straight and next to each other in the rows of prayer. If this is followed, Satan is blocked; if it is not, it allows Satan to pass through the people who are praying. The Messenger of Allah (peace be upon him) said,

$$\text{أَقِيمُوا صُفُوفَكُمْ لَا يَتَخَلَّلُكُمْ كَأَوْلَادِ الْحَذَفِ قِيلَ يَا رَسُولَ اللَّهِ وَمَا أَوْلَادُ الْحَذَفِ قَالَ سُودٌ جُرْدٌ تَكُونُ بِأَرْضِ الْيَمَنِ}$$

"Straighten your rows, [stand shoulder to shoulder, be flexible with respect to your brother,] and close up the gaps, for the devil enters through such gaps like the *hadhaf*." He was asked, "What are the *hadhaf*?" He answered, "Small black lambs found in Yemen."[1] In another hadith he said, "Stand close together in your rows, bring them close to one another. By the one in whose hand is my soul, I can see Satan passing through the gaps in the rows like a bunch of small black sheep."[2]

---

[1] This was recorded by Ahmad in his *Musnad* and by al-Haakim with a *sahih* chain. See *Sahih al-Jami*, vol. 1, p. 384.
[2] This was recorded by Abu Dawud at-Tayalisi with a *sahih* chain. See *Sahih al-Jami*, vol. 1, p. 384.

# How Does Satan Get to the Souls of Humans?

## The secret whispering

Satan is able to reach the thought and the heart of the human. He does it in such a way that the human does not perceive it or recognize it. He has been helped in this manner by the nature in which he has been created. This is the thing known as the "whisper" or thought that enters a humans mind. Allah informs us of that when He calls him,

$$\text{مِن شَرِّ ٱلْوَسْوَاسِ ٱلْخَنَّاسِ ۝ ٱلَّذِى يُوَسْوِسُ فِى صُدُورِ ٱلنَّاسِ}$$

"the mischievous whisperer, who whispers into the hearts of mankind" (*al-Naass* 4-5). Ibn Katheer says in his commentary to this verse, "Satan perches and lurks at the heart of the human. If he is neglectful, Satan whispers into his heart. If he is remembers Allah, Satan withdraws."

And it is confirmed in *Sahih al-Bukhari* that the Prophet (peace be upon him) said,

$$\text{إن الشيطان يجري من الإنسان مجرى الدم}$$

"Satan flows in the children of Adam like the flowing of the blood."

It was that secret whispering that misled and deceived Adam and lead him to eat from the tree.

$$\text{فَوَسْوَسَ إِلَيْهِ ٱلشَّيْطَٰنُ قَالَ يَٰٓـَٔادَمُ هَلْ أَدُلُّكَ عَلَىٰ شَجَرَةِ ٱلْخُلْدِ وَمُلْكٍ لَّا يَبْلَىٰ}$$

"But Satan whispered to him, saying: O Adam! Shall I show you the tree of immortality and power that wastes not away?" (*Taha* 120).

And, also, Satan may take the shape of a human, and may talk to humans and order them to do things or not to do things. We shall discuss this presently.

# 4
# [The Capabilities of Satan][1]

## The Forms Devils Can Take

Sometimes Satan does not approach humans by way of whispering into his soul. Instead, he appears to them in the shape of a human; his voice can be heard but his body cannot be seen. Or he might take on a strange shape. Sometimes the jinn appear in front of humans and inform them that they are jinn. Sometimes they falsely claim to be angels. Sometimes they call themselves "invisible men" while at other times they claim to be from the world of the spirits.

All of these things have been related from people throughout the ages. Sometimes the devils speak directly to a person while at other times they speak through a medium or channeler, using the tongue of that person for a while. Sometimes, they may respond to humans in writing.

They can do much more than that. They have been known to carry humans through the wind and take them from place to place. Or they may bring the person something he desires. But this is only done with the evildoers who do not believe in Allah as the Lord of the Heavens and the Earth or those people who do sinful acts. Many times, such people appear like the most pious of people but in reality they are the most misguided and corrupt people. Many of the past and present have related such incidents and they cannot be denied since the reporting of such occurrences has been widespread and continuous (*mutawaatir*).

---

[1] Actually, the author gave no title to this chapter. This title is suggested by the translator.—JZ

Included among those reported events is what ibn Taimiya recorded concerning al-Hallaaj: "He was a magician, and sometimes devils would serve him. He was with some of his companions on Abu Qabis Mountain. They asked him for some sweets. He went off to a place close by and brought a plate of sweets. Later it was determined that those sweets had been stolen from a store in Yemen and a devil had carried it to that place."

And ibn Taimiya also wrote,

> Things like that happen to many, besides al-Hallaj, who live evil lives. We know of many such people during our time and during other times. Like the man who is now [during ibn Taimiya's time] in Damascus. Satan used to carry him from Salihiya Mountains to villages around Damascus. He would be carried through the air to the windows of houses and enter the houses with the people seeing him. He would come at night to the Small Gate [one of the six gates around Damascus at that time] and he and his companions would be seen there. And he is one of the most wicked people. One of them was in a fortified prison in a city called Al-Shahida. He would go through the air to the top of a mountain and people would see him. A devil used to carry him. He was a highway robber.
>
> Most such people are leaders of evil. One of them was called al-Barsha Abu al-Majib. His tent was pitched for him once on a dark night. Bread was made in the manner of an offering. They did not mention Allah. And there was none among them who would mention Allah nor had they any book containing Allah's name. Then al-Barsha rose in the air. They watched him and heard him speak to Satan and heard Satan speak to him. Whoever laughed or stole some of the bread would be hit without knowing who hit him. Then Satan informed them of some of things they had asked about. Then he ordered them to sacrifice a cow, horse or similar animal. [He told them] to strangle the

animal and not to mention the name of Allah upon it. When they would do that, he would then fulfill their needs.

Ibn Taimiya also mentioned a Sufi shaikh

who said about himself that he used to commit adultery and sodomize boys. He said, "A black dog with two white spots between his eyes would say to me, 'So and so will come to you about an oath he made by you and I have fulfilled his need on your behalf.' Then the person would come with that oath and that disbelieving *shaikh* would already tell him about it."

And ibn Taimiya mentioned from the same man, "If anyone desired me to change anything, like glue, then I would speak until I lost my senses and then I would find the glue in my hand or my mouth and not know who put it there." And he said, "When I walked at night, I would have a black staff with a light in front of me." Ibn Taimiya said, "When that shaikh repented and started to pray, fast and avoid the forbidden acts, the black dog left him. And the alterations stopped and he could not produce glue or anything else."

Ibn Taimiya also mentioned another shaikh who would send his devils to possess certain people. The family of those people would come to the shaikh asking him to rescue their relatives. Then that shaikh would tell his devils to leave that person. The family would then pay that shaikh lots of money for his services. Sometimes the jinn would bring the shaikh money and food that they had stolen from people. Some people had some figs. The shaikh asked his devils for some figs and they brought those figs to him. When the owners went to their containers, they found the figs gone.

Ibn Taimiya mentions another person who was busy in acquiring knowledge. The devils came to him to deceive him. They said to him, "We have made the prayer no longer obligatory on you. And we will bring you whatever you need." Then they would bring him sweets or fruits. This continued until he met some true scholars of the sunnah who asked him to repent. Then he paid the owners of the sweets for the sweets he had eaten while being tempted by the devils.[1]

In *Majmu al-Fatawa*, ibn Taimiya explained some of the ways of the devils in tempting people. He wrote,

> I know some people whom the plants would talk to and tell them of their beneficial ingredients. Actually, Satan who had entered the plant was the one talking. And I know people to whom the bushes and rocks would say, "Welcome, o devoted servant of Allah." If they read "The Verse of the Throne" ( *al-Baqarah* 255) all of that would stop. I know of some people who go bird hunting and the sparrows and others say to them, "Take me so the poor can eat me." A Satan had entered the bird and spoken in the same way he enters humans and speaks from them. And some people are in their houses with the doors locked and see themselves outside while they did not open the door and vice-versa. Similar is the case with the city gates. Jinn take them in and out of them quickly. Lights will shine for them. Or a person who he was seeking would appear while actually it was Satan appearing like his friend. If they recite "The Verse of the Throne" over and over, all of that stops.[2]

And ibn Taimiya wrote,

> I know of people who are spoken to by something that says, "I am from the commands of Allah." And he tells the person that he is the Mahdi that the Prophet gave glad tidings of. And he performs supernatural acts for him. For example, if he even thinks of flying with birds or locusts through the air or if he desires them to go to the right or left, they do whatever he wishes. Of if he thinks to get some cattle up or have them sleep or leave, it happens for him without any apparent movement on his part. And they

---

[1] All of the above quotes are from ibn Taimiya, *Jaami al-Rasaail*, pp. 190-194.
[2] *Majmoo al-Fatawa*, vol. 11, p. 300.

take him to Makkah and back. Someone will be brought to him in a beautiful form and he will be told that it is one of the noble angels who has come to visit him. The man will say to himself, "How [can the angel] look like a beardless youth." Then he will look up again and find that he has a beard. It will be said to him, "The sign that you are the Mahdi is that you have a specific birthmark." He will look and he will see it. All of that is from the plots of Satan.

Ibn Taimiya also wrote,

The people of misguidance and heresies, those who are ascetic and worshippers but not according to the manner prescribed by the *shariah*, sometimes have strong influence that draws many to the places of Satan in which it is prohibited to pray. This is because the devils descend upon them and the devils talk to them about some matters in the same way they talk to the fortune tellers. In the same manner, they enter the statues and idols and talk to the worshipper of the idols. And they help them in some of their needs in the same manner they help magicians. In a similar fashion, they help the worshipper of idols, the sun, the moon and the planets when they worship them in a manner they think that are deserving of, of sanctifying them, to dressing and lighting incense for them and so on. Devils, that they call the "spirits of the planets", descend upon them and meet some of their needs.[1]

## Those who are served by the devils get close to them by way of sinful acts

Those who believe that they have been granted special powers and consider themselves special devotees of Allah are actually just being served by the devils. There is no doubt that they get close to the devils

---

[1] *Majmoo*, vol. 19, p. 41.

by way of what they love of disbelief and idolatry. Ibn Taimiya says that many of those people write the Word of Allah in impure substances and they invert the letters of the Quran, either the words of *surah al-Fatiha*, *surah al-Ikhlas* or other verses. And they write the Word of Allah in blood or other impure substances. And they write or make other statements that are pleasing to Satan.[1]

If they say or write what is pleasing to the devils, then the devils aid them in satisfying some of their desires, such as transforming water or transporting them in the air to some places. Or they might steal wealth from other treacherous people who do not mention Allah's name over it and bring it to some of their selected friends and so on.

## "Invisible men"

It is mentioned in the explanation to the Creed of at-Tahaawi,

There are some devils that the people call invisible men. Some people converse with them. They perform for the people some "miracles" that make the humans believe that they are close friends of Allah. Some of them aid the polytheists against the Muslims. Some say that the Messenger ordered them to kill the Muslims along with the polytheists because the Muslims were sinful.

The commentator to the Creed noted,

In reality they are the brothers of the polytheists. The people of knowledge are in three groups with respect to invisible men. (1) One group denies the existence of such invisible men. But the people have witnessed them. And it is confirmed that some trustworthy people have witnessed them and have related what they saw. And if they would were to see them and confirm their existence they would submit to them. (2) A group that admits their existence and accepts it as a will of Allah. They believe, therefore,

---

[1] *Majmoo*, vol. 19, p. 35.

that there is a hidden path to Allah other then the path of the Prophets. (3) A group that rules out the existence of patrons of Allah outside of the framework of the Messenger but they believe both groups have received help from Allah. These people give glorification to the Messenger, being ignorant of his religion and laws.

Then he says, making clear what they and their followers are:

The truth of the matter is that they are all followers of the devils. The "invisible men" are nothing but jinn who are called men, as Allah says, "Indeed men of the humans used to invoke the protection of men of the Jinn..." (*al-Jinn* 6). And the humans have company with them and witness and see them. Sometimes they cannot be seen but it is not the case that they always keep themselves hidden from mankind. Those who think that they are humans are mistaken and ignorant.

Then he explains the reason for the differences of opinion about them and the reasons for the existence of three groups mentioned above,

The problem lies in not differentiating between the patrons of Satan and the patrons of Allah. It is obligatory to compare the actions of the people (or of the invisible men) and their statements to the book of Allah and the sunnah of the Prophet (peace be upon him). What agrees with these two guides is correct and what disagrees with them is wrong. No matter what a person does and exposes of his deeds, he will not be a believer or devotee of Allah, even if he flies in the air or walks on water, as long as he does not stick to the Book and Sunnah.[1]

The human must always have some balance that can be used to distinguish between the devotees of the Merciful and the devotees of Satan and between the righteous and the impious. Otherwise, he will himself stray. That standard is the book of Allah and the sunnah of the

---

[1] *Sharh al-Aqeeda al-Tahaawiya*, pp. 571-572

Prophet (peace be upon him). If a person adheres to them, it is fine and good. If not, then he is not upon anything sound or praiseworthy, even if we see him resurrecting the dead or performing alchemy. Ibn Taimiya said,

> The one who cannot distinguish between the Godly situations and Satanic situations will have truth resembling falsehood in his eyes. One whom Allah does not enlighten his heart and give him the reality of faith and following of the Quran will not know the path of truth from falsehood. He will confuse the two situations, in the same way people were confused by Musailama the liar of Yemen and other liars who claimed to be prophets.[1]

Ibn Taimiya has written an important book that clearly differentiates between the servants of Allah and the servants of Satan. After reading this book the affair should be clear to the reader. Its name is *Al-Furqan bain Auliya ar-Rahman wa Auliya ash-Shaitan*.[2]

## The Ruling about being served by the jinn

It is clear that Allah granted the Prophet Solomon a dominion that no one will be given after him, due to his supplication. If a human is being obeyed by the jinn, not by mastery over them, but by their own pleasing, is this considered permissible? Ibn Taimiya has written a response to this question:

> Jinn, with humans, are in different situations. If one orders the jinn to what Allah and His Messenger has ordered from the worship of only Allah and obedience to Him and His Prophet, and he also orders mankind to the same, then that person is from the most virtuous of the

---

[1] *Jaami al-Rasaail*, p. 197.
[2] That book has been translated into English: *The Criterion between the Allies of the Merciful and the allies of the Devil* (Birmingham, England: Idarah Ihya-us-Sunnah, 1993).—JZ

patrons of Allah. And he is acting as the successor of the Prophet (peace be upon him) and his lieutenant.

If a person uses the jinn for activities that are permissible and he also orders them to what is obligatory for them and prevents them from what is prohibited for them, then he is similar to a king that behaves in the same manner. Then the most he can become is a devotee of Allah among the general devotees of Allah, like the comparison between a Prophet who was given rule and a worshipping messenger of Allah: like Solomon and Joseph with respect to Abraham, Moses, Jesus and Muhammad, the blessings of Allah and peace be upon all of them.

If he uses the jinn for activities that have been prohibited by Allah and His Messenger, as idolatry, or killing one who has no right to be killed, or being an enemy of the people without fighting them, such as harming others or making them forget knowledge and other acts of oppression, or committing lewd acts— that is, he uses them to help him in sin and transgression and idolatry— he is a disbeliever. If he uses them for acts of disobedience then he is a sinner, either a *faasiq* (wicked evildoer) or a sinner who is less than that.

If the person is completely ignorant of Islamic law and uses the jinn for what he believes to be noble deeds, such as having the jinn take him to the pilgrimage, listen to innovations or take him to Arafat, then this does not fulfill the requirement of the pilgrimage, and similar other activities. The person is mislead and has been duped by such actions.[1]

---

[1] *Majmoo*, vol. 11, 307.

## Making the Spirits Appear [Through Seances and Channeling]

Talk about the appearance of spirits had become widespread these days. Many people who are considered wise and prudent believe in this falsehood.

The alleged appearing of the spirits have come through many means. Some of it is just clear fabrication simply through deception, trickery, psychological influence, scientific instruments and so on. In other cases it is done through the use of the jinn and devils.

Dr. Muhammad Muhammad Hussain has written a book entitled *al-Roohiya al-Hadeetha* in which he uncovers much of the deception that is performed under the name of this activity. The charlatans never perform their acts except under a very dim red light that approaches darkness. They make bodies appear. Sounds and movements come that darkness. Even the one who is watching closely cannot determine where people are sitting or where voices are coming from. Similarly, he cannot distinguish the different aspects of the room, such as its walls, doors or windows.

In that book, Dr. Muhammad discusses *al-Khibaa* (a separate chamber) which is a room that is cut off from the people present or in the corner or a room covered by a thick curtain. This is the place where the medium sits and it is from his hands that the alleged bodies appear. In the darkness of the room, it is that dark corner from where the spirits and voices come. And when they return they also return to that same place. It is not permitted for the people present to touch or look into the spirit or shape that has appeared.

The author states that the spiritualists will never be at a loss, in such a dark environment, for any scientific instruments they need to perform their tricks.

Deceiving humans by such deception is an old and well-known trick that the devils have always used to mislead mankind. They seek the people's credibility and honor in the same way that they seek their wealth. Ibn Taimiya discussed a group of people of his time who were called al-Bata'ihiya. They claimed that they had knowledge of the unseen and that the truth was unveiled to them. They claimed that they could see and show people the "invisible men". Then some of their deception was discovered. They used to send some women to some of the houses to find out the inner secrets of the household and then they would claim that such was some of the special knowledge that they were privy to.[1]

They promised one man, who was hoping to be a ruler, to show him some of the "invisible men". They made a long plank of wood. They set up a long platform on a mountain some distance away. This made it look like people were walking in the air. The deceived one will look at them from a distance and will see a people on the mountain, raised above the earth. They took from that man a great deal of money and then their deception was made clear to him.

They deceived another man called Qafjaq. A man would enter a grave and talk from the grave and he would think it was the dead speaking. They took him through a small gate in the cemetery to a man they claimed was al-Sharani from the hills of Lebanon. They did not bring him close to him but kept him far away so his blessings would return to him. They asked him for a great deal of money. Qafjaq said, "The shaikh knows the unseen and he knows that in all of my wealth, I do not have as much as he asked for." So Qafjaq got close and tore off the hair of the person and found that the faker was covering himself with a sheepskin.

Dr. Muhammad Muhammad Hussain also makes it clear that the mediums or channelers—those people whom the spiritualists claim are naturally disposed to make the actual contact with the spirits and it is through them that they appear and speak—are usually deceiving fakes and liars. Most of these mediums are not of good character, nor are they religious. In fact, the spiritualists do not require any character or religion in their mediums. He mentioned an incident that happened to him personally that made it clear that these mediums are nothing but deceivers and liars.

---

[1] Ibn Taimiya, *Majmoo al-Fatawa*, vol. 11, p. 485.

He also explained how some of those present are also involved in the scheme. And they are very careful just to pick participants who are not sharp enough to figure out the deception that is going on.

## The use of the jinn and devils

Dr. Muhammad Muhammad Hussain uncovered much concerning the first method of the spiritualists in their claims to bring forth the spirits. This is the method of trickery, falsehood, psychological deception and scientific tricks.

But I must point to the second method, that of using jinn and devils. I believe that the majority of such claims of presenting the spirits are done through this method.

### Making the spirits appear is an ancient claim

The claim of making the spirits appear is not of recent invention, but it is an ancient claim indeed. We have already discussed how some people had connections with the jinn. In fact, it is recorded in books of trustworthy people that some people claimed that the spirits of the dead had reappeared after the death of the person. Ibn Taimiya wrote, "From those people [that is, those people of satanic influence involved in idolatry, polytheism, magic and so forth] are those who believe that if one of them dies, he returns to them after his death and talks to them, pays their debts, returns their pledges and advises them. He appears to them in the shape that he was in during his life. It is a Satan who appears in his form and they think it is actually him."[1]

---

[1] Ibn Taimiya, *Jaami al-Rasaail*, pp. 194-195.

## A modern day experience

This experiment took place with the author Ahmad Izzudin al-Bayanuni. He mentioned it in his book *Kitab al-Iman bi-l-Malaika*. I eagerly decided to quote the complete text of what he wrote:

The people of the East and the West have preoccupied themselves with the claim of making the spirits appear. There have been many articles written about it, written in different languages, published in Arabic as well as non-Arabic magazines. Books have been written about it. Much research has been done lately on this topic. Many experiments have been performed. After all of that, the intelligent people have concluded that the raising of the spirits is nothing but falsehood and forgery, a call to disbelief and wickedness.

What they claim to be the appearing of the spirits of people who have passed away is nothing but fakery and forgery. The spirits that appear are nothing but devils that are playing with and duping humans.

In reality, there is no one who is capable of making the spirits appear. After the spirit leaves the body it goes to reside in the realm called *al-Barzakh* which is the interval between this worldly life and the life of the hereafter. Therein the person is either in bounties or punishment. They are preoccupied there with a great affair which would prevent them from appearing before the humans.

I [al-Bayanuni] was called to such an act of these spiritualists. And I experienced my own lengthy experience. This experience made it clear to me that it is nothing but falsehood, forgery and deception. It is just the playing of the devils. They present that to the people to mislead them and to deceive them and to make humans follow them.

## The beginning of the experience

I had known for more than ten years of a person who claimed that he was using the jinn to do good deeds in the service of mankind. And that was done through a person who was a medium. He claimed that he achieved that through recitations and lengthy invocations which took up a great deal of time. He was instructed in thorough incantations by someone who claimed he was knowledgeable in that area.

The medium came to me one day telling me that so and so of the jinn had called for me to discuss something important and there was a great matter in store for me.

I went to the appointment, trusting in Allah and very happy about it, in order to learn new information through this experience.

## How did the deception begin?

The first deceiving step that they took with me, in the process of bringing forth the spirits, was to have me ask Allah for forgiveness, glorify him and other acts of *dhikr*. This would make a person believe, at first glance, that he is meeting with spirits who are pure, holy and truthful.

I entered the house of the medium and we were alone together in a room. The medium sat on the bed. And we began— obviously under his guidance with asking forgiveness and sanctifying Allah— until he became like in a trance and I laid him down on his bed. I covered him with a covering in the way I was told to do. Then in a low voice, his companion greeted me. His knowing me and his like for me were obvious. He introduced me to himself. He claimed to be a created being. He was not from the angels or the jinn but was of another creation, a different species. He came into being by Allah's saying, "Be" and he was.

The person of the voice claimed that the jinn only appeared through his command. And that between him and receiving the command from Allah there was only four intermediaries, with the Angel Gabriel being the fifth.

He began to praise me. He said that they will cut off any meetings they have with other humans and they shall only meet with me. Because, they claimed, I was a special person of this age. And this was a special sanction from Allah and it was Allah who had chosen me for that. And they made me a glittering promise full of amazing things.

I accepted this new experience and false call with trust in Allah and asking Allah to protect me from error and to guide me to the clear truth, enlightened by the light of knowledge and following the path of steadfastness and praising Allah.

At the end of the first meeting, he promised me a second meeting. Then the person himself instructed me to make some special incantations to awake the medium from his absence. That was done. And the medium was sitting. His eyes opened as if he had been wakened from a deep sleep and did not know what had transpired.

I went back for the second appointment also. Then we had many meetings, one after another, for a long time. During every meeting, they renewed their good promise to me and described a great future for me and the great blessings that the nation would receive at my hands.

## The situation develops

The situation developed further. Many "spirits" came to visit me in every meeting. Some with invocations being made before the meeting while others without it. While eating or drinking tea with the medium, the medium would fall asleep with his head down at the promised time. And the "spirits" would appear, some claiming to be angels or from the jinn or companions of the Prophet or saints. They would always speak with reverence and respect. They would invoke blessings for my visit and point to a blessed future. Then they would leave and others would come.

## Who were those visitors?

I was visited by beings that claimed to be angels, jinn, Abu Huraira, scholars, "saints", such as Abu al-Hasan al-Shaadhili, well-known and accepted scholars, such as al-Shaikh Ahmad al-Tirmaaneeni, and some scholars that I had met before and had known of their deaths, including my father (may Allah have mercy on him).

They gave me glad tidings of my father's visit at a specific time. I looked forward to this meeting with anxiety. When it was time for the meeting, they requested me to read *surah al-Waqiah* aloud. I read it. When I finished reciting it, they said, "Your father will appear after a few moments. Listen to what he says and do not ask him about anything."

## The beginning of my vigilance

After a few minutes, there came someone who claimed to be my father. He greeted me. He showed his happiness for meeting me. And he was happy with me for meeting those spirits. He advised me to assist the medium and his family and to take care of them in the best way as he had no other means of making money except through this way.

He ended his speech with "the prayers on the Prophet Abraham". And I knew that my father was passionately fond of saying the prayers upon the Prophet (peace be on him), especially in "the prayer of Abraham".

The most amazing thing was that his accent was exactly the same as my father's.

He said *salaam* and left.

Then I began to ask myself, "Why did they advise me not to ask him about anything?" For a secret reason no doubt. The secret reason became clear to me at that moment. It was not my father. It was his "partner" from the jinn, the one who accompanied him throughout his life. He came to me in the form of my father and imitated his most particular characteristics.

They advised me not to ask him about anything because the "partner" from the jinn, no matter to what extent he knows and remembers about my father, he is not able to remember every detail that a son knows about his father. They feared that if I asked him something of that nature, he would not be able to respond and the matter would become clear.

With others, I would meet them and not know who they were until they were about to leave and then they would say, "I am so and so," greet me and leave immediately.

There was also a secret reason for that: If any of them would tell me who they were, and he was well-known for being knowledgeable, I could discuss a diffecult topic with him and he would not be able to respond. Again, the matter would then be uncovered.

One time someone came and debated with me saying that the face of the woman is not *aurah* [or from the private parts that must be covered] and need not be covered. I refuted him and he responded to me with a response that had no aspect of knowledge in it. The argument became heated between us. I said to him, "How do you respond to those jurists who say that the face of the woman is *aurah* and she must cover out of fear of *fitnah* [temptation and sin]?" The argument ended without any benefit. Then he told me that he was Shaikh Ahmad al-Tarmaaneeni and he left. It became clear to me that he was undoubtedly a liar because Shaikh al-Tarmaaneeni was a leading Shafi scholar and the leaders of the Shafi school say that all of the woman is *aurah*, even if she is an aged, gray-haired woman. If he really was the shaikh he said he was and he had discovered some new knowledge in the world of *barzakh*[1] he would have informed me about it and shown me its evidence. But it was all a lie and deception. Its intention was misguidance. And Allah— and all praises are due to Allah— refused except to guide me and confirm me on the truth and guidance. A woman uncovering her face, especially in times like these with moral laxity and a sick society, is something no knowledgeable or religious person would agree to.

## The reality becomes uncovered

The reality of the situation became more and more uncovered meeting after meeting and experience after experience. Finally, I was certain that all of it were lies and forgeries. It had no root in righteousness and no standing in religion.

Even the medium, who I was advised to help and treat generously, was known not to pray and he was not ordered to perform his prayers. His beard was shaven and no one ordered him to let it grow.

---

[1] *Barzakh* is the existence from death until one is resurrected.

Certainly, he devours the wealth of the people through falsehood and deceiving promises. There is no source of income for him except through that evil means.

A man came to me after he heard that I had some relation with that medium and complained to me about his deception. He took 300 Syrian riyals from him and the man was a poor person who was very much in need of that money. I insisted that the medium return the money to him. He did so, in his and his devils' hope that I would continue to meet with them.

The medium and his family base most of their entire lives on lying.

## Conclusions

Those spirits, after everything became clear to me, tried to threaten me. But that did not shake my heart whatsoever. And all praises are to Allah.

I used to record what they used to say to me. These recordings filled two large files. I recorded most of what they said to me.

When it became unquestionably clear to me that it was all fake, without any other way to explain it, I made my final judgment about them and burned the two files that were filled with lies and forgeries.

Those spirits who claimed to be Companions of the Prophet, saints and pious people were all devils. No intelligent believer should be deceived by them.

All of the ways that are taken to make the spirits appear are nothing but lies and falsehood. It does not matter if it is through a channeler or medium, as in the experience I had, or through a table or tea cup, that some people have experienced and mentioned to me. All of them end in the same result that I reached.

A wonderful thing is that I have seen other people write on this topic and the conclusion of the intelligent people who experienced these things is the same conclusion I arrived at. They concluded that those spirits are nothing but the "partners" of humans from among the jinn, as Allah had guided me to. And all praise is to Allah.

I have fulfilled, by these words, the obligation of advising others. And Allah is the Guide to the Straight Path.[1]

## The gravity of this call

This claim of those people that the spirits appear is an attempt on the part of the devils, both jinn and human, to ruin the religion of the people. Those beings that appear are nothing but devils that come and speak in words that would destroy and demolish religion. They propound new principles and teachings that are completely opposed to religion. In one such meeting, the spirit (Satan) claimed, by the tongue of the channeler, that the Angel Gabriel was present at that meeting. When they did not know who Gabriel was, he told them, "You don't know Gabriel, the one who revealed the Quran to Muhammad? He is blessing this gathering." Dr. Muhammad Muhammad Hussein quoted a magazine entitled *Aalim al-Ruh* ("The World of the Spirit"). It had an article entitled, "The Speech of the Great Spirit Wyatt Hook". It stated,

> We must become united in this movement, in this new religion. We must have love between us. We must have the ability to compromise and understand one another... My message [the spirit that is speaker here, that is Satan] is to nurse the rejected and help mankind free himself from Allah [and that is the truth as his message is one of disbelief in Allah]. Humans are a god garbed in the elements of the earth [this is what they pump up humans with, they lie to them in order to mislead them]. And he does not know what is in his power. He has not sensed his angelic and divine parts... Spiritualism will be more powerful than any other thing to establish this new religion that can encompass the entire world.

And he also quoted from that magazine the introduction of a new order or system that is built upon the above goal.

---

[1] This ends the excerpt that is taken from al-Bayanuni's work.

That new order will be for every human being and through it they will make clear for us a new way of life and they shall give us a new concept of Allah and His will. They will give us spiritual peace and comfort and the happiness of soul and heart. They will break down the barriers between society and individual and between beliefs and religions. Membership in that order will be without reference to country, color, religion or political persuasion.

These spirits allege that they are messengers that are sent from Allah. Dr. Muhammad Muhammad Hussain mentions that Muhammad Farid Wajdi related that one of those spirits (or devils), said, "We are messengers from Allah in the same way that messengers were sent before us. Except that our teachings are more advanced than their teachings. Our god is their god. Except our god is more apparent than their god. He has less human characteristics and more godly ones. Do not submit to any belief or ideology. Do not accept any belief without thought nor any teaching that is not based on reason."

They allege that the messengers and prophets were nothing except intermediaries of the highest rank of intermediaries. The miracles that were performed at their hands were nothing but what the spirits manifest, like what manifests itself in the seances. They claim that they can repeat any of the miracles ascribed to Jesus. Some newspapers ran a large add claiming that one of the spiritualists in America could perform all of the miracles of Jesus, such as returning sight to the blind, allowing the mute to speak and so on. Furthermore, that alleged doctor is a child of only ten years old, called Michel. When he comes to a sick person, he simply puts his fingertips on the person and recites some invocations and words and the miracle happens. They say that that child inherited his spiritual blessings from his father. And he never accepts any money for what he does.[1]

That child inheriting those blessings from his father reminds us of a story that is told in some parts of Palestine. It is said that one man,

---

[1] See *Jaridat al-Qabs al-Kuwaitiya*, Nov. 17, 1977.

who was seen to be pious and holy, used to perform extraordinary acts. He used to— during that time they had no planes or cars— go to *Hajj* during the Night of Arafat. The pilgrims would witness him there and he would even deliver some letters to his relatives and friends. He would also take letters from them for their relatives and return on the same night. Many people believed he was noble and pious although he never performed any of the rites of the pilgrimage and would not stay in Mina for the prescribed time or perform the throwing of the stones. Then Allah willed that his falseness be discovered and shown to the people. When death came to him, he called his oldest son and told him that on the night of Arafah a camel will come to take him to Arafah every year. When the camel came, he rode it for some time and then it stopped and started talking to the son. He told him that he was a Satan that his father had worshipped and prostrated to. That is why he used to perform those services for him. When his son refused to prostrate to Satan and sought refuge in Allah from him, Satan left him in the desert. Allah gave him the ability to return to his home and unveil the truth about his father, the disbeliever.

This story was also alluded to by al-Bayanuni in his book about the angels in a more abridged fashion.

## Is it possible to make the spirits appear?

The magazine *Scientific American* offered a large financial prize for anyone who could offer proof that spirits do appear. That prize is still available as no one has been able to win it, although there are a great number of spiritualists and their likes in America. In addition to that, there is another prize that is being offered by the American magician Denger for the same purpose and no one has won that prize either.

But what is the Islamic position with respect to bringing back the spirits of the dead? When one studies the texts related to this point, he will conclude with certainly that such an act is absolutely impossible. Allah has informed us that the spirit is from the unseen which man cannot possibly fathom or reach.

$$\text{وَيَسْأَلُونَكَ عَنِ الرُّوحِ قُلِ الرُّوحُ مِنْ أَمْرِ رَبِّي وَمَا أُوتِيتُم مِّنَ الْعِلْمِ إِلَّا قَلِيلًا}$$

"They ask you concerning the spirit. Say: The spirit is by command of my Lord, and of knowledge you have been vouchsafed but little" (*al-Israa* 85).

And Allah has informed us that He takes the souls of the dead when they die,

$$\text{اللَّهُ يَتَوَفَّى الْأَنفُسَ حِينَ مَوْتِهَا وَالَّتِي لَمْ تَمُتْ فِي مَنَامِهَا ۖ فَيُمْسِكُ الَّتِي قَضَىٰ عَلَيْهَا الْمَوْتَ وَيُرْسِلُ الْأُخْرَىٰ إِلَىٰ أَجَلٍ مُّسَمًّى}$$

"Allah receives the souls at the time of their death, and that (soul) which dies not in its sleep. He keeps that soul for which He has ordained death and dismisses the rest till an appointed term. Lo! Herein are portents for people who take thought" (*al-Zumar* 42). After death, Allah puts angels in charge of the souls that either punish it if he were an ungrateful unbeliever or gives it bounties if he were a pious person.

The Prophet (peace be upon him) has made clear to us how the angel of death takes the soul at the time of death and what happens to it after that. If the souls are held by Allah and in the charge of strong guardians, it is not possible that they escape from them and come to the people and talk to them and play with the minds of humans.

Some of the mediums claim that the spirit of some righteous person, martyr or prophet has come to them. How could it be that they would leave the bounties of paradise to come to this world to come to the dark rooms of the mediums? Allah has informed us that the martyrs are alive with their Lord.

$$\text{وَلَا تَحْسَبَنَّ ٱلَّذِينَ قُتِلُواْ فِى سَبِيلِ ٱللَّهِ أَمْوَٰتًۢا ۚ بَلْ أَحْيَآءٌ عِندَ رَبِّهِمْ يُرْزَقُونَ}$$

"Think not of those who are slain in the way of Allah, as dead. Nay, they are living. With their Lord they have provision" (*ali-Imraan* 169).

The Prophet (peace be upon him) has informed us that the souls of the martyrs are in the bellies of green birds in paradise; they eat from the fruits of paradise and drink from its streams. And they are hanging from the Throne of the Lord. How do these liars of today claim that their spirits are appearing before them? "This is a grave sin that comes from their mouths and they say nothing but a lie."

## A conjecture and a reply

Some people may ask, "How is it that these spirits know the deeds and the character of the persons who they claim to be?"

We have stated that the one who claims he is a spirit is a devil. Perhaps that devil is the "partner" that accompanied that human through his life. We mentioned the texts that state that every human has a devil who accompanies him. That devil accompanies him and knows many aspects related to his character, habits, attributes, friend, relatives and so forth.

It is very easy for them to answer the questions put to them because they have such knowledge. If one asks, "How do you explain the scientific answers that they sometimes give?" We reply, "We have already mentioned that devils and jinn have such knowledge that allows them to respond and benefit us." But this knowledge is used to mislead mankind. They only benefit us to the point that we trust them. Then they mislead us in such a way that destroys our worldly life and our life in the Hereafter.

## The devils leave those who follow them

Those spiritualists who claim that they make the spirits appear and can cure people by them are nothing but liars; and the "spirits" are nothing but devils. Sometimes Satan even leaves such people and disgraces and humiliates them. In *al-Qabas*, a Kuwaiti newspaper (6/12/1978), there was an article about a medium in England by the name of Peter Goodwin. He had come into spiritual powers by which he was able to perform many miracles, such as cure those it was difficult to cure, find lost items and so forth. And he had mastery over the spirits to have them help mankind.

Peter Goodwin, by his unique powers, was able to be in many places at one time. For example, his friends saw him in London, while, at the same time, some others saw him in Liverpool and still others saw him in Manchester. And during the whole time yet another group stated that he was not in any of those places but he was actually sitting at home with his family.

Sometimes his body would appear at different times in one and the same place. For example, he would be sitting among his friends, then he would enter upon them again and sit with them. Then again for a third and fourth time, sitting and talking with them. So there would be five Peter Goodwins at one meeting and he would be talking to them or some of them.

But then Peter lost all of that and became like a normal person, without the ability to cure, find lost items, predict the future or control the spirits to serve mankind.

His downfall began last year when he began to use his spiritual powers that Allah had granted him for material gain. He now looks to his near past and says, "What happened to me was not in the reckoning. The spirits became angry with me and have afflicted me by leaving me."

## The beginning of his plight

Last year, he decided that he would open centers for spiritual healing throughout all of Britain. He wanted to open a center in every big city in Britain. For that purpose, he placed advertisements in the evening newspapers. He was looking for trainees for spiritual research in a full-time or part-time course. The cost would be between 40 to 50 British pounds.

He received some applicants for the position. One of the applicants he received was a twenty-nine year old writer, Rubin Lacy, a sixty-five year old woman, Jean Bartlett, and man in his thirties named Arthur Jeffrey. Peter Goodwin began holding interviews until he began to tire. Rubin Lacy stated,

> We found when we came to the appointment that Peter Goodwin was not there. Instead, the one who conducted the interview was a woman in her fifties who was assisted by a young man and woman, very beautiful. They distributed a questionnaire to us and asked us to fill it out. Among the questions it included were, "Have you ever witnessed a spirit before?" "Do you believe in spiritual remedies?" "Do you take drugs?" "Have you ever been in a mental hospital?" The woman told us that Peter Goodwin was planning on opening up a medical center in every city in England and that he would train us in spiritual healing so we would be able to work in those centers. Then he would send us clients. We would charge five sterling pounds for one session. And we would cure approximately forty per week— on the condition that we would give Peter Goodwin half of the first five thousand sterling pounds we make and we would be able to keep the rest. Most of the people began to debate this issue. Some of the people did not like what they heard so they left the room without completing the remainder of the questionnaire.

## What did an eyewitness say?

After all of that, some of the respondents were selected and they were allowed to meet Peter Goodwin in another room. He met with the first person for twenty minutes. Successively his interviews grew shorter until he saw the last one for only about five minutes. Then he chose some of them for him to train.

One of the persons he chose was Jean Bartlett who was a retired interior decorator. Her husband was Arthur Bartlett. Jean stated,

> I could not comprehend anything that Peter was trying to teach me. He would always start to get confused during the training. At the end of the training, he had stopped giving lectures in person but would just record what he had intended to say and give them the cassettes to listen to. He talked about the limits that humans can reach in life. One time, he asked us to make a figure out of clay that resembled a human. And he taught us to recite some incantations to it. But all of that did not result in anything.. Peter Goodwin gave us some more comments but we did not understand anything from him.

Peter had also chosen Arthur Jeffrey and his wife Angela. Angela narrated their experience,

> At the beginning, we got the feeling that there was a scientific atmosphere prevailing in his lectures. But Goodwin was always confused. He began to lose his powers little by little. After some days, he became like a normal person, like us. He did not have any miraculous abilities. We felt that since he no longer did anything amazing in front of us. In fact, he began to record his lectures and we would listen to the tapes without seeing him. For that reason, we all stopped attending his lectures and paying the fees we used to pay, which were ten sterling pounds for each lecture.

From his office, Peter Goodwin, the one who lost the trust of the spirits, stated,

> I was planning on developing the spiritual powers of my students. Then I was going to give them a diploma for that so they could go and work. They would benefit from it and would benefit others and I would benefit. And although I received many spiritual messages telling me that I must not use my great spiritual gift from God for the purposes of gaining economic rewards, I did not listen. The result was that I began to lose my spiritual powers until they left me completely. How did that happen? Until now I do not know.

## Our Comments to this Event

1. This man claimed that he brought forth the spirits but he has no proof for this claim. But there is proof that they were simply devils who were playing with him as he asked the people to make a statue and read some specific incantations. These are things that are pleasing to Satan and angering to Allah.

2. If it were the case that Satan was helping him, then it is very possible that he may have been seen at many places at one time since the devils have been given the ability to resemble humans.

That happened in the past and it continues to happen. We have already related that Satan came to the polytheists in the form of Maalik ibn Suraaqa during the battle of Badr. Ibn Taimiya narrated many such incidents. I shall recount some of what he wrote to make it clear to the reader that this is something very old. Ibn Taimiya stated,

> Some of my Companions told me that they had sought my help during their harshest times. One of them was afraid of the Armenians while the other feared the Tartars. Both of them mentioned that they sought my aid and then saw me flying in the air defending them from the enemies. I informed them that I was unaware of that. I never

defended them. But that was Satan who comes in the form of humans to deceive them when they associated partners with Allah [by calling on ibn Taimiya's aid instead of Allah's].

He also said, "This happened to more than one of our companions and *shaikh*s with respect to their friends. One of them prays for aid from his Shaikh and he sees his shaikh coming and fulfilling his need. The Shaikh then tells him, 'I was not aware of that.' And it becomes clear that it was a devil."

He also wrote,

> I told some of our companions when they mentioned to me that when they sought aid in two people that they believed in, they saw them coming in the air and telling them, "Make your heart good and we will defend you and do such and such for you." I said to them, "Does that tell you anything?" They said, "No." I said, "That shows you that they were devils. For devils, if they tell humans the truth about any issue or story they then commit many lies with it as the jinn used to do with the soothsayers."

3. The devils of Peter Goodwin abandoned him in the same way that the devils who appeared like shaikhs abandon the people they promise to defend and help. The same was true for Satan who abandon the monk after he promised to help him. This is to disgrace and humiliate the person who was just previously honored and respected by everybody.

4. Peter was under the impression that this power had come from God, but this is a lie that has no proof for it.

## The Jinn and the Knowledge of the Unseen

It is spread among many people that the jinn know the unseen. And the jinn do their best to spread this wrong notion among humans. But Allah has shown the falsity of their claim in the story of the Prophet Solomon. Solomon was given power over the jinn who worked on his behalf. After his death, his body stayed erect, leaning on a staff, and the jinn continued to work. They were not aware that he had died until some crawling creatures ate away the staff he was resting on. Then Solomon fell and it was made clear to the people that the jinn are liars when they claim to know the unseen. Allah says,

$$\text{فَلَمَّا قَضَيْنَا عَلَيْهِ ٱلْمَوْتَ مَا دَلَّهُمْ عَلَىٰ مَوْتِهِۦٓ إِلَّا دَآبَّةُ ٱلْأَرْضِ تَأْكُلُ مِنسَأَتَهُۥ ۖ فَلَمَّا خَرَّ تَبَيَّنَتِ ٱلْجِنُّ أَن لَّوْ كَانُوا۟ يَعْلَمُونَ ٱلْغَيْبَ مَا لَبِثُوا۟ فِى ٱلْعَذَابِ ٱلْمُهِينِ}$$

"And when We decreed death for him [Solomon], nothing showed his death to them save a creeping creature of the earth which gnawed away his staff. And when he fell the jinn saw clearly how, if they had known the unseen, they would have not continued in despised toil" (*Saba* 14).

We have already mentioned how they stole messages from the heavens and how the number of guards in the heavens were increased after the Prophet Muhammad (peace be upon him) was sent. After that the jinn were confounded.

## Fortune tellers and diviners

By that we know one of the greatest mistakes that the masses make when they believe that some people, like fortune tellers and soothsayers, know the unseen. We see them going to them and asking them about things that were stolen or crimes that were committed. And they ask them about things that have not happened yet to themselves and their children. Both the questioner and the questioned will be thwarted. The knowledge of the unseen rests only with Allah. Allah does not disclose any of it except to whom He chooses of his righteous servants:

$$\text{عَالِمُ ٱلْغَيْبِ فَلَا يُظْهِرُ عَلَىٰ غَيْبِهِۦٓ أَحَدًا ۝ إِلَّا مَنِ ٱرْتَضَىٰ مِن رَّسُولٍ فَإِنَّهُۥ يَسْلُكُ مِنۢ بَيْنِ يَدَيْهِ وَمِنْ خَلْفِهِۦ رَصَدًا ۝ لِّيَعْلَمَ أَن قَدْ أَبْلَغُوا۟ رِسَٰلَٰتِ رَبِّهِمْ وَأَحَاطَ بِمَا لَدَيْهِمْ وَأَحْصَىٰ كُلَّ شَىْءٍ عَدَدًۢا}$$

"He is the Knower of the Unseen, and He reveals unto none His secret, Save unto every messenger who He has chosen, and then He makes a guard to go before him and a guard behind him that He may know that they have indeed conveyed the messages of their Lord. He surrounds all their doings, and He keeps count of all things" (al-Jinn 26-28).

To believe that a certain person has the knowledge of the unseen is a sinful and wrong belief that goes against the authentic Islamic belief that only Allah has the knowledge of the unseen.

To go to some people to ask for a verdict that involves the unseen is a very great sin. It is recorded in *Sahih Muslim* and *Musnad Ahmad*, on the authority of one of the wives of the Prophet (peace be upon him), that the Messenger of Allah (peace be upon him) said,

$$\text{مَنْ أَتَى عَرَّافًا فَسَأَلَهُ عَنْ شَيْءٍ لَمْ تُقْبَلْ لَهُ صَلَاةُ أَرْبَعِينَ لَيْلَةً}$$

"Whoever goes to a diviner and asks about something, his prayer will not be accepted for forty days."

To believe in what they say is disbelief. Abu Huraira reported, as recorded in *Musnad Ahmad*, that the Prophet (peace be upon him) said,

$$\text{مَنْ أَتَى كَاهِنًا أَوْ عَرَّافًا فَصَدَّقَهُ بِمَا يَقُولُ فَقَدْ كَفَرَ بِمَا أُنْزِلَ عَلَى مُحَمَّدٍ}$$

"Whoever goes to a diviner or soothsayer and confirms what they have said, then he has disbelieved in what was revealed to Muhammad."[1]

---

[1] Recorded by Ahmad in his *Musnad* and by al-Haakim. According to al-Albani, it is *sahih*. See al-Albani, *Sahih al-Jaami*, vol. 2, p. 1031.—JZ

In *Sharh al-Aqeeda at-Tahaawiya* it states, "The astrologers fall under the category of diviners according to some scholars while others only say that its meaning applies to them also. And if that is the case for the one who asks the question, what (do you think) will be the case with respect to the one who is being asked?" Meaning that if the one who just asks the question will not have his prayer accepted for forty days and if the one who confirms what the diviner says becomes an unbeliever, what do you think is the ruling concerning the diviner or soothsayer?

## Questioning the diviner for the purpose of testing him

Ibn Taimiya is of the opinion that to question the diviner in order to test him, uncover his true situation and distinguish between his false and true statements is permissible. His proof is in the hadith that is in the two books of *Sahih*s: The Prophet (peace be upon him) questioned ibn Sayaad. The Messenger of Allah (peace be upon him) asked him, "What comes to you?" He answered, "Sometimes a truthful person and sometimes a liar comes to me." He then asked him, "What do you see?" He answered, "I see a throne upon the water." The Prophet (peace be upon him) said, "I have concealed something from you." He said, "It is *al-Dukh*." The Prophet (peace be upon him) said, "May you be disgraced. You will never raise above your rank. You are nothing but a brother of the soothsayers." You can see that the Prophet (peace be upon him) asked him those questions to show his true situation to the people.

## Astrologers

These are the people who use the stars or the celestial bodies to predict the affairs of the earth. This is a practice that is prohibited by the Book and the sunnah. In fact all of the messengers of Allah have prohibited it.

وَلَا يُفْلِحُ ٱلسَّاحِرُ حَيْثُ أَتَىٰ

"And a wizard shall not be successful to whatever point of (skill) he may attain" (*Taha* 69). And Allah also said,

أَلَمْ تَرَ إِلَى ٱلَّذِينَ أُوتُوا۟ نَصِيبًا مِّنَ ٱلْكِتَٰبِ يُؤْمِنُونَ بِٱلْجِبْتِ وَٱلطَّٰغُوتِ

"Have you not seen those unto whom a portion of the Scripture has been given, how they believe in idols (Ar., *jibt*) and false deities (Ar., *taaghoot*)" ( *al-Nisa* 51). Umar ibn al-Khattab said that the *jibt* is magic.[1]

## A Misconception

Some people allege that the astrologers, soothsayers, fortune tellers and others are sometimes truthful. Their being truthful in many situations is just a form deception of mankind. As they usually make a general statement that can be interpreted in numerous ways. When the event occurs, they interpret their statement in the way that would make it seem correct.

Other times when they are correct, it is the result of acumen and a keen eye. Other times it comes from the jinn who meet them and give them some news they stole from the heavens. In the two *Sahih*s and in *Musnad Ahmad* it is related from Aisha that the Messenger of Allah (peace be upon him) was asked about diviners. He said, "They have nothing." They said, "But sometimes they give some words that turn out to be true." He answered her, "Those words of truth are from what the

---

[1] Quoted from *Sharh al-Aqeeda al-Tahawiya*, p. 568.

jinn stole. He says them into the ears of his patron and mixes with it one hundred lies."

If the information they give that is correct is related to something similar to the name of a thief or knowing the name of a person and his family members before the first meeting with him, this could all be done through some trickery. This could be done by having an assistant who gets information from the people or is able to listen to their discussions before the time of the meeting. Or it could be from the acts of the devils as devils knowing about things that happened in the past is not something strange or marvelous.

## The soothsayers are the messengers of Satan

Ibn al-Qayyim has written,

Fortunetellers and soothsayers are messengers of Satan. This is so because the polytheists hasten to them. They rush to them in anticipation when anything important is happening and they believe in their words. They take them as the decider of their affairs and they are pleased with their rulings. This is the same behavior that the followers of the messengers [of Allah] have towards the messengers. They believe that [these fortune tellers] have knowledge of the unseen. They inform them about the unseen things that no one else knows about. So for the people who make idolatry through them, they are in the place of messengers. In reality, the fortune tellers and soothsayers are truly the messengers of Satan. He sends them to his party of polytheists and makes them appear like truthful messengers until his party responds to them, in order to take them away from the messengers of Allah. They consider their messengers to be the truthful ones who have knowledge of the unseen. Since there is such a great difference and contradiction between the two, the Messenger of Allah (peace be on him) said, "Whoever goes to a fortuneteller and believers in what he says, he has disbelieved in what has been revealed to Muhammad."

So people are of two categories: followers of the fortune tellers and followers of the [true] messengers [of Allah]. One person cannot be of both the latter and the former. In fact, the further he goes from the Messenger (peace be on him) by the amount he gets closer to the fortune teller. And he denies the Messenger by the amount that he believes in the fortuneteller.[1]

Whoever studies the history of the different peoples in the world will recognize that the diviners and magicians have been given a position similar to that of the messengers. But they are messengers of Satan. It was the soothsayers and magicians that their people listened to. They determined what would be lawful and what would be prohibited. They took the people's wealth. And they ordered the people to perform different types of rituals and worship that were pleasing to Satan. And they ordered the cutting off of family relations and violating people's honor. Al-Aqqad has discussed these topics in his book *Iblees*.

## The Obligation of the Muslim Nation Towards Them

What the astrologers, fortune tellers, magicians and diviners claim is a great misguidance that should not be taken lightly. It is to be rejected and stopped. It is an obligation upon those whom Allah has given His religion and taught them His book and the sunnah of His Prophet to eradicate this misguidance through speech, by showing the falsity of their claims with clear proofs. And those who have power must use that power to physically stop those who claim the knowledge of the unseen, such as fortune tellers, soothsayers, palm readers, people who read tea cups and so on. They must be stopped from spreading their diseases in the magazines and newspapers. Anyone who shows their material publicly must be punished for the evil that they do. Allah

---

[1] Ibn al-Qayyim, *Ighaatha al-Luhfaan*, vol. 1, p. 271.

blamed the Children of Israel for failing to prevent the wrong that they saw among themselves,

$$كَانُواْ لَا يَتَنَاهَوْنَ عَن مُّنكَرٍ فَعَلُوهُ$$

"They did not prevent the evil that was being done" (*al-Maaidah* 79). And the Prophet has said, as Abu Bakr narrated and is recorded in the books of *Sunan*,

$$إن الناس إذا رأوا المنكر لا يغيرونه أوشك أن يعمهم الله بعقابه$$

"Verily, if a people see an evil and do not put an end to it, then Allah might afflict them all with a general affliction."[1]

## Jinn and Unidentified Flying Objects

Many times we hear about the sightings of unidentified flying objects (UFOs). Perhaps a week cannot go by without hearing of one person or a group of people who have reported a sighting. They are seen either flying through the skies or stationed for a time on earth. Some people have reported a creation different from that of humans emerging from the vehicles. Some have even claimed that the creatures have asked them to join them on the vessels and so on.

This claim has not just been made by unknown or obscure people but even well-known and famous people have made such claims, such as the ex-President of the United States, Jimmy Carter, who claimed to have witnessed a UFO in Georgia in 1973.

He began a special study of the existence of other creatures who have began to invade earth. He even had a discussion with a scientist who believes in other creatures. Along with President Carter was Frank Price, his scientific advisor. Then Carter watched a film detailing the

---

[1] Recorded by Ahmad and ibn Majah. According to al-Albani, it is *sahih*. See al-Albani, *Sahih al-Jaami*, vol. 1, p. 398.—JZ

most recent researches on creatures that live in outer space. The one who presented that film was the Head of the Department of Astronomy of Cornell University, Carl Sagan. Sagan is the expert that the Space Administration turns to with any question concerning creatures living in outer space.[1]

It was also reported in a Kuwaiti journal that Mao Tse Tung believed that beings other than humans lived on other planets. The author of that report mentioned that about 61% of the American youth are convinced that UFOs do exist and, according to American newspapers, about a half a million Americans have actually witnessed such UFOs. Some of them even had direct contact with the UFOs.

Recently film producer Steven Spielburg made a movie entitled *Close Encounters of the Third Kind* which cost 22 million dollars to produce. This film was made after he collected together all of the information about the sighting of and contacts with UFOs. The film was first shown in the White House and the first person to see it was the President. After that film came out, the Space Administration was convinced that it is a must to research this matter more. In 1979, they devoted one million dollars for such research. They started a secret project called SITY and they set up special instruments to determine if there were creatures invading the earth from outer space.

## After the above, we can conclude the following

1. There is no scope to deny the existence of strange creatures that are not human. Sightings of such creatures have come through continuous reporting over the past twenty centuries, in fact over the last one hundred centuries. I researched this topic for some time and found an article reporting such on a weekly basis or even more often.[2]

2. People are confused concerning the exact explanation for what these beings and flying objects might be, especially since the speed

---

[1] See *Jarida al-Siyasa al-Kuwaitiya*, no. 3399, May 12, 1977.
[2] The most recent event occurred in Kuwait where more than one person said he saw a UFO. The Kuwaiti newspapers reported that incident.

of their vehicles seems to be much greater than what humans have been able to manufacture.

3. I am certain that those beings are from the species of the jinn that reside on this earth and which we have been discussing throughout this book. We have already mentioned their superior abilities, including their speed of movement above the speed of sound or light. Similarly, they have been given the ability to take on different shapes and they are able to appear in front of humans in different shapes.

And by that, by the grace of Allah, it has been made clear to us the reality of these beings. We can feel the loss and confusion of those people who do not have the knowledge that we possess. Therefore, we can spend our mental and monetary resources on researches that will be beneficial.

Some people have asked about the reason why these beings and UFOs seem to be appearing in our times while they did not appear in past times. The response is that the jinn use, in their schemes, whatever happens to be the mode of the day. During this time, scientific progress is the fad of the day. Therefore the jinn mislead them by the use of this medium that interests them. Today people are beginning to explore space and the possibility of life in outer space. [Hence, the jinn are appearing in the form of UFOs and space creatures in order to mislead and deceive mankind.]

# 5
# THE WEAPONS OF THE BELIEVER IN HIS WAR AGAINST SATAN

## 1. Caution and care

This evil enemy of the human is always anxious to mislead mankind. He does this through a number of means, many of which we have discussed in the previous chapters. One must beware of this enemy. One must be aware of his goals and his stratagem in order to be victorious over him. If man is heedless about these affairs, then Satan can attack him through any means that he pleases. Ibn al-Jauzi made an exceptionable parable about this battle between man and Satan. He said in *Talbees*,

> The heart is like a fort that is surrounded by a wall and the wall has gates from which it can be torn down. In it lies the mind. The angels frequent that fort and next to that fort are places where the desires lie. And the devils enter into this surrounding area without being prevented from doing so. And the war exists between the inhabitants of the fort and the inhabitants of the surrounding areas. The devils never stop circling the fort and looking for an opening where the guard is heedless and from where he can tear down the fort. It is obligatory for the guards to be completely aware of all of the gates of the fort that must be guarded as well as all of its weak points from which destruction can come. The guard cannot take a break because the enemy never takes a break. A man said to

al-Hasan al-Basri, "Does Iblees sleep?" He answered, "If he were to sleep we could then have a rest."

The fort is lit by the remembrance of Allah and faith in Him. In it is a polished looking glass through which [the guardians] can then see anything that passes by. The first thing that Satan does is to blow smoke into the fort to make its walls black. This causes rust and damage in the fort. Sound thought repels Satan and remembrance of Allah cleans the looking glass. The enemy has carriages and sometimes they are able to enter the fort. The guards may come upon them and force them to leave. Perhaps they may enter due to the heedlessness or carelessness of the guards. Perhaps, due to the smoke and the rust, Satan enters through any way and he is not perceived. Perhaps the guard is injured by the heedlessness or is taken prisoner and led to the following of the desires. And perhaps he becomes like the jurist who does evil.[1]

## 2. Sticking to the Book and the sunnah

The greatest thing that can be used as a defense against the devils is sticking to the Book and the sunnah, by one's knowledge and by one's actions. The Book and the sunnah present the straight path, and it is Satan who struggles to steer us from this straight path. Allah says in the Quran,

$$\text{وَأَنَّ هَٰذَا صِرَاطِي مُسْتَقِيمًا فَاتَّبِعُوهُ وَلَا تَتَّبِعُوا ٱلسُّبُلَ فَتَفَرَّقَ بِكُمْ عَن سَبِيلِهِۦ ذَٰلِكُمْ وَصَّىٰكُم بِهِۦ لَعَلَّكُمْ تَتَّقُونَ}$$

---

[1] Ibn al-Jauzi, *Talbees*, p. 49.

"And He (commands you, saying:) This is My straight path, so follow it. Follow not other ways, lest you be parted from His way. This has He ordained for you, that you may ward off evil" (al-Anaam 153). The Prophet (peace be upon him) explained this verse. He once drew a straight line with his hand and said, "This is the straight path of Allah." Then on its left and on its right he drew other lines and he said, "These paths all have Satan calling (people) to them." And then he recited the above verse.[1]

If the person follows what has come from Allah in his beliefs, actions, words, worship, law, and so on, and avoids what He has forbidden, then he will be protected from Satan. Allah says in the Quran,

$$يَٰٓأَيُّهَا ٱلَّذِينَ ءَامَنُوا۟ ٱدْخُلُوا۟ فِى ٱلسِّلْمِ كَآفَّةً وَلَا تَتَّبِعُوا۟ خُطُوَٰتِ ٱلشَّيْطَٰنِ إِنَّهُۥ لَكُمْ عَدُوٌّ مُّبِينٌ$$

"Oh you who believe, Come, all of you, into submission (unto Him); and follow not the footsteps of Satan. Lo! He is an open enemy for you" (al-Baqara 208). The Arabic word al-silm in that verse refers to Islam while some say it means obeying Allah and Muqaatil says it refers to all acts in which there is righteousness. From that we see that it is an order to apply all of the branches of Islam and all the aspects of its laws according to one's abilities; and the verse prohibits the following of the footsteps of Satan. Whoever enters completely into Islam is far away from the steps of Satan. Whoever does not follow any part of Islam has, in fact, followed in some of the footsteps of Satan. Therefore any kind of allowing what Allah has prohibited or vice-versa is a following of Satan. Eating any forbidden and foul foods is all part of following in the footsteps of Satan that has been declared prohibited for us.

---

[1] This was recorded by Ahmad, al-Haakim, who called it *sahih*, and al-Nasaai.

$$\text{يَٰٓأَيُّهَا ٱلنَّاسُ كُلُواْ مِمَّا فِى ٱلْأَرْضِ حَلَٰلًا طَيِّبًا وَلَا تَتَّبِعُواْ خُطُوَٰتِ ٱلشَّيْطَٰنِ إِنَّهُۥ لَكُمْ عَدُوٌّ مُّبِينٌ}$$

"O mankind! Eat of that which is lawful and wholesome in the earth, and follow not the footsteps of the devil. Lo! he is an open enemy for you" (*al-Baqara* 168).

Sticking to the Book of Allah and his sunnah in one's words and actions will rebuke Satan and will greatly infuriate him. It is recorded in *Sahih Muslim*, *Musnad Ahmad* and *Sunan Ibn Majah* on the authority of Abu Huraira that the Prophet (peace be upon him) said,

$$\text{إِذَا قَرَأَ ابْنُ آدَمَ السَّجْدَةَ فَسَجَدَ اعْتَزَلَ الشَّيْطَانُ يَبْكِي يَقُولُ يَا وَيْلَهُ أُمِرَ ابْنُ آدَمَ بِالسُّجُودِ فَسَجَدَ فَلَهُ الْجَنَّةُ وَأُمِرْتُ بِالسُّجُودِ فَأَبَيْتُ فَلِيَ النَّارُ}$$

"When the son of Adam reads a verse of prostration and then prostrates, Satan departs from him and cries, saying, 'Woe to me. The son of Adam was ordered to prostrate and he did so and, therefore, he will be granted paradise. I was ordered to prostrate and disobeyed and, therefore, I will get the hell-fire.'"

## 3. Taking refuge and shelter in Allah

The best way to take shelter from Satan and his soldiers is to seek refuge and aid in Allah from the accursed Satan. Allah has power over Satan. If the slave seeks refuge in Him, how can Satan get to him? Allah says,

$$\text{خُذِ ٱلْعَفْوَ وَأْمُرْ بِٱلْعُرْفِ وَأَعْرِضْ عَنِ ٱلْجَٰهِلِينَ ۝ وَإِمَّا يَنزَغَنَّكَ مِنَ ٱلشَّيْطَٰنِ نَزْغٌ فَٱسْتَعِذْ بِٱللَّهِ ۚ إِنَّهُۥ سَمِيعٌ عَلِيمٌ}$$

"Keep to forgiveness and enjoin kindness, and turn away from the ignorant. And if a slander from the devil wounds you, then seek refuge in Allah. Lo! He is Hearer, Knower" (*al-Araaf* 199-200).

Allah even ordered the Messenger (peace be upon him) to seek refuge from the suggestions of the devils and from having them present with him.

$$\text{وَقُل رَّبِّ أَعُوذُ بِكَ مِنْ هَمَزَٰتِ ٱلشَّيَٰطِينِ ۝ وَأَعُوذُ بِكَ رَبِّ أَن يَحْضُرُونِ}$$

"And say: My Lord! I seek refuge in You from suggestions of the evil ones. And I seek refuge in You, my Lord, lest they be present with me" (*al-Muminoon* 98-99). This invocation is asking that we don't fall prey to what they whisper to us and we do not follow such whispers up. Allah has ordered us to seek refuge in Him from the Satanic enemy from which there is no other escape, since he does not accept acts of kindness and courtesy. He only desires the destruction of humans due to his enmity for them.

Ibn Katheer, in his commentary to the Quran, states

> This means to seek shelter in Allah and to adhere to Him in the face of any possible evil. The meaning of "I seek refuge in Allah from the outcast Satan," is to seek shelter in the protection of Allah from the outcast Satan, such that he will not harm one in one's religion or worldly life. [It is seeking refuge in Allah such that] Satan should not prevent one from doing what one has been ordered to do or to push one to do some act that one has been prohibited

to do. Verily, Satan does not turn from the person except through the aid of Allah. The devils from among the humans can be dealt with in a kind fashion, as has been ordered by Allah. And this kind treatment may stop them from the evil that they plan on doing. But such bribery will not work with the devils from among the jinn because they are a different type of creation. He does not accept bribes nor is he affected by kind behavior. This is because he is evil by nature. The only source that can help one against him is his Creator.

The Prophet (peace be upon him) would often seek refuge in the Lord from Satan, in different ways and on many different occasions. After the opening invocation of the prayer he used to say, "I seek refuge in Allah, the Hearer, the Knower, from the accursed Satan and from his 'puffing up,' 'spitting,' and 'evil suggestion.'" The four compilers of the *Sunan* related that hadith. These words are interpreted in the following manner: 'puffing up' means death by strangling[1]; 'sputtering' means pride; and the latter refers to poetry.

## Seeking refuge upon entering bathrooms

When one enters the lavatories, one should seek refuge from the male and female devils. It is reported in the two *Sahih*s that Anas ibn Malik related that whenever the Prophet (peace be upon him) would enter the place to relieve oneself, he would say,

اللَّهُمَّ إِنِّي أَعُوذُ بِكَ مِنَ الْخُبُثِ وَالْخَبَائِثِ

"Oh Allah, I seek refuge in You from the male and female evil jinn." It is recorded in *Musnad Ahmad* and *Sunan Abu Dawud*, with a *sahih* chain, that Zaid ibn Arqam related that the Prophet (peace be upon him) said,

---

[1] This is what al-Ashqar wrote. Most authorities say it means "madness". See, for example, Majd al-Din ibn al-Athir, *al-Nihaaya fi Ghareeb al-Hadith* (n.c.: al-Maktab al-Islami, n.d.), vol. 5, p. 273.— J.Z.

$$\text{إِنَّ هَذِهِ الْحُشُوشَ مُحْتَضَرَةٌ فَإِذَا دَخَلَ أَحَدُكُمْ فَلْيَقُلِ اللَّهُمَّ إِنِّي أَعُوذُ بِكَ مِنَ الْخُبُثِ وَالْخَبَائِثِ}$$

"These privies are frequented by jinn. So when one of you enters the privy, he should say, 'I seek refuge in Allah from the male and female evil jinn.'"

## Seeking refuge during the time of anger

A hadith states that during the Prophet's time there were two men who were caught by extreme anger such that it appeared to the narrator of the hadith that one of them was going to cut off the other's nose due to his anger. The Prophet (peace be upon him) said, "I know a statement, that if he were to say it what troubles him of anger would leave him." The people asked, "What is it, oh Messenger of Allah?" He replied, "Oh Allah, I seek refuge in You from the accursed Satan." (This was recorded by al-Bukhari, Muslim, Abu Dawud and Ahmad, and the wording is that of Ahmad.)

The Prophet (peace be upon him) taught one of his companions to say,

$$\text{اللَّهُمَّ فَاطِرَ السَّمَوَاتِ وَالْأَرْضِ عَالِمَ الْغَيْبِ وَالشَّهَادَةِ لَا إِلَهَ إِلَّا أَنْتَ رَبَّ كُلِّ شَيْءٍ وَمَلِيكَهُ أَعُوذُ بِكَ مِنْ شَرِّ نَفْسِي وَمِنْ شَرِّ الشَّيْطَانِ وَشِرْكِهِ وَأَنْ أَقْتَرِفَ عَلَى نَفْسِي سُوءًا أَوْ أَجُرَّهُ إِلَى مُسْلِمٍ}$$

"Oh Allah, Creator of the Heavens and the Earth, the Knower of the Seen and the Unseen, There is no God Besides You, Lord of everything and Master over it, I seek refuge in You from the evil of my own soul, and from the evil of Satan and his partners that they may perpetrate harm against me or pass that on to another Muslim."[1]

---

[1] This was related by at-Tirmidhi with a *sahih* chain. *Sahih al-Jaami*, vol. 6, p. 56.

## Seeking refuge during the time of sexual intercourse

We have also been encouraged to seek refuge at the time that a man goes to his wife, by saying,

$$\text{بِاسْمِ اللَّهِ اللَّهُمَّ جَنِّبْنَا الشَّيْطَانَ وَجَنِّبِ الشَّيْطَانَ مَا رَزَقْتَنَا}$$

"In the name of Allah. Oh Allah, keep us away from Satan and keep Satan away from what You provide us." Should it be that a child shall come from them, Satan will never harm it. This was recorded by al-Bukhari and Muslim.

## [Seeking Refuge Upon Entering a Valley or a Strange Land][1]

When a person enters a valley or a strange land, it is necessary for him to seek refuge in Allah and not in the jinn and the devils as the people used to do during the days of ignorance. They used to say, "I seek refuge in the leader of this valley from the foolish ones of his people." The result was that they would magnify the jinn and then the jinn would harm them. Allah relates,

$$\text{وَأَنَّهُ كَانَ رِجَالٌ مِّنَ ٱلْإِنسِ يَعُوذُونَ بِرِجَالٍ مِّنَ ٱلْجِنِّ فَزَادُوهُمْ رَهَقًا}$$

"And indeed individuals of humankind used to invoke the protection of individuals of the jinn, so that they increased them in revolt (against Allah)" (*al-Jinn* 6). In other words, the jinn increased their transgression. But the Muslim has been shown by the Prophet (peace be upon him) what to say instead, upon reaching a new place or valley,

---

[1] This subtitle is not in al-Ashqar's published edition but it is obvious that it or something like it is needed here.— JZ

$$\text{لَوْ أَنَّ أَحَدَكُمْ إِذَا نَزَلَ مَنْزِلاً قَالَ أَعُوذُ بِكَلِمَاتِ اللَّهِ التَّامَّةِ مِنْ شَرِّ مَا خَلَقَ لَمْ يَضُرَّهُ فِي ذَلِكَ الْمَنْزِلِ شَيْءٌ حَتَّى يَرْتَحِلَ مِنْهُ}$$

"If one of you reaches a place (to stay), he should say, 'I seek refuge in the perfect word of Allah from the evil of what He created,' in that case no harm will come to him from that place until he mounts to leave from there." This was related by Ibn Majah with a *sahih* chain.[1]

## Seeking refuge in Allah from Satan upon hearing the braying of a donkey

The Prophet (peace be upon him) said, "If a donkey brays, then seek refuge in Allah from the outcast Satan."[2] Previously we stated that if a donkey brays at night it is because he has seen a Satan.

## Seeking refuge in Allah before reciting the Quran

Allah says,

$$\text{فَإِذَا قَرَأْتَ الْقُرْآنَ فَاسْتَعِذْ بِاللَّهِ مِنَ الشَّيْطَانِ الرَّجِيمِ ۞ إِنَّهُ لَيْسَ لَهُ سُلْطَانٌ عَلَى الَّذِينَ آمَنُوا وَعَلَى رَبِّهِمْ يَتَوَكَّلُونَ}$$

"And when you recite the Quran, seek refuge in Allah from Satan, the outcast. Lo! he has no power over those who believe and put their trust in their Lord" (*al-Nahl* 98-99). Ibn al-Qayyim discussed the wisdom behind seeking refuge in Allah from Satan while reading the Quran. He stated,

---

[1] Actually, Muslim has recorded virtually the same hadith.—JZ
[2] This was recorded by at-Tabaraani in his *Mujam al-Kabeer* with a *sahih* chain. See al-Albani, *Sahih al-Jaami*, vol. 1, p. 286.

1. The Quran is a healing for whatever is in the heart; it removes whatever comes from Satan, be it his evil whisperings, lusts or evil desires. It is the antidote to what Satan has put into the heart. So first the person is asked to reject whatever is in his heart from the acts of Satan. Therefore, the medicine will find the heart free and can take its proper place and have its proper affect. As is said in poetry, "Her desire came to me before I knew the desire/And it met my heart empty so it took root therein." So this healthy medicine comes to the heart and cleans it from what can damage it. And it becomes successful therein.

2. The Quran is the source of guidance, knowledge and good in the heart of the reader, in the same way that water is the source that brings forth plants. Satan is a fire that burns down the plants, one by one. For every good plant that springs in the heart, Satan attempts to destroy it and burn it down. And Allah orders us to seek refuge in Him in order for Him to ruin what Satan is attempting to do. The first point stated above deals with the benefits of the Quran while this point actually deals with the preservation and remaining of the Quran in the heart.

3. The angels descend upon the one who reads the Quran and listen to its recitation. This has been related in a hadith in which Usaid ibn Hudhair was reciting the Quran and he saw a canopy with lamps in it. The Prophet (peace be upon him) told him that those were angels. And the devils are the opposite of the angels and are their enemies. The one who reads the Quran has been ordered to ask Allah that he should be put far away from his enemy, the devils, until he is in the midst of only angels. This situation cannot possibly be occupied by both the angels and the devils at the same time.

4. Satan tries to disturb the one who reads the Quran with his steeds and feet until the reader is void of the meanings of the Quran. The reader should try to ponder over and understand the words of Allah. Satan tries to come between his heart and the meaning of the Quran. Thus the reader is not able to benefit from the Quran. Therefore we have been ordered to seek refuge from this Satan when we are about to read the Quran.

5. The reader of the Quran is in a private conversation with Allah. And Allah listens closer to His words when recited in a pleasant way than a singer listens to her song. The song of Satan is poetry and music. The reader has been ordered to seek refuge from Satan so Satan will be removed from the private conversation and Allah will listen to the person's recital.

6. Allah has stated that whenever He sent a Messenger or a Prophet, Satan has always tried to interfere in what he is preaching by bringing words or ideas that do not originate with Allah. The early scholars all agreed that this meant that when one is reciting, Satan throws some words or such into the recital. If this was done with respect to the Prophets, what must be the case with respect to others? This is why the reciter sometimes will make mistakes. And why he sometimes gets confused and cannot recite properly. Or his mind and his heart becomes confused. When he begins to recite, he might find one of these, if not all of them, occurring.

7. Whenever a person contemplates the doing of a good deed, Satan becomes even more anxious in his attempts to come between the person and the good deed, to prevent the person from doing the good deed. [Therefore, we are

asked to seek refuge in Allah in order for Satan to be prevented from stopping us from this good deed.]¹

## Invocations for one's children and family

The Prophet (peace be upon him) used to pray for his grandsons, al-Hasan and al-Husain, by saying,

أُعِيذُكُمَا بِكَلِمَاتِ اللَّهِ التَّامَّةِ مِنْ كُلِّ شَيْطَانٍ وَهَامَّةٍ وَمِنْ كُلِّ عَيْنٍ لَامَّةٍ وَيَقُولُ هَكَذَا كَانَ إِبْرَاهِيمُ يُعَوِّذُ إِسْحَقَ وَإِسْمَعِيلَ

"I seek refuge for you two by Allah's perfect word, from every Satan and evil suggestion (Ar., *haama*) and from every evil eye (*laama*)." Then he said, "This is how my father Abraham used to invoke for Ishmael and Isaac." Recorded in the two *Sahih*s.² Abu Bakr al-Anbari said, "*Al-Haamat* is the singular of *al-hawam*. It is used for every evil inspiration. And *al-lamat* is *al-mulama* but it is stated in the text as *lamat* to match with *hamat* and be easier on the tongue."³

## The best of invocations are the last two surahs of the Quran

The best words to make invocations with are *surah al-Falaq* and *surah al-Nass*. Uqbah ibn Amr narrated that the Prophet said, "The people did not make invocation like these two: 'Say, 'I seek refuge in the Lord of Daybreak,' and 'Say, 'I seek refuge in the Lord of Mankind.'" (Recorded by al-Nasaai.)

---

¹ Ibn al-Qayyim, *Ighaatha*, vol. 1, p. 109.
² This is what Dr. al-Ashqar wrote but the hadith, with a slightly different word order, is only in *Sahih al-Bukhari* but not in *Sahih Muslim*. Al-Tirmidhi has recorded it exactly as above.— J.Z.
³ Quoted from ibn al-Jauzi, *Talbees Iblees*, p. 47.

## A great understanding

One of the early scholars said to his student, "What would you do if Satan entices you to sin?" He said, "I would struggle against him." "And if he returns?" "I would struggle against him," the student repeated. "And if he returns again?" The student again says, "I would struggle against him." The scholar told him, "This can take forever. What if you are passing by some sheep and their watchdog starts barking at you, preventing you from passing, what would your action be?" The student answers, "I would wear it down by struggle and repel it." The teacher then says, "This is a lengthy process. If you go instead to the owner of the sheep, he will be able to make the dog desist."[1] This is a great lesson narrated by ibn al-Jauzi and that is that seeking refuge and shelter with Allah is the strongest way to refute Satan and to get far away from him. This is what the mother of Mary did when she said,

وَإِنِّىٓ أُعِيذُهَا بِكَ وَذُرِّيَّتَهَا مِنَ ٱلشَّيْطَٰنِ ٱلرَّجِيمِ

"Lo! I crave your protection for her and for her offspring from Satan the outcast" (*ali-Imraan* 36).

## A Misconception

Some people say, "We seek refuge in Allah but we still feel Satan coming to us and urging us to evil or preoccupying us while we are in the prayers." The reply to this is that seeking refuge in Allah is like a sword that is in the hands of a warrior. If his arm is strong, he is able to penetrate and kill his enemy. If his arm is weak, he may leave no mark at all on his opponent, even if it is a very sharp sword. The same is the case with seeking refuge from Satan. If one is pious and God-fearing, this invocation becomes like a fire that burns Satan. If the person is of

---

[1] Quoted from ibn al-Jauzi, *Talbees*, p. 48.

weak faith, one whose faith is mixed with evil, then this weapon hardly harms Satan whatsoever. Ibn al-Jauzi has drawn the following parallel,

> The likeness of Iblees with a pious person and with one of weaker faith is like the [following two men]: A man who sits to eat a meal. A dog comes to partake of the food. The man shouts at the dog and he flees. And there is another man for whom a dog comes to eat from his plate and he also shouts at the dog, but it has no affect. The first man is like a pious man whom Satan comes to but is repelled by his invocation. The second is like one whose faith is mixed with evil, when he seeks refuge in Allah, Satan does not leave him. And we seek refuge in Allah from Satan.[1]

Therefore, the Muslim who wants safety in Allah from Satan and his plots must work to increase his faith and he must turn to Allah for help and security. And there is no power or strength except Allah.

## 4. Being busy with the remembrance of Allah

Remembrance of Allah is one of the greatest acts that will save the person from Satan. We shall present the hadith in which John came to the Tribes of Israel with five commands. One of them was, "And I order you to make remembrance of Allah for its example is like that of a man who is being chased quickly by an enemy until he reaches a protected fort. He then protects himself from the enemy. Similarly, the servant does not protect himself except by the remembrance of Allah." Ibn al-Qayyim said that if that were the only benefit of the remembrance of Allah, then the slave should always be remembering Allah and never let his tongue leave from His remembrance. The person does not protect himself from his enemy except through the remembrance of Allah. Satan does not enter unless one becomes neglectful and falls into his ambush. But if he remembers Allah again, Satan will be defeated, humiliated and

---

[1] Ibn al-Jauzi, *Talbees Iblees*, p. 48.

made small like a small sparrow or a small fly. This is why it is called the withdrawing whisperer. In other words, it whispers into the souls of men, but when Allah is remembered it is turned away. Ibn Abbas said that Satan perches in the heart of the son of Adam. If he is forgetful or neglectful, Satan whispers to him. If he remembers Allah, Satan withdraws.[1]

According to ibn al-Qayyim, the devils enclose humans and are their greatest enemies. What do you think of a person who is surrounded by his greatest enemies who are bent on his destruction. All of them attack him with whatever evil and harm they can. The only way to be safe is to be safe from all of them, and that is through the remembrance of Allah.[2] And ibn al-Qayyim records the hadith that was related by Abdurahman ibn Samra. He said that the Prophet (peace be upon him) went out to them. He stood among them and said,

> I saw something amazing yesterday. I saw a man from my community having the angel of death coming to him to take his soul. Then came good dealings with his parents (to intercede for him) and the angel of death left him. And I saw a man whose punishment in the grave was being laid out for him. Then came his ablutions and he was rescued by them. Then I saw a man from my community who had been surrounded by devils. Then came the remembrance of Allah and the devils were driven away from him. And I saw a man of my community who was surrounded by the angels of punishment, then there came his prayers and he was rescued from their hands. And I saw a man from my community who was panting from thirst. When he got close to them, he was prevented from every jug of water and they were taken away from him. Then came his fasting of the month of Ramadhan and, therefore, he drank and was satisfied. I saw a man from my community and I saw prophets sitting in groups. Every time the man went to the circles he was driven away. Then

---

[1] Ibn al-Qayyim, *al-Waabil al-Sayib*, p. 60.
[2] Ibn al-Qayyim, *al-Waabil al-Sayib*, p. 144.

came his washing from major defilement, and they took him by his hand and sat him besides me. And I saw a man from my community, in front of him was darkness, behind him was darkness, on his right was darkness, and on his left was darkness, and above him was darkness, and below him was darkness. And he was lost in the darkness. Then there came his pilgrimage and lesser pilgrimage and they took him out of the darkness and entered him into light. And I saw a man from my community who was being burned by a fire. Then there came his charity and it formed a cover between him and the fire. And it provided a shade over his head. And I saw a man from my community who was talking to the believers, but they would not talk to him. Then there came his keeping of family relations and it said, 'Oh gathering of Muslims, he kept together family ties so speak with him.' Therefore, the believers talked to him and they shook his hand. And I saw a man of my community who was encircled by the angels who throw the disbelievers into Hell. Then there came his ordering the good and forbidding the evil, so he was rescued from their hands. And he was entered among the angels of mercy. And I saw a man from my community who was kneeling and between him and Allah there was a curtain. Then there came his good character and he was taken by his hand and permitted to be with Allah. And I saw a man from my community whose recorded deeds were taken from his left hand. Then there came his fear of Allah and he took his papers and had them placed on his right side. And I saw a man from my community who had a very light weight on the scale. Then there came his young children who had died and his weight was increased. I saw a man from my community who was on the brink of the hell-fire. Then there came his hope in Allah and he was rescued from it and he moved on from it. I saw a man from my community who was thrown in the fire. Then there came his tears that he cried out of fear of Allah and he was rescued from that. And I saw a man from my community standing along a path that was shuddering in the same way that a limb of a palm tree shudders on a stormy night. Then there came his good thoughts about Allah and the shuddering was stopped. And I saw a man from my community crawling on the path [over the hell-fire]. Sometimes he was crawling on it and sometimes he was hanging from it. Then there came his prayers upon the Prophet and he was made to stand on his feet and he passed over it. And I saw a man from my community who came to the doors of paradise and they were closed in front of him. Then there came his testifying that there is no god except Allah and the doors were opened for him and he entered into paradise.

[Ibn al-Qayyim then stated,]

This hadith was recorded by al-Haafidh Abu Musa al-Madeeni in his book *At-Targheeb fi al-Khisaal al-Manjiya wa at-Tarheeb min al-Khilaal al-Mardiyya*. In fact, this hadith is the basis of his book and the rest of the work is just a commentary on this hadith. He says that this hadith is very good. It was related by a Amr ibn Bariz, Ali ibn Zaid ibn Jadaan and Hilal Abu Jabalah from Saeed ibn al-Musayyab. Ibn Taimiya also thought highly of this hadith. It is reported to me that he used to say, "Supporting narrations show that it is authentic."[1]

The important portion of the hadith [for our purposes] is, "I saw a man from my nation who had been surrounded by

---

[1] This lengthy hadith was recorded by al-Tabaraani and al-Hakim al-Tirmidhi. Its chain is weak according to Nur al-Din al-Haithami and al-Iraqi. Ibn al-Jauzi stated that the hadith is not authentic. Al-Suyooti, al-Munaawi and al-Albani have all determined that it is weak. See Abdul Rauf al-Munawi, *Faidh al-Qadeer Sharh al-Jami al-Sagheer*, (Beirut: Dar al-Marifa, 1972), vol. 3 p. 26; Muhammad Nasir al-Din al-Albani, *Dhaeef al-Jami al-Sagheer wa Ziyadatuhu* (Beirut: al-Maktab al-Islami, 1988), pp. 302-3, hadith no. 2086.— J.Z.

devils. Then came the remembrance of Allah and the devils were driven away from him."

This is consistent with the hadith of al-Harith al-Ashari which states, "I order you to the remembrance of Allah. It is like a man who is being quickly chased by his enemies until he finds a safe fortress to be in and he has protected himself from them." In the same way, the remembrance of Allah protects one from Satan.

The person never completely protects himself from Satan except through the remembrance of Allah. At-Tirmidhi records on the authority of Anas ibn Malik that the Prophet (peace be upon him) said, "Whoever says (meaning, upon leaving his house), 'In the name of Allah. I trust in Allah. There is no power or might except in Allah,' it is said to him, 'You have been guided, defended and protected.' And he will be protected from Satan. And Satan will say to another devil, 'What can we do with a man who has been guided, defended and protected?'" This was also related by Abu Dawud and an-Nasai. At-Tirmidhi said the hadith is *hasan*. And it is confirmed that the Prophet (peace be upon him) said, "Whoever repeats one hundred times in a day, 'There is no god except Allah, the One who has no partner, Whose is the dominion and the Praise, and who has power over all things,' will be protected from Satan until the evening." And Sufyan mentioned from Abu az-Zubair on the authority of Abdullah ibn Dhamra that Kaab said that when a man leaves his home and says, "In the name of Allah," an angel will say, "You have been guided." And if he says, "I trust in Allah," the angel says, "You have been protected." And when he says, "There is no power or might except in Allah," the angel says, "You have been guarded." Then the devils say to each other, "Go back, you have no way to him. How could you have a way to someone who has been sufficed, guided and guarded?"

Abu Khilaad al-Misri said, "When a person embraces Islam, he enters into one fort. When he enters the mosque, he has entered into two forts. And whoever sits in an assembly that is making remembrance of Allah, he has entered into three forts."

Al-Haafedh Abu Musa related in the above-mentioned book that Abu Imraan al-Jauni related that Anas said that the Prophet (peace be upon him) said, "If a person lies on his side in his bed and says, 'In the name of Allah,' and recites surah al-Fatiha, then he will be safe from the evil of the jinn and humans and of everything."[1]

In *Sahih al-Bukhari* it is related from Muhammad ibn Sireen on the authority of Abu Huraira that he was put in charge of the zakat and a man came and started taking from the food. [This hadith was mentioned earlier.] On the third occasion, Satan told Abu Huraira, "I will teach you some words by which Allah will benefit you..." He taught him to read the verse of the throne upon going to bed. The Prophet (peace be upon him) commented that he had told the truth although he is a liar.

Al-Haafedh Abu Musa records from Abu al-Zubair on the authority of Jaabir that the Messenger of Allah (peace be upon him) said, "When a person goes to his bed, an angel and a devil are promptly with him. The angel says, 'Seal your day with good.' And the devil says, 'Seal your day

---

[1] As-Syuti mentions it in *al-Jaami al-Kabeer* and traces it back to al-Bazzaar and al-Dailami. Al-Haithami said in *al-Majma*, "In its chain is Ghassan ibn Ubaid and he is weak. Ibn Hibban declares him to be trustworthy. The rest of the narrators are from the two *Sahihs*." (These comments were made by the 'editor' of ibn al-Qayyim's book *al-Waabil as-Sayib*.)

with evil.' If he remembers Allah until he is overcome with sleep, the angel drives the devil away and he spends the night guarding him. When he gets up, the angel and Satan are promptly with him. The angel says, 'Begin the day with good.' The devil says, 'Begin the day with evil.' If the person says, 'Praise be to Allah, the one who gave my soul life after its death and He did not kill it in its sleep. Praise be to Allah, the One who clings on to [the soul] that has had death determined for it and sends the others [back to the person] again for a determined period. Praise be to Allah, the One who holds the heavens and the earth from perishing. And if they were to perish, none would be able to hold them after him. Praise be to Allah, the One who holds the skies from falling on the earth, except by His permission.'[1] Then the angel drives away Satan and protects him during the day."[2]

And in the two *Sahih*s, it is recorded from Ibn Abbas that the Messenger of Allah (peace be upon him) said, "When one of you goes to his wife and says, 'In the name of Allah. Oh Allah, ward off Satan from us and ward off Satan from what you shall provide us,' then if they are given a child from that union, Satan will never harm it."[3]

---

[1] In *Mawarid al-Dhamaan* and in *Majma al-Zawaid*, it states, instead of the last sentence quoted above, "If he then lies on his bed, he will enter paradise." In *Mustadrak* by al-Haakim, it states, "If he is strangled by an animal, he will die as a martyr. And if he stands to pray, he prays among the virtuous." (These comments were quoted from the editor of *al-Waabil al-Sayib*.)

[2] The meaning of this hadith has been recorded by Ibn Hibban (#2362, as it states in *Muwaarid*) and al-Haakim (vol. 1, p. 548). Al-Haakim declared it *sahih* and al-Dhahabi agreed with him. Its narrators are trustworthy. Al-Haithami mentioned it in *Majma al-Zawaid* (vol. 10, p. 120) and stated, "Recorded by Abu Yala. And its narrators are from the *Sahih* save Ibrahim ibn al-Hajjaj al-Shaami and he is trustworthy." Actually the correct name is Ibrahim ibn al-Hajaj al-Sami, with a *sin* instead of a *shim*. (From the editor of *al-Waabil al-Sayib*.)

[3] Recorded by al-Bukhari (vol. 13, p. 321) in the "Book of *Tauheed*", Chapter: Asking by the names of Allah, "Book of the Beginning of Creation", Chapter: Attributes of Iblees and his soldiers, and in "The Book of Supplications", Chapter:

Al-Haafez Abu Musa also related that al-Hasan ibn Ali said, "I am the guarantor for anyone who relates these twenty verses that Allah will protect him from every oppressive devil and from every rebellious devil and from every harming predatory animal and from every assaulting robber. The verses are: the verse of the throne, three verses from *surah al-Araaf*, from 'Verily, your Lord is Allah who created the Heavens and the earth' (*al-Araf* 54-57), the first ten verse of *al-Saffaat*, three verses from *surah al-Rahmaan* (verses 33-35), and the ending of *surah al-Hashr* (verses 21-24)."

Muhammad ibn Abaan said: While a man was praying in the mosque, something by his side startled him. It said, "You will face no harm from me. I came to you for the sake of Allah. Go to Urwah and ask him, 'What do you say to seek refuge from Iblis?'" He (Urwah) said, "Say: I believe in Allah, the Great, the One. And I have disbelieved [and denied] the false gods and idols. And I stick to the firm handhold that has no break to it. And Allah is all-hearing, all-seeing. Allah is sufficient and suffices. Allah hears him who calls upon Him. And there is no end beyond Allah."

Bishr ibn Mansur said: Wuhaib ibn al-Warid said: A man went to the cemetery during part of the night. He said, "I heard a sharp voice. Then a bed was brought and laid out. Something came until it sat upon it. His soldiers gathered around him. Then he screamed, saying, 'Who will rid me of Urwah ibn al-Zubair?' None of them responded to him until one of them said, 'I will take care of him for you.' He turned toward Madinah and I was watching. Then he

---

The supplication for the Married Person. And recorded by Muslim, number 1434, in "The Book of Marriage", Chapter: What is Recommended to be said at the Time of Intercourse. (From the editor of *al-Waabil al-Sayib*.)

returned soon. He said, 'There is no way to get to Urwah.' And he said, 'Woe to you, I found that he said some words in the morning and in the evening. With those words, we cannot get to him." The man continued saying, "When the morning came, I told my family to prepare my trip for Madinah. I came to Madinah and asked about Urwah until I was guided to him. He was an old man. I said, 'What is it that you say in the morning and in the evening?' He refused to tell me. Then I told him what I had seen and heard. He answered, 'I do not know except that I say in the mornings, "I have believed in Allah, the Great and disbelieved in the false gods and idols. And I cling to the firm handhold that has no break in it. And Allah is all-hearing, all-knowing." In the mornings, I say it three times. And in the evenings, I say it three times.'"

Abu Musa recorded on the authority of Muslim al-Bateen that the Angel Gabriel said to the Prophet (peace be upon him), "Verily an *afreet* (devil) plots against you. So when you go to bed, say, 'I seek refuge in the perfect words of Allah which neither the pious nor the corrupt can exceed, from the evil of what descends from the sky and the evil of what ascends to it, and from the evil of what the earth sheds and the evil of what comes forth from it, and from the evil of the trials of night and day, and from the visitations of night and day, except for one that comes knocking with good, Oh Most Merciful One.'"[1]

---

[1] Its chain is broken. Malik recorded it in *al-Muwatta* (vol. 2, pp. 951-2) in "The Book on Hair", Chapter: Taking Refuge, on the authority of Yahya ibn Saeed in *mursal* form. Al-Zurqaani said in *Sharh al-Muwatta*, "Al-Nasaai recorded it with an unbroken chain from Muhammad ibn Jafar from Yahya ibn Saeed from Muhammad ibn Abdul Rahman ibn Saad ibn Zaraarah from ibn Abbas al-Salami from ibn Masud." Al-Zurqaani said, "Hamzah al-Kanaani al-Hafedh said, 'That is not what is considered strong. The correct view is that it is *mursal*.'" Al-Suyooti said, "Al-Baihaqi recorded it in *Al-Asma wa al-Siffat* with the chain Dawud ibn Abdul Rahman al-Attaar from Yahya ibn Saeed who said: I heard a man from al-Sham narrate from ibn Masud who said, 'During the night of the jinn, one of the *afreet* found in his

It is also stated in the *Sahih* that Satan flees from the call to prayer.

Suhail ibn Abu Saleh said: My father sent me to the Tribe of Haaritha and with me was a young boy, my companion. Someone called his name out from behind a wall. He looked over the wall and did not see anyone. When I mentioned that to my father, he said, "If I knew that you would encounter such a thing, I would not have sent you. But if you ever hear a voice, make the call to prayer as I heard Abu Huraira narrate from the Messenger of Allah (peace be on him) who said, 'When the call to prayer is made, Satan flees and he loudly emits gas.'" Another narration states, "If he hears the call to prayer, he turns and loudly passes wind until he cannot hear the call..."[1]

Al-Haafez Abu Musa also recorded from the hadith of Abu Raja that Abu Bakr related that the Prophet (peace be upon him) said, "Be excessive in saying 'There is no god but Allah,' and in asking forgiveness, for Satan says, 'I destroy them by sins and they destroy me by saying, "There is no god but Allah," and by asking forgiveness. When I see that among them, I destroy them by their desires until they reckon that they are guided and they no longer ask for forgiveness.'"[2]

---

hand a blaze...'" Al-Zurqaani said, "There is some question about that. The Night of the Jinn is when they listened to the Quran. It is not the same as the Night of the *Israa*. They are two different hadith even though the supplication is the same in both of them." (From the editor of *al-Waabil al-Sayib*.)

[1] Recorded by al-Bukhari in "The Book of the Call to Prayer", Chapter: The Virtue of Making the Call to Prayer, and by Muslim in "The Book of Prayer", Chapter: The Virtue of the Call to Prayer and Satan's Fleeing upon Hearing it. (From the editor of *al-Waabil al-Sayib*.)

[2] Al-Haithami mentions this hadith in *Majma al-Zawaaid* and ascribes it to Abu Yala. Al-Haithami said, "Its chain contains Uthman ibn Matr and he is weak." (From the editor of *al-Waabil al-Sayib*.)

He also mentions from Ibrahim ibn al-Hukm from his father on the authority of Ikrima who said: While a man was traveling, he passed by a man who was sleeping. He saw two devils with that man. The traveler heard one of the devils say to his companion, "Go and destroy that sleeping person's heart." When he came close to him, he returned and said, "He fell asleep with some verses so we have no path to him." The other devil went to the sleeper to confirm it. When he came close to him, he returned. He said, "You are correct." Then they both left. The traveler went to wake the person who was sleeping to inform him of what he had seen from the devils. He asked the sleeper, "Tell me upon what verses you slept?" The man said, "On this verse, 'Lo! Your Lord is Allah Who created the heavens and the earth in six Days, then mounted He the Throne. He covers the night with the day, which is in haste to follow it, and has made the sun and the moon and the stars subservient by His command. His verily is all creation and commandment. Blessed be Allah, the Lord of the Worlds' (*al-Araaf* 54)."

Abu al-Nadhr Haasim ibn al-Qaasim said, "I saw [some jinn] in my house...[1] It was said, "O Abu al-Nadhr, move from our neighborhood." That was difficult for me, so I wrote to ibn Idrees, al-Muhaarabi and Abu Usaamah in Kufah. Al-Muhaarabi wrote back to me, "There was a well in Madinah and they would cut the rope for the bucket. A group of riders stopped there and they complained to them about that. They called for a container of water and they said these words [given below] and then they poured that water into the well. A fire came out of the well. It was extinguished at the top of the well." Abu al-Nadhr said, "So I took a container of

---

[1] There is something missing in his words. From the context it seems that those whom he had seen said to him, "O Abu al-Nadhr..."

water and then I stated those words. I went to the corners of the house and sprinkled that water over them. They cried out to me, 'You are burning us. We will move from you.' Those words were, 'In the name of Allah, we begin our evening in the name of Allah, the One for whom nothing is prevented; by the power of Allah that no one can possibly reach or which never does any wrong; and by Allah's authority, the forbidding, we seek a covering; and by all His excellent names, I am a seeker of refuge from the deceivers and from the evil of the devils of both man and jinn; and [I seek refuge] from the evil of every open and hidden [evil]; and [I seek refuge] from what comes out in the night and takes root in the day and what takes root in the night and comes out in the day; and from the evil of what is created, both animate and inanimate; from the evil of Iblees and his soldiers; from the evil of every walking creature whose forelock You have taken; verily, my Lord is on a straight path; I seek refuge in Allah from whatever Musa sought refuge from, and Jesus and Abraham who fulfilled his covenant; and from the evil of what is created, both animate and inanimate; from the evil of Iblees and his solders and the evil he wants. I seek refuge in Allah, the All-Hearing, the All-Knowing, from the accursed Satan. In the name of Allah, the Compassionate, the Merciful. 'By those [angels] arranged in rows, by those [angels] who drive the clouds, by those [angels] who bring the Book, verily, your God is indeed one, Lord of the heavens and of the earth, and of all that is between them, and Lord of every point of the sun's risings. Verily, We have adorned the near heaven with the stars and to guard against every rebellious devil. They cannot listen to the higher group for they are pelted from every side, outcast. And theirs is a constant torment, except such as snatch away something by stealing, and they are pursued by a flaming fire of piercing brightness' (*al-Saaffaat* 1-10)."

This is some of what is related in reference to the Prophet's statement to the person, "One protects himself from Satan through the remembrance of Allah."[1]

I would like to end this topic with a hadith that was not mentioned by ibn al-Qayyim. This hadith shows that remembering Allah in every affair will make Satan despised, belittled, disparaged and defeated. Imam Ahmad related that Tameema heard from one of the companions of the Prophet (peace be upon him) who related that he was riding behind the Prophet (peace be upon him) and the Prophet's donkey stumbled. The companion said, "Perish Satan!" The Prophet said, "Do not say, 'Perish Satan,' for in that case you give him some honor and he said, 'By my strength it fell down.' If you said, 'In the name of Allah,' Satan would have been belittled until he became like a fly." Ibn Katheer said only Ahmad related it and it has a good chain.[2]

---

[1] Although ibn al-Qayyim and al-Ashqar (may Allah reward them both) found these reports to be important enough to reproduce them in their respective works, one must very careful in how one deals with such reports. The general principle is true and there can be doubt about that: the remembrance of Allah repels Satan. However, some people may conclude from these reports that there is something special about what these different people had said or recited of the Quran. This special status can only be known from the Quran itself or from the Prophet (peace be upon him). Especially worrisome is the narration where the person saw two jinn who had attempted to get to a person who was sleeping but because he had read a certain verse, the devils could not get to him. What is known from the Prophet (peace be upon him) is that reciting "the verse of the Throne" protects one from Satan during one's sleep. One may ask: Why did those jinn appear to those humans? This could have been simply another attempt on the devils' part to mislead mankind. That sleeping person did not read "the verse of the Throne" but he read a different verse. Based on this story, some people may recite that verse and neglect reading "the verse of the Throne" and that may have been the goal of those evil devils in the first place. Allah knows best. The point is that nothing special can be said about certain verses or words of *dhikr* unless such special status can be proven through the Quran and sunnah.—JZ

[2] Ibn Katheer, *al-Bidaayah*, vol. 1, p. 65.

## 5. Sticking to the Muslim community

What makes the Muslim even farther away from Satan and his tricks is living in the lands of Islam and choosing for oneself a pious group of companions that will support him along the truth and encourage him to it. They will keep him from evil deeds and will remind him of good deeds. Unity and togetherness adds strength to strength and is a special strength. The Prophet (peace be upon him) said,

فَإِنَّ الشَّيْطَانَ مَعَ الْوَاحِدِ وَهُوَ مِنَ الِاثْنَيْنِ أَبْعَدُ مَنْ أَرَادَ بُحْبُوحَةَ الْجَنَّةِ فَلْيَلْزَمِ الْجَمَاعَةَ

"Certainly, Satan is with the one and is farther away from the two. Whoever of you desires the felicity of paradise, should stick to the community."[1] And "community" means the community of the Muslims with their *imam*. And there is no value in a community in Islam except for those communities that stick to the Book of Allah and the sunnah of the Prophet (peace be upon him). And it is stated in a hadith,

مَا مِنْ ثَلَاثَةٍ فِي قَرْيَةٍ وَلَا بَدْوٍ لَا تُقَامُ فِيهِمُ الصَّلَاةُ إِلاَّ قَدِ اسْتَحْوَذَ عَلَيْهِمُ الشَّيْطَانُ فَعَلَيْكُمْ بِالْجَمَاعَةِ فَإِنَّمَا يَأْكُلُ الذِّئْبُ الْقَاصِيَةَ

"There are not three persons in a city or desert except that they must establish the prayer, otherwise they are overcome by Satan. Stick to the community for the wolf eats the sheep that is remote from the pack."[2]

Abu Dawud also recorded in his *Sunan* from Muaawiya ibn Abu Sufyaan, that the Prophet (peace be upon him) said,

---

[1] This was recorded by at-Tirmidhi who called it *hasan sahih*. Its narrators are all trustworthy and the hadith is *sahih* as it has many chains.
[2] This has a *hasan* chain. It was recorded by Abu Dawud, al-Nasaai and others.

$$\text{أَلَا إِنَّ مَنْ قَبْلَكُمْ مِنْ أَهْلِ الْكِتَابِ افْتَرَقُوا عَلَى ثِنْتَيْنِ وَسَبْعِينَ مِلَّةً وَإِنَّ هَذِهِ الْمِلَّةَ سَتَفْتَرِقُ عَلَى ثَلَاثٍ وَسَبْعِينَ ثِنْتَانِ وَسَبْعُونَ فِي النَّارِ وَوَاحِدَةٌ فِي الْجَنَّةِ وَهِيَ الْجَمَاعَةُ}$$

"Verily the people before you of the Book split up into seventy-two groups. This nation will split up into seventy-three groups. Seventy-two of them will be in the fire. One of them will be in paradise: the one of the community."[1]

# 6. Uncovering designs and plans of Satan[2]

It is upon the Muslim to discover the way of Satan in misleading mankind and to uncover Satan's ways and to show them to the rest of mankind. The Quran does this, as did the Prophet (peace be upon him). They did so in the best manner possible. The Quran showed us the way in which Satan deceived Adam. And the Prophet (peace be upon him) informed his companions about how the devils listened to the news of the skies and passed that on to the diviners and soothsayers along with a hundred lies to go with it. He clarified that for them in order for them not to be deceived by something similar to it. He also explained to them how Satan whispers to them in order to ruin their prayers and worship. He also explained to them how Satan makes them think that their ablutions had become invalid when that was not really the case. He also described to them how the devils separate a man from his wife. He also told them how Satan makes one think about who created this and that until he thinks about who created Allah.

---

[1] This was recorded by Abu Dawud with a good chain.
[2] If the reader desires to know the details of the plans, plots and conniving of Satan and how he deceives people in their religion with respect to beliefs, acts of worship and deeds, and how he toys with the Jews, Christians, Magians and idol worshippers, then he must read the following two books: *Talbees Iblees* by ibn al-Jauzi and *Ighaatha al-Luhfaan* by ibn al-Qayyim.

## 7. Differing from Satan

Satan appears in the form of a sincere advisor and claims that he is giving sincere advice to humans. It is incumbent upon the person to do the opposite of what he orders and to say to him, "If you were to advise anyone, you should advise yourself. You have put yourself in the Hell-fire. And you have earned the wrath of Allah. How can anyone advise another when he does not advise himself?" Al-Haarith ibn Qais said, "If Satan comes to you while you are praying, and says, 'You are showing off,' then rebuke him and make it even longer!"[1] This was his insight, may Allah have mercy on him. If we are aware that there is some act that is pleasing to Satan or is one of his characteristics, then we must act in a contrary manner. For example, if Satan eats with his left hand, then we must eat with our right hand. The Prophet (peace be upon him) said,

لِيَأْكُلْ أَحَدُكُمْ بِيَمِينِهِ وَلْيَشْرَبْ بِيَمِينِهِ وَلْيَأْخُذْ بِيَمِينِهِ وَلْيُعْطِ بِيَمِينِهِ فَإِنَّ الشَّيْطَانَ يَأْكُلُ بِشِمَالِهِ وَيَشْرَبُ بِشِمَالِهِ وَيُعْطِي بِشِمَالِهِ وَيَأْخُذُ بِشِمَالِهِ

"Each of you should eat with his right, drink with his right, take with his right and give with his right for Satan eats with his left, drinks with his left, gives with his left and takes with his left."[2] Also Satan drinks with us if we drink standing; therefore the Prophet (peace be upon him) taught us that we should drink sitting.

Also the Prophet (peace be upon him) told us that we should take a short nap at midday because Satan does not do so. He said, "Take a short nap because Satan does not take a short nap."[3]

The Quran has warned us about extravagant spending. It has counted the one who spends extravagantly as a brother of Satan. This is true because Satan loves the wasting of wealth and its spending where it

---

[1] Quoted in *Talbees*, p. 38.
[2] This was recorded by ibn Majah with a *sahih* chain. See al-Albani, *Sahih al-Jaami*, vol. 5, p. 81.
[3] This was recorded by Abu Nuaim in *al-Tibb* with a *hasan* chain. See al-Albani, *Sahih al-Jaami*, vol. 4, p. 174.

is not needed. And under the heading of extravagance comes the owning of more furniture and bedrooms than one needs. The Prophet (peace be upon him) said,

فِرَاشٌ لِلرَّجُلِ وَفِرَاشٌ لِامْرَأَتِهِ وَالثَّالِثُ لِلضَّيْفِ وَالرَّابِعُ لِلشَّيْطَانِ

"Bedding for the man, bedding for his wife, bedding for a guest, and the fourth bedding is for Satan."[1]

Concerning this aspect, the Prophet (peace be upon him) has also instructed us about the food that we drop. We should not leave it for Satan. We should remove the dirt from it and eat it. He (peace be on him) said,

إِنَّ الشَّيْطَانَ يَحْضُرُ أَحَدَكُمْ عِنْدَ كُلِّ شَيْءٍ مِنْ شَأْنِهِ حَتَّى يَحْضُرَهُ عِنْدَ طَعَامِهِ فَإِذَا سَقَطَتْ مِنْ أَحَدِكُمُ اللُّقْمَةُ فَلْيُمِطْ مَا كَانَ بِهَا مِنْ أَذًى ثُمَّ لِيَأْكُلْهَا وَلَا يَدَعْهَا لِلشَّيْطَانِ فَإِذَا فَرَغَ فَلْيَلْعَقْ أَصَابِعَهُ فَإِنَّهُ لَا يَدْرِي فِي أَيِّ طَعَامِهِ تَكُونُ الْبَرَكَةُ

"Verily, Satan is present with you in every affair, he is even present with you when you take your meals. So if a portion of food should fall, then wipe off any dirt that may be upon it and eat it and do not leave it for Satan. And when one is finished, he should lick his fingers for he does not know wherein may lie the blessings." This was related by Muslim in his *Sahih*.[2]

## The transportation of the devils and their lodging

The transportation in the form of camels, horses and donkeys in the olden days, and in the form of cars and other similar vehicles in the

---

[1] This was recorded by Ahma al-Nasai and Abu Dawud with a *sahih* chain. See al-Albani, *Sahih al-Jaami*, vol. 4, p. 8. [Actually, it was also recorded by Muslim.—JZ]
[2] See al-Albani, *Sahih al-Jaami*, vol. 2, p. 75.

present day are for the benefit of mankind. However, if the owner of a car does not have use for it and passes by a people who need it for transportation and he does not allow them to use it, then it is a vehicle of the devils. It is stated in a hadith,

$$\text{تَكُونُ إِبِلٌ لِلشَّيَاطِينِ وَبُيُوتٌ لِلشَّيَاطِينِ فَأَمَّا إِبِلُ الشَّيَاطِينِ فَقَدْ رَأَيْتُهَا يَخْرُجُ أَحَدُكُمْ بِجُنَيْبَاتٍ مَعَهُ قَدْ أَسْمَنَهَا فَلَا يَعْلُو بَعِيرًا مِنْهَا وَيَمُرُّ بِأَخِيهِ قَدِ انْقَطَعَ بِهِ فَلَا يَحْمِلُهُ وَأَمَّا بُيُوتُ الشَّيَاطِينِ فَلَمْ أَرَهَا}$$

"There will be camels for the devils and houses for the devils. As for the camels of the devils, I have already seen them. One of you goes out with an animal that he has made fat and passes by his brother who is in need of a lift, and he does not give him a ride. As for the houses of the devils I have not seen them yet."[1] Perhaps the meaning of the houses of the devils in that hadith are the modern day automobiles. People ride them and are always passing up their brothers who need rides without stopping for them.

The horses and animals that are counted among the horses of Satan are those on which bets and wagers are made. The Messenger of Allah (peace be upon him) said,

$$\text{الْخَيْلُ ثَلَاثَةٌ فَفَرَسٌ لِلرَّحْمَنِ وَفَرَسٌ لِلْإِنْسَانِ وَفَرَسٌ لِلشَّيْطَانِ فَأَمَّا فَرَسُ الرَّحْمَنِ فَالَّذِي يُرْبَطُ فِي سَبِيلِ اللَّهِ فَعَلَفُهُ وَرَوْثُهُ وَبَوْلُهُ وَذَكَرَ مَا شَاءَ اللَّهُ وَأَمَّا فَرَسُ الشَّيْطَانِ فَالَّذِي يُقَامَرُ أَوْ يُرَاهَنُ عَلَيْهِ وَأَمَّا فَرَسُ الْإِنْسَانِ فَالْفَرَسُ يَرْتَبِطُهَا الْإِنْسَانُ يَلْتَمِسُ بَطْنَهَا فَهِيَ تَسْتُرُ مِنْ فَقْرٍ}$$

"Horses are of three kinds: the horses of the Merciful One (Allah), the horses of Satan, and the horses of man. The horse of the most Merciful is the horse that is dedicated to fighting in the way of Allah. Therefore, its

---

[1] Recorded by Abu Dawud with a *sahih* chain. See al-Albani, *Silsilat*, vol. 1, p. 148.

feeding, dung, urine and everything related to it are considered good deeds. The horse of Satan is that horse on which the people bet and gamble. The horse of man is that which is used for breeding and which is a protection against poverty."[1]

## Haste is from Satan

A characteristic loved by Satan is haste which leads humans to make mistakes. The Prophet (peace be upon him) said, "Deliberateness is from the Merciful and haste is from Satan."[2] It is obligatory upon us to differ from Satan in this characteristic and to act in a manner that is pleasing to the Merciful one. The Messenger of Allah also said to one of his companions,

إِنَّ فِيكَ خَصْلَتَيْنِ يُحِبُّهُمَا اللَّهُ الْحِلْمُ وَالْأَنَاةُ

"You have two characteristics that Allah and His Messenger love: clemency and deliberateness."[3]

## Yawning

From among the actions loved by Satan is yawning. It is for this reason that the Prophet (peace be upon him) ordered us to restrain yawns as much as possible. He said,

التَّثَاؤُبُ مِنَ الشَّيْطَانِ فَإِذَا تَثَاءَبَ أَحَدُكُمْ فَلْيَرُدَّهُ مَا اسْتَطَاعَ فَإِنَّ أَحَدَكُمْ إِذَا قَالَ هَا ضَحِكَ الشَّيْطَانُ

---

[1] This was recorded by Ahmad with a *sahih* chain. See al-Albani, *Sahih al-Jaami*, vol. 3, p. 137.
[2] This was recorded by al-Baihaqi in *Shuab al-Iman* with a *hasan* chain. See al-Albani, *Sahih al-Jaami*, vol. 3, p. 57.
[3] Recorded by Muslim.—JZ

"Yawning is from Satan. If one of you yawns, restrain it as much as you can. If one of you says, 'Ah!' while yawning, Satan laughs at him." (This hadith was recorded by al-Bukhari and Muslim.) This is because yawning is a sign of laziness. Satan is pleased and rejoices when the human becomes lazy. Due to laziness, his actions and sacrifices that raise him in Allah's sight become less.

## 8. Repentance and seeking forgiveness

Quick repentance and returning to Allah whenever one is seduced by Satan aids the servant against the plans of Satan. This is a characteristic of the pious servants of Allah. Allah says,

إِنَّ ٱلَّذِينَ ٱتَّقَوْا۟ إِذَا مَسَّهُمْ طَٰٓئِفٌ مِّنَ ٱلشَّيْطَٰنِ تَذَكَّرُوا۟ فَإِذَا هُم مُّبْصِرُونَ

"Lo! those who ward off evil, when a glamour from the devil troubles them, they do but remember (Allah) and behold they then see [what is right]" (*al-Araaf* 201). This verse as been explained as being in reference to thinking about or actually committing sins. They then remember the punishment of Allah and the reward from Allah in case of good deeds and Allah's promise, so they repent and return quickly to Him and they seek refuge in Him. "And behold they then see," means that they stand by the right and correct what they have done. This points to the fact that Satan plots to make the person blind from the truth and his eyes and heart become covered by desires and doubts.

The Prophet (peace be upon him) said,

إِنَّ الشَّيْطَانَ قَالَ وَعِزَّتِكَ يَا رَبِّ لَا أَبْرَحُ أُغْوِي عِبَادَكَ مَا دَامَتْ أَرْوَاحُهُمْ فِي أَجْسَادِهِمْ قَالَ الرَّبُّ وَعِزَّتِي وَجَلَالِي لَا أَزَالُ أَغْفِرُ لَهُمْ مَا اسْتَغْفَرُونِي

"Verily, Satan said, 'By your honor, Oh Lord, your servants will never be free from my seductions as long as their souls are in their bodies.' And the Lord said, "By My Honor and Grandeur, I will not stop to forgive those who ask for my forgiveness.""[1]

That is the case for those servants who return to Allah soon after their deed and repent. In this matter they have a perfect example in their father Adam. When Adam ate from the tree, he was given words of repentance from his Lord and he repented. Adam and his wife both turned to Allah, saying,

$$\text{قَالَا رَبَّنَا ظَلَمْنَا أَنفُسَنَا وَإِن لَّمْ تَغْفِرْ لَنَا وَتَرْحَمْنَا لَنَكُونَنَّ مِنَ ٱلْخَٰسِرِينَ}$$

"Our Lord! We have wronged ourselves. If You forgive us not and have not mercy on us, surely we are of the lost" (al-Araaf 23).

As for the devotees and allies of Satan, Allah says about them,

$$\text{وَإِخْوَٰنُهُمْ يَمُدُّونَهُمْ فِى ٱلْغَىِّ ثُمَّ لَا يُقْصِرُونَ}$$

"Their brethren plunge them further into error and cease not" (al-Araaf 202). "Their brethren" here refers to the brothers of the devils among the humans, as in the verse,

$$\text{إِنَّ ٱلْمُبَذِّرِينَ كَانُوٓا۟ إِخْوَٰنَ ٱلشَّيَٰطِينِ}$$

"Lo! The squanderers were ever brothers of the devils" (al-Israa 27). They obey and listen to the devils and accept what they order. And "plunge them further into error," means that they adorn the sins and make them look good, as in the verse,

---

[1] This was recorded by Ahmad in his *Musnad* and by al-Hakim in his *Mustadrak*. See al-Albani, *Sahih al-Jaami*, vol. 2, p. 72.

$$\text{أَلَمْ تَرَ أَنَّا أَرْسَلْنَا ٱلشَّيَٰطِينَ عَلَى ٱلْكَٰفِرِينَ تَؤُزُّهُمْ أَزًّا}$$

"Do you see not that We have set the devils on the disbelievers to confound them with confusion" (*Maryam* 83).

## 9. To put an end to the suspicious aspects and the questionable matters by which Satan enters into the soul

You should never allow yourself to be in a doubtful or questionable situation. When that is the case, you should tell others about what is happening, to make the matter clear to them. And you should not to allow Satan to whisper into the souls of the Muslims. On this matter, the Prophet (peace be upon him) has set a perfect example for us. Earlier we mentioned the hadith from al-Bukhari and Muslim in which Safiya bint Hayy came to visit and talk to the Prophet (peace be upon him) while he was making seclusion in the mosque. She got up to go back home and the Prophet (peace be upon him) also got up to walk her back home. Her apartment was in the house of Usama ibn Zaid. Two men of the Ansar passed by. When they notice the Messenger of Allah (peace be upon him), they passed by quickly. The Messenger of Allah informed them that that was his wife Safiyyah bint Hayy. They glorified Allah, implying that they could not have any suspicion with respect to the Messenger of Allah and he told them, "Satan flows in the human like the flowing of the blood. I was afraid that he would forge some evil lie in your hearts or say something to you."

Al-Khattabi said, "From the beneficial points of that hadith is that it is preferable for a person to be cautious concerning any disliked act that may lead to doubts or bring some thought to the hearts. He should himself show to the people that he is free of any suspect act." It has been related that al-Shafi said that the Prophet (peace be upon him) feared that something would occur to them in their hearts and they would think about it and be led astray or out of Islam. Hence, the Prophet (peace be on him) said that to them out of apprehension for them and not for himself.[1] Allah has guided us to speak well among each other in order to prevent Satan from putting enmity and hatred between us. Allah says in the Quran,

وَقُل لِّعِبَادِى يَقُولُواْ ٱلَّتِى هِىَ أَحْسَنُ إِنَّ ٱلشَّيْطَانَ يَنزَغُ بَيْنَهُمْ

"Tell My bondsmen to speak that which is kindlier. Lo! Satan sows discord among them. Lo! Satan is for man an open foe" (*al-Israa* 53). Some people are very lax with respect to this order from Allah. They speak to their brother in some ambiguous fashion or call him by a nickname that he does not like and from that Satan enters to cause discord between them instead of love and closeness.

## The cure for being possessed

Previously it was mentioned that Satan is the cause of what is known as possession or the "touch of the jinn." Here we shall try to make clear the cause of possession and its cure.

### The causes of being possessed

Ibn Taimiya explained,

> Possession of the human by the jinn can occur from desires, lusts, passions and zealousness in the same way that a human is in accord with another human... And it also occurs, and this is the majority case, due to hatred and revenge. For example, one of the humans harms a jinn or the jinn thinks that the human was trying to harm them

---

[1] Quoted in ibn al-Jauzi, *Talbees*, p. 46.

by urinating on some jinn or throwing hot water on them or a human might kill a jinn, even though the human may not have realized that. Among the jinn is ignorance and wrongdoing and, therefore, they get revenge from humans above and beyond what is just. And it could occur from the horseplay or simply evil acts of the jinn in the same way the evil is done by the foolish of the humans.[1]

## Our obligation towards them

We mentioned that the jinn have been ordered to worship according to the prescribed law. If a Muslim is able to contact a jinn, in the same way that a human speaks to a jinn that has taken over a human body, the Muslim must seek to enforce the Islamic law upon the jinn, that is, encourage the jinn to good and so on.

If the possessed is from the first type above, due to desires, lust or passion, then it is a great lewd act that has been prohibited by Allah for humans and jinn. This is true even if it is with the approval of the other party— therefore, what must obviously be the ruling if the other party does not like it? It is a lewd and oppressive act. One must tell the jinn that and inform him that it is a prohibited act and provide evidence against such an act such that the ruling is clear to him. And inform him that this is the rule of Allah and His Messenger that was sent to all the beings: jinn or human.

If it is from the second type, where some human had harmed them, if the human was not aware of that, then inform the jinn that the human was acting in ignorance and that he did not intend to harm the jinn. Therefore he does not deserve the punishment that is being given to him. If the action occurred in the person's house or on his property, then inform the jinn that the person was just acting in a manner that was permissible to him. And the jinn need not live in a place that belongs to a human without the human's permission for they are allowed the dilapidated and abandoned buildings.

---

[1] Ibn Taimiya, *Majmu*, vol. 19, p. 39.

Ibn Taimiya said,

If the jinn is wronging the human, then inform the jinn of the rule of Allah and His Messenger and provide evidences for him to establish the proof against him. And order him to the good and forbid him from doing the evil, in the same manner that one treats another human. As Allah says, "We never punish until We have sent a messenger" (*al-Israa* 15). And He says, "O you assembly of the jinn and humankind. Came there not unto you messengers of your own who recounted unto you of My tokens and warned you of the meeting of this your Day?" (*al-Anaam* 130).[1]

## Prohibition of killing the snakes of the houses

Ibn Taimiya said, "It is for this reason that the Messenger of Allah (peace be upon him) forbade the killing of the snakes in the house without first giving them proper warning three times." We have already mentioned the hadith on this question. Ibn Taimiya mentions the hadith and then explains the reasoning behind it,

> To kill a jinn without any right is not permissible in the same way that it is not permissible to kill a human without any due right. Oppression or wrongdoing is forbidden under any circumstance. It is not allowed for anybody to wrong another, even if the other person is an unbeliever. Allah says, "Let not hatred of any people seduce you that you act unjustly. Deal justly, that is nearer to your duty. Observe your duty to Allah" (*al-Maaida* 8). The snake in the house could be one of the jinn. So it should be given three warnings and if it leaves, [fine. If not, then] kill it. If it is a jinn, it may have come as a snake to frighten the humans. This provocation means it is allowed to be

---

[1] Ibn Taimiya, *Majmu*, vol. 19, p. 42.

repelled, even if this implies killing it. Otherwise, killing it for no proper reason is not permissible.

## Abusing the jinn and striking them

Ibn Taimiya mentions that it is obligatory to aid one's brother who is being wronged. The one who is a victim of possession is being wronged. But aid is also only done with justice, as Allah has ordered. If one does not drive away the jinn with exhortation, proof and consultation, then it is allowed to abuse, strike or curse the jinn in order to drive it away. This is what the Prophet (peace be upon him) did with the devil who put a flame of fire in his face, he said, "I seek refuge in Allah from you, and I curse you with the curse of Allah." He said that three times.

Ibn Taimiya also mentioned that one may be forced to strike the jinn in order to try to drive it away. One may strike the possessed numerous times as the strikes will harm the jinn and not the human who is being harmed, until the person comes to and he will not have felt a thing. There will be no mark left on the person himself. It has been the case that some have been struck three hundred to four hundred times on the leg, such that had it been a human he would have been killed. But it is the jinn that is being hit and screams. Ibn Taimiya has related that he himself has done and witnessed such an act on many occasions.

## Using *dhikr* and Quranic reciting as help against the jinn

The best thing that can be used against the jinn in the case of possession is the mentioning of Allah and reciting of the Quran, especially the verse of the throne (*al-Baqara* 255), "For whoever reads it, Allah will not stop to have a protector for him and Satan will not come close to him until the morning." This is in a hadith from *Sahih al-Bukhari* that was presented earlier.

Ibn Taimiya wrote,

The numerous people who have experienced these events all confirm the amazing effectiveness of this verse in warding of devils and breaking their spells. It has a great effect in repelling devils from humans, from the possessed and from those picked out by devils, such as wrongdoers, people with bad tempers, those who follow their desires and lusts, musicians and those who become ecstatic through whistling and clapping. If these verses are read over them with sincerity to Allah, the devils will leave. It will put an end to the mirages created by the devils. It will also disclose the falseness of those, the brothers of the devils, who perform miraculous acts. The devils inspire their devotees with some knowledge that the ignorant think are miracles that Allah grants His pious servants. In fact, they are simply Satan's acts of deception over his devotees, of those whom have earned Allah's wrath and those who have gone astray.[1]

## The Messenger (peace be upon him) drove away the jinn from the possessed

The Prophet (peace be upon him) did this on more than one occasion. In *Sunan Abu Dawud* and *Musnad Ahmad* it is recorded on the authority of Umm Abbaan bint al-Waazi ibn Zaari ibn Aamr al-Abdi on the authority of her father, that her grandfather went to the Messenger of Allah (peace be upon him) and with him was his son (or the son of his sister) who was possessed. Her grandfather said, "When we came to the Messenger of Allah (peace be upon him), I said, 'My son (or the son of my sister) is possessed. I want you to pray to Allah for him.'" The Messenger of Allah (peace be on him) said, "Bring him to me." So I went to get him from the group of riders. I took off his traveling clothes and put nicer clothes on him. Then I took him by his hand to the Messenger of Allah. The Messenger of Allah (peace be on him) said,

---

[1] Ibn Taimiya, *Majmu*, vol. 19, p. 55.

"Bring him closer to me and turn his back to me." So the Messenger of Allah grabbed his garment from top to bottom and struck him with such force in the back that I could see his armpit. He said, "Leave, oh enemy of Allah. Leave, oh enemy of Allah." After that the look of the boy changed to a healthier one. Then the Prophet sat the boy in front of himself and called for water and wiped the boy's face with some and made a supplication for him. After the Messenger of Allah's supplication, there was no one in his group who was better than him.[1]

In the *Musnad* it is also related from Yala ibn Marra that he said, "I have seen three things from the Prophet that no one saw before me nor after me. I went with him on a journey and we came upon a place on the trip where we found a woman sitting and with her was her boy. She said, 'Oh, Messenger of Allah, this boy is afflicted with a calamity and, therefore, we are afflicted by it. It afflicts him, in one day, I do not know how many times!' The Prophet asked for the boy to be given to him. The boy was lifted up to him. The Prophet placed the boy between himself and the saddle front. He opened the boy's mouth and blew in it three times, saying, 'In the name of Allah, I am a slave of Allah, be driven away, oh enemy of Allah.' Then he gave the boy back and said, 'On our way back we shall meet you here and you tell us what has happened.' We left and on the way back we found the woman in the same place with three sheep. The Prophet said, 'What has happened to your boy?' She said, 'By the One who has sent you with the truth nothing (of that nature) has occurred to him until now! So take these sheep.' The Prophet said, 'Go down and take one from her and leave the rest.'"

The Prophet (peace be upon him) made the jinn leave by ordering, striking and cursing. But by themselves they are not sufficient. One must also possess a strong faith and a good relationship with Allah to have a strong effect on the jinn as the following story will demonstrate.

---

[1] By a quick scan of both *Musnad Ahmad* and *Sunan Abu Dawud*, this translator could not find this hadith in either work.—JZ

## Imam Ahmad ordered the jinn to leave and they responded

It is related that Imam Ahmad was sitting in his mosque. There came to him one of his companions from the caliph al-Mutawakil. The man said to Ahmad, "In the house of the commander of the Believers, there is a slave-girl who is possessed. He sent me to you for you to pray for her recovery." Ahmad gave him a pair of wooden shoes and said, "Go to the house of the commander of the believers and sit at the head of the slave girl and say to the jinn, 'Ahmad has said to you, 'Which do you prefer: leaving this slave-girl or being struck by these shoes seventy times?'" The man went with the shoes to the slave girl and he did as he was instructed. He heard from the tongue of the slave-girl, "Listening and obedience is for Ahmad. If he were to order us to leave Iraq, we would leave it. He obeys Allah and for whoever obeys Allah, everything is obedient to him." It left the slave girl. She became better and afterwards she gave birth to children. Then Ahmad died and the jinn returned again to the slave girl. The commander called the same companion again to come. He came with the same shoes and said to the jinn, "Leave or else I will strike you with this shoe." The jinn said, "I will not leave nor will I obey you but Ahmad ibn Hanbal obeyed Allah and we were ordered to obey him."

## What the Healer Must Be Like

It is necessary that the one who is trying to cure the possessed be of strong faith and full of conviction that the remembrance of Allah and Quranic recitation will have an effect on the person and the jinn. The stronger the faith, the stronger the effect on the jinn. Perhaps the person is stronger than the jinn in faith and, therefore, he drives the jinn out. Perhaps the jinn is stronger and, therefore, he does not leave. Perhaps the person is weak in faith and the jinn has intended him harm. So the person must continue to make supplications and invoke the aid of remembrance of Allah and Quranic recitation, in particular the verse of the Throne.

## Incantations and invocations

Ibn Taimiya stated,

Concerning curing the possessed by means of incantations and invocations, there are two types: One type is where the meaning of the incantation is clear. It is within what Islam allows to be said by any person, such as prayers to Allah and mentioning His name and His speech to His creation and so on. This type is allowed to be used as an incantation in the case of possession as is confirmed in the *Sahih* that the Prophet (peace be upon him) said, "What is permissible in incantations is what does not contain any polytheism." And he also said, "If one of you is able to aid his brother, then he should do so."

If the incantation contains statements that are forbidden, such as elements of some type of polytheism, or they have no understandable meaning to them, which might imply some words of disbelief, then it is not allowed for anyone to use such an incantation. This is the ruling even if the jinn should leave after its use because Allah and His Messenger have prohibited it due to its harm being greater than its benefit.[1]

He also mentioned at another place[2] that many of those people who use the polytheistic incantations are unable to repel the jinn. Many times they are not able to overpower the jinn when they ask them to kill or capture a jinn that has possessed a human. The jinn deceives them and only makes it seem like they killed or captured that jinn.

---

[1] Ibn Taimiya, *Majmu*, vol. 24, p. 277.
[2] Ibn Taimiya, *Majmu*, vol. 19, p. 46.

## Conciliation to the jinn

Some people endeavor to please the possessing jinn by performing animal sacrifices to them. That is an act of polytheism that Allah and His Messenger have prohibited. It is related that the Prophet (peace be on him) prohibited sacrificing to the jinn.

Some people allege that this falls under the category of using something that is forbidden as a medicine. But this is a grave mistake on their part. Actually, Allah never places a cure in something that is forbidden. Even if one accepts the opinion that it is permissible to use forbidden objects, such as dead carrion or pork as medicine, this cannot be used as a proof that it is permissible to make sacrifices to the jinn. About using forbidden things as medicine, there is a dispute among the jurists, but there is no difference of opinion about the illegality of using polytheism and disbelief as medicine; this is forbidden by all the scholars. There is no dispute on this point.

# The reality of the struggle

To end this section, I would like to reproduce ibn al-Qayyim's important discourse on the reality of the struggle and its nature. He said,

> Allah chose man from among His creation and honored him, selected him and made him the seat of the aspects of faith, oneness of Allah, sincerity, love and hope in Allah. But He also tested man with desires, enmity and heedlessness. He also tested man by his enemy Iblees that never lets up.[1]

Then he wrote,

> He [Satan] enters upon the person through the doors of his own soul and nature. Therefore, his soul is inclined towards him. Because he gets to the person through the

---

[1] Ibn al-Qayyim, *al-Waabil al-Sayib*, p. 21.

things he loves. So he works with the soul and the person's desires against the person. Hence, there are three controlling conspirers. They make the person's limbs act out their commands, as the limbs are simply instruments for the execution of acts. It is the person's will, which is controlled by those three [mentioned above], that drives them. The case of the limbs is just to obey what they have been ordered to do. This is the affairs of the slave. But because of His Lord's mercy, Allah, the All-Powerful, the Merciful, has sent another soldier to help him and has given him another force to fight off that force that seeks his destruction. He has sent His messengers to him. He has revealed His book for him. And He has helped him with an honorable angel to oppose his enemy Satan. If Satan orders him to do something, the angel orders him to follow the command of his Lord. And he shows him the destruction that will be the result of following the enemy. Sometimes one force is successful and sometimes the other force is. The person who is given victory is the one whom Allah supports. The one who is preserved is the one whom Allah guards. He makes for him, in opposition to the soul that commands the person to do wrong, the soul that is filled with tranquillity. When the soul orders to evil, the tranquil soul keeps him from it. If the evil commanding soul tries to keep him from good, the tranquil soul orders him to do it. Sometimes the person will obey this one and sometimes he obeys the other. That is the normal case. Perhaps one of them may have a complete control over him such that the other never has any control over him.[1]

---

[1] These different aspects of the soul are based on the Quranic verses, "Lo! the human soul enjoins unto evil," (*Yusuf* 53) this is the lower self of man that incites to evil. And, "But ah! Thou soul at peace! Return unto thy Lord, content in His Good Pleasure" (*al-Fajr* 27-28).— J.Z.

Against those desires that lead one to follow Satan and the instigating soul, Allah made light, vision and intelligence that lead one to reject the following of the desires. Every time he wants to follow desires, the intellect, vision and light call out in warning, "Be aware, be aware. One who destructs and ruins is in front of you. You are the hunted for the criminals."

Sometimes he obeys the advisor and his guidance and the right way is made clear to him. And sometimes he follows the guide of desires and he breaks away from the path. His wealth is taken and his clothes are stolen. And it is said, "Do you see from where you have come?" The strange thing is that he knows from where he has come. And he knows the path that he has been cut off from and the path that he has taken. But he insists on following it and his guide has made him firm in it and has ruled over him and has overpowered him. If he were to make it weakened by going against it, warning it when it calls him, fighting it when it wants to take him, he would be able to control himself from it. But he himself gives himself over; he gives it his hand. He is like a person who puts his hand into the hand of his enemy. He gives him glad tidings and then metes him out a painful punishment. He seeks help but it does not help him. This is how he becomes a prisoner to Satan, lusts and the instigating soul. Then he seeks rescue from it and he is not able to be rescued. When the person has been tried with what he has been tried with, he is supported by soldiers, numbers and fortresses [such as words of *dhikr*]. It is said, "Fight your enemy and struggle against him. These are the soldiers and take whichever of them you wish. These are the fortresses and use any of them you will. And cling to them until death and the matter is soon and the time of clinging will be short indeed." It is as if a great king has sent for you and taken you to his residence. You are made to rest from that struggle. You are separated from your enemy. You go wherever you wish within that noble residence [of Paradise]. And your enemy is imprisoned in the harshest conditions in front of your eyes.

He has entered into that prison [Hell] that he wanted to leave you in and its gates have been closed upon him. He despairs of any rescue. You are in the midst of those things that your soul desires and that are pleasing to your eyes. This is the reward for your patience during that short span of time and your clinging to guard posts in the battlefield. It was only but a short span of time that was then finished, as if there were no hardship at all. If the soul becomes weak and forgets about what a short span of time it is and how quickly it will be finished, he should ponder Allah's words, "On the day when they see that which they are promised (it will seem to them) as though they had lived but an hour of daylight" (*al-Ahqaaf* 35). "On the Day when they behold it, it will be as if they had but lived for an evening or the morning thereof" (*an-Naaziaat* 46). And, "He will say: How long did you stay on the earth, counting by years? They will say: We stayed but a day or part of a day. Ask of those who keep count. He will say: You tarried but a little if you only knew" (*al-Muminoon* 112-114) And, "The day when the Trumpet is blown. On that Day We assemble the guilty white-eyed (with terror), murmuring among themselves: You have lived but ten (days). We are best aware of what they utter when their best in conduct say: You have lived but a day" (*Taha* 102-104). One time the Prophet (peace be upon him) was addressing his companions while the sun was just over the top of the mountain, close to setting, and he said, "There is not left of this world, compared to what has already past, save as much as is left of this day compared to what has passed." (Recorded by Ahmad in his *Musnad*, at-Tirmidhi in his *Sunan*. Al-Tirmidhi called it *hasan sahih*.) The intelligent, sincere person must ponder over this hadith for his own well-being. He must realize what little is to be achieved of what is left of this world and realize that he is in a world of deception and dreams. He has traded the eternal happiness and everlasting bounties for a measly price that is worth nothing. If he were to seek the pleasure of Allah and the life of the Hereafter, he would be given a wonderful and great bounty. As it states in a report, "Son of Adam, sell this world for the hereafter, and you will profit by both. And do not sell the hereafter for this world, as then you will lose both of them."

One of the early scholars said, "Son of Adam, you are in need of your portion of this world, but you are much more in need of your portion in the hereafter. If you start with your portion in this life, you will lose part of your portion in the Hereafter. Be careful about your portion of this life. But if you start with your portion of the Hereafter, you will be successful also in your portion of this life."

Umar ibn Abdul Aziz said in his speech, "O people, you have not been created without a purpose. Nor have you been left without guidance. You are promised a day in which Allah will judge between you and separate you. And the servant who has been barred from the mercy of Allah that encompasses all things and thrown out of His paradise that is as wide as the heavens and the earth will be miserable and frustrated. Tomorrow, safety and security will be for the one who fears Allah and is conscious of Him. He who purchased a big thing by a small thing. He who purchased an everlasting thing for a fleeting one. He who buys happiness in the place of misery. Do you not see that you are in the way of those who are to die. And you leave behind you those who will remain. Everyday people are dying in front of you and going to meet Allah. And you throw them in their graves. Their loves and hopes have come to an end. The means have come to an end. They have left their friends and are facing the account."

The point is that Allah gives us, in this short period, soldiers and resources to protect ourselves from our enemies. He has even shown us what protects ourselves from our own enemies and how to free ourselves if we are made prisoner by them. Imam Ahmad recorded in his *Musnad* and at-Tirmidhi in his *Sunan*, from the hadith of al-Haarith al-Ashari, that the Prophet (peace be upon him) said, "Verily, Allah ordered John the son of Zakariya with five commands, that he must act by and order the children of Israel to act by. And he was about to be slow in delivering them. Jesus said to him, 'Allah ordered you to five commands, to act by them and to order the children of Israel to act by them, so either you order them or I will order them.' John said, 'I fear that if you beat me to it that I shall be swallowed up and punished.' So John gathered the people in Bait al-Maqdis. The mosque was filled. John sat in his place and said, 'Allah has ordered me by five commands, to act by them and to order you to act by them...'" The fifth of those was, "And I order you to remember Allah as it is like a person who is being quickly followed by his enemies until he takes refuge in a fort and he protects himself from them. Similarly, the servant cannot protect himself from Satan except by the remembrance of Allah." (Al-Tirmidhi called the hadith *hasan sahih*.)

He also ordered the people to prayer. "And I order you to prayer. And if you pray, do not turn away for Allah sets His face to the face of the servant in prayer as long as he does not turn away." The turning away that is prohibited in the prayer is of two types: (1) Turning the heart away from Allah to something other than Allah. (2) Turning the sight or the face away. Both of them are prohibited. Allah does not stop facing the slave as long as the slave stays in his prayer and does not turn away from Allah. If his face or heart turns away, Allah turns away from him. The Prophet (peace be upon him) was asked about turning away in the prayer and he said, "This is what Satan steals from the prayer of the person."[1] In a report it is stated that Allah says, "Are you turning to something better then Me? Something better than Me?" One who does such an act is like a person who receives an audience with a king and during the conversation he is looking to his left and to his right. His heart has left the king and he does not understand what the king said. This is because his heart is not present with the king. What does that person expect the king would do to him? At the least, he would expect the king to turn away from him in anger due to the way be behaved. Isn't that much less than the case of the person who turns away from Allah during the prayer and earns Allah's anger? Such a worshipper is not equal to the one whose heart is conscience and turning to Allah in the prayer and in whose heart he realizes the greatness of the One he is standing before. His heart is filled with awe. His neck is in submission to Him. He is ashamed to turn towards something else in front of Allah or that Allah would turn from him. The difference between one who does such an act in the prayer and one who does not do so is like the difference between the heavens and the earth. Hasaan Ibn Atiya said, "Two people participate in the

---

[1] Recorded by Ahmad in *al-Musnad* (vol. 6, pp. 106-7), al-Bukhari (vol. 2, p. 194) in "The Book of the Call to Prayer", Chapter: Turning During the Prayer, Abu Dawud (number 910) in "The book of Prayer", Chapter: Turning during the Prayer, al-Tirmidhi (number 590) in "The Book of Prayer", Chapter: What has been narrated concerning turning during the prayer and al-Nasaai (vol. 3, p. 8) in "The Book of Forgetfulness", Chapter: Stern warning concerning turning during the prayer, from the hadith of Aisha. (From the editor of *al-Waabil al-Sayib*.)

same prayer but there is a difference between them in merit like the difference between the heavens and the earth. That is because one of them sets his heart to Allah while the other is not thoughtful and is heedless. When the person turns his thoughts to some other creation similar to himself, between him and His Lord there is a curtain. He does not turn to Allah or come close to him. What do you think of the Creator's reaction towards him?"

If one stands in front of the Creator and between them there is a partition, which is the secret whispers, desires and the soul that is infatuated with them, then how can this really be a meeting? When a servant stands for prayer, Satan becomes jealous of him as the person is standing in the most honorable of settings. Satan comes close to him and tries to seduce him. He makes it hard for the one who is trying to pray and uses all of his devices and weapons to distract the person. He never stops returning to the slave and pestering him and trying to make him forget what he is supposed to be doing and saying. He disturbs him with his steeds and legs until the person takes the prayer lightly. When he takes the prayer lightly, he abandons it. If the servant can fight that off and disobey Satan and stand for the prayer, Satan then gets between the person and his own heart and he mentions to him in the prayer things that did not come to his mind beforehand, perhaps making him think that he has forgotten something important. The person despairs from that. Satan mentions that to him in the prayer in order to make his heart preoccupied with other things and to take him away from Allah. Therefore, the man stands in prayer without his heart. He did not receive from his standing in front of Allah and getting close to Him what the person receives whose heart is attuned to Allah's presence in the prayer. Then he leaves the prayer in the same way that he entered it, with his mistakes, burdens and sins. And the prayer did not aid him in eradicating those sins. For the prayer only wipes out the evil deeds if the prayer is performed correctly, with humbleness to Allah, and standing in front of Allah in body and soul. In that case, the person will feel the affects of the prayer, feeling lighter as if weights had been taken off of him. He finds the prayer to be spirit and life. And he wishes that he had never finished the prayer because in the prayer he finds the sweetness of his eyes and his true pleasure. In the prayer, he finds the paradise of his heart and the rest from this world. When he returns to this world from the prayer he feels like he is in a tight cell of a prison until he returns to the prayer. He gets rests in the prayer and does not rest from the prayer. Those who truly love Allah say, "We pray to get rest in our prayer," as their *imam*, leader and prophet said before them, "Oh Bilal, give us rest by the prayer." He did not say, "Give us rest from the prayer!" He also said that the pleasure of his eyes lies in the prayer. The one for whom the prayer is the pleasure of his eyes, how can his eyes be pleased without it and how can he bear not being in the prayer.

It is related that when a servant stands to pray Allah says, "Raise the partition between us." But when he turns away, Allah says, "Lower it again." This turning away has been explained as the turning away of the heart. If one turns one's attention to something else, the partition comes back between him and Allah. Then Satan enters and presents to the person the affairs of this world. He shows it to him like in a mirror. If the person does not turn away from Allah, Satan does not have the ability to come between the person and Allah. Only when the partition comes down does Satan enter. If one flees to Allah and makes his heart aware of Allah, Satan flees. If he turns away, Satan becomes present. And this is how the person and how the enemy of Allah behaves with respect to the prayers.

## How can a person make his heart observant during the prayer?

[Ibn al-Qayyim also wrote,]

The person can make his heart attuned to the prayer and the remembrance of Allah if he is able to conquer his lusts and desires. If not, his heart will be conquered by his lusts and his desires have taken him prisoner. In that case, Satan will have found a place to sit and lurk. How can a person then become free of his secret whispering and thoughts?

The hearts are of three kinds: A heart which is free of any faith or goodness. This is the heart of the wrongdoer (to his own soul). Satan can take a rest from whispering into such a heart because it is his home or land. He decides within it whatever he pleases. He is completely established in that heart.

The second type of heart is a heart which is somewhat lit by the light of faith. Its lamp is there. But there is also the darkness of lusts and desires within the same heart. Satan comes to this heart and must also leave it at times. In such a heart, Satan is at war. Such a heart has different circumstances in different people. Some hearts of this nature are victorious over Satan the majority of the time, while others are losers to Satan the majority of the time. While others run about fifty-fifty.

The third type of heart is a heart which is filled with the light of faith which completely removes the lusts and their veils as well as the darkness from them. Faith is a type of radiance that burns the whispering whenever it comes close. It is like the stars in the heavens; if Satan approaches, then meteors are thrown at them and burn them. The heavens are not more inviolable than the believer. Allah protects the believer to a greater degree than He protects the heavens. The heavens are the places of worship for the angels and the place from whence comes the revelation and in it are the lights of obedience to Allah. But the heart of the believer contains the unicity of Allah, love for Allah, cognizance of Allah and faith in Allah. In it are their lights. It has the right to be guarded and protected from the schemes of its enemies. Nothing will pass to it save that it will be guarded from it.

Here is an excellent analogy: There are three types of houses. The home of the king that contains his treasures, jewels, and so on. The home of the common man that contains his treasures and provisions. But his provisions are not like that of the king. And an empty house that does not contain anything. If a thief was coming to one of these houses to steal something, which one would he come to? If you said the empty house, then your answer does not make any sense because in that house there is nothing to steal. It was said to Ibn Abbas, "The Jews allege that they receive no mischievous whispering during their prayers." He replied, "What is Satan to do with a heart that is ruined?" If you said the house of the king, that is an impossibility. It is too difficult to get into as there are always guards present that are watching the house. It would not be possible for the thief to enter therein. How will the thief even be able to get close to it? The only solution that is left for the thief is to go to the house of the common man. Therein is what will attract him.

Ponder this analogy. Let your heart think about it. This analogy perfectly describes the conditions of the three types of hearts. The heart that is void of faith and goodness is the heart of the unbeliever and the hypocrite. That is the house of Satan. He protects himself therein and has peace there. He takes it as his abode. There is no treasure or provision for him to steal from there as it all belongs to him. Therefore there is no need for the mischievous whispering either.

As for the heart that is filled with the presence of Allah and His grandeur, love for Him, protection from Him and so forth, no devil would be able to steal anything from it. The best a devil could ever do is take advantage of one of those rare moments where the person is negligent, as this happens to all people and he is human. It is the custom of man that forgetfulness, heedlessness and similar aspects sometimes occur to them.

Wahb ibn Munabbih narrated that in some of the previous divine books it was recorded that Allah said, "I do not reside in houses as they cannot encompass Me. And what thing can encompass Me when the heavens are filled by My Throne? But I am in the heart of the faithful one who leaves everything besides me." And that is the meaning of another report, "My heavens and My earth do not encompass me, but the heart of my believing slave encompasses me."[1] A heart has the [belief in the] oneness

---

[1] Al-Sakhawi stated in *al-Muqaasid al-Hasana*, "Al-Ghazali mentioned it in *Ihya* with the text, 'Allah said, "[The heavens and earth] do not encompass me]".' And he mentioned it with the wording, "The heart of my believing, soft-hearted, composed slave encompasses Me." Al-Sakhaawi said, "Al-Iraqi said, 'I do not find any source for it.' And ibn Taimiya said, 'It is recorded among the *Israaeeliyat* [stories that have their source in the Jews or Christians] and it has no known chain back to the Prophet (peace be on him). And it is recorded from al-Zarkashi that some of the scholars called it a *baatil* ("false") hadith and that it was fabricated by atheists.

of Allah, knowledge of Allah, love for Him, belief in him and affirmation of His promises in it as well as desires of the soul and its character and callers to desires.

The heart is between those two calls. Sometimes it tends to the call of faith, cognizance and love of Allah alone. But at other times it tends to the call of Satan and lusts. That type of heart is coveted by Satan. But Allah gives support to whomsoever He wills, "Victory comes only from Allah, the Mighty, the Wise" (*ali-Imraan* 126). But that heart cannot be overtaken by Satan except through the use of his weapons. Satan enters into it and he finds his weapons there [in the person's heart] and he takes them and fights with them. Satan's weapons are the lusts, doubts, deceptions and false hopes that are found in the heart. Satan finds these within the heart and uses them against the heart. But if the person has a stronger faith, it will be able to fight off Satan and overcome him. Otherwise the place is for Satan. There is no power or might except Allah. If the person permits Satan to enter, and he opens the door to his house and allows him to come in and use those weapons to fight himself with, then he can only blame himself...

---

Al-Ajaluni recorded that statement and approved of it. (From the editor of *al-Waabil al-Sayib*.)

# 6
# The Wisdom Behind the Creation of Satan

Satan is the fountainhead of evil and harm. He is the leader for the destruction of this life and the next. He raises his banner at every time and in every place. He calls people to disbelief and disobedience of the Merciful. Is there, then, any wisdom behind his creation? If yes, what is that wisdom? Ibn al-Qayyim has responded to this question in *Shifa al-Aleel* under the heading, "In the creation of Satan and his troops there is a wisdom that none can completely grasp save Allah."

## 1. The effects of fighting against Satan and his supporters leads to the perfection of worship

From this wisdom is the perfection and completion of the servitude by the Prophets and the servants of Allah by their struggling against the enemy of Allah and his party and by opposing Satan and his supporters. This also includes their angering Satan and his supporters. [Another important aspect is] their seeking refuge in Allah from Satan and their fleeing to Allah in order to seek refuge from Satan's evil and machinations. From all of that accrues such welfare in this world and the hereafter which would not have occurred without it. It also leads to the reaching of lofty positions of worship that would not have been reached without Satan's existence.

## 2. By the existence of Satan, the slaves of Allah become fearful due to their sins

The creation of Iblees has made the angels and humans fearful of their sins since they have witnessed what has become of Satan after his great sin. His fall from the rank of rule to that of the devils was great and complete. Of course, the angels who witnessed that event attained a new worship of Allah and a different submission to Him and fear of Him. They are like the slaves of a king who witness a slave being greatly humiliated. Those who witness that action will definitely be the most fearful and cautious in front of that king.

## 3. Allah has made him a lesson for those who reflect

Satan is a lesson for all who differ from the commands of Allah and who, out of pride, do not obey Allah and who perform acts of disobedience. This is in the same way that our father Adam is an example for all of those who make mistakes as was his repentance and his return to Allah. The fathers of the jinn and mankind were tested by their sins. One father is a lesson for all of those who continue in their sinful ways without repenting while the other is a lesson for anyone who sins and returns to his Lord. The signs of these two great examples are filled with wisdom and lessons.

## 4. Allah has made Satan a test and trial for His slaves

Satan is a quarrelsome creature by which Allah tests His creatures, thereby distinguishing those who are pure from those who are evil. Allah created the humans from the earth. Some of them are smooth and some are rough. Some of them are good and some are evil. Therefore, there must be something that makes their make-up apparent. The Prophet (peace be upon him) said,

إِنَّ اللَّهَ تَعَالَى خَلَقَ آدَمَ مِنْ قَبْضَةٍ قَبَضَهَا مِنْ جَمِيعِ الْأَرْضِ فَجَاءَ بَنُو آدَمَ عَلَى قَدْرِ الْأَرْضِ وَالسَّهْلُ وَالْحَزْنُ وَالْخَبِيثُ وَالطَّيِّبُ

"Allah created Adam from a handful which he took from all of the earth. So the children of Adam are corresponding to the earth, some are smooth, some are rough, some are good and some are bad."[1] What was in the original source is also in the creation. It is part of Allah's wisdom for these differences to exist and be exhibited. There must be a reason for these differences to come about. The creation of Satan is the instigator who makes it clear which of His creation are what. Iblees shows the difference between the good and the evil in the same way that the Messengers and Prophets from Allah also performed a similar trial. Allah says,

$$مَّا كَانَ ٱللَّهُ لِيَذَرَ ٱلْمُؤْمِنِينَ عَلَىٰ مَآ أَنتُمْ عَلَيْهِ حَتَّىٰ يَمِيزَ ٱلْخَبِيثَ مِنَ ٱلطَّيِّبِ$$

"It is not (the purpose) of Allah to leave you in your present state till He separates the wicked from the good" (*ali-Imraan* 179). The messengers were sent to the humans who are responsible for their actions. Some of the people are good and some are evil. The messengers join the good to the good and the evil to the evil.

It is the infinite wisdom of Allah that mixes these two groups of beings together in this world of trial and test. Then, in the everlasting world, they will be separated and one group will go to one abode while the other will go to the other abode, according to Allah's great wisdom and overriding decree.

## 5. The creation of Satan demonstrates the complete ability of Allah to create opposites

From the wisdom of creating Satan is Allah's showing that He is completely capable of creating the likes of Gabriel and the angels as well as Iblees and the devils. This is one of the greatest signs of His ability and power. He created opposites such as the heavens and the earth, light

---

[1] This is an abridgment of a hadith found in Ahmad, al-Tirmidhi, Abu Dawud and elsewhere. According to al-Albani, it is *sahih*. See al-Albani, *Sahih al-Jaami*, vol. 1, p. 362.—JZ

and darkness, paradise and hell, water and fire, hot and cold, good and evil and so on.

## 6. Opposites show the virtues of their opposites

Part of this wisdom is to show the complete goodness of one of the two opposites. Opposites show the good points of their opposites. If there was nothing that was ugly, we would not recognize what is beautiful. If it were not for poverty, we would not recognize the value of affluence.

## 7. Trials are a way to the actualization of thankfulness

From the wisdom of creating Satan is that Allah loves that thanks to Him should be actualized and realized. There is no doubt that His patrons are harmed by the existence of Iblees and his soldiers. Their being tested by him leads to a type of thankfulness that would not exist without Iblees' existence. Compare how many times Adam gave thanks to Allah while he was in the garden before he was expelled from there and how thankful he was after his tribulation; he gave true thanks and repented to Allah and that was accepted from him.

## 8. In the creation of Iblees rests many aspects of worship

Such worship includes the love of Allah, trust in Him, patience, being pleased with Allah and so on. These types of worship are most beloved to Allah. These types of worship are realized through struggle (*jihad*) and the submitting of one's self to Allah and to put one's love for Allah before anyone else. And *jihad* is the apex of worship and most beloved to Allah. These types of worship are fully actualized due to the creation of Iblees and his party. No one can enumerate all of the benefits of this aspect except Allah.

## 9. The creation of Satan makes Allah's signs clear as well as the wonderfulness of His power

In creating those beings that oppose His messengers, deny them and fight against them, Allah has opened the door to a way in which He has demonstrated many of His clear signs, power, wonderfulness of His creation and detail. These great signs make the existence of Iblees and his soldiers more beloved to Allah than their non-existence. These great signs include the flood at the time of Noah, the splitting of the sea, the rod, Moses' hand, saving Abraham from the fire and many other signs that prove His power, knowledge and wisdom that would not have occurred without the creation of those beings that oppose Him.

## 10. Iblees' creation from fire is a sign

Fire and related matters can be used for burning, overpowering others or corruption. But it also contains radiance and light. Allah is the one who brings out both of these aspects from it. In the same way, He made from the clay of the earth good and evil, soft and rough, red, black and white humans. This is a clear evidence and sign of His ability and Power. And they are signs that show that,

$$\text{لَيْسَ كَمِثْلِهِۦ شَيْءٌ وَهُوَ ٱلسَّمِيعُ ٱلْبَصِيرُ}$$

"There is nothing like Him, and He is the Hearer, the Seer" (*al-Shoora* 11).

## 11. Iblees' creation makes apparent the meaning of many of Allah's names

Many of Allah's attributes appear through the creation of Iblees, such as the Debaser, the Elevator, the Honorer, the Humiliator, the Judge, the Just, the Avenger, and so on. These names evoke their attached meanings that appear through His rulings such as His attributes of goodness, sustaining, mercy and so on. It is a must that both of these types of names be evident in this world.

## 12. The creation of Satan makes apparent Allah's complete rule and control over the affairs of this creation

Allah has complete rule and authority over this creation. His complete ability means His ability to administer the creation in any way, including the aspects of punishment, reward, humiliation, justice, grace, honoring and belittling. Both types of creation (good and bad) must be present for all of these aspects to be displayed.

## 13. Iblees' existence is from the completeness of Allah's wisdom

The All-Wise is one of Allah's names. Having wisdom is one of His attributes. This requires that He put everything in its proper place, for which nothing else would be proper, and with proper proportions. He has decided to make exact opposites, that have no common characteristics whatsoever. Would His Wisdom be complete except by that? Therefore, the existence of both types of creation is from His Infinite Wisdom in the same way as it is a sign of His Infinite Power.

## 14. Praise to Allah for what He has hindered and subdued

He is praiseworthy in everyone of His aspects, in His justice, hindering, subduing, elevating, and humiliating. In the same way He is praiseworthy for His granting, honoring, and elevating. His praise is complete in both aspects. He praises himself for both of those. The angels, messengers and servants also praise Him. All of this necessitates His complete praise. In His creation is perfect wisdom in the same way that for Him is perfect praise. It is not permissible to deny His praise in the same way that one cannot deny His wisdom.

## 15. By Iblees' creation, Allah shows His servants His calmness and patience

From the wisdom of the creation of Satan, Allah loves to show His servants His calmness, patience, mercy, generosity, and so on. In order for that to be exhibited, it was necessary to create beings that associate partners with Him, oppose His rule, strive to oppose Him and work to anger Him. Some even compete with Allah in His lordship. Still Allah grants them good things, health, provisions, and so forth. And He calls them to follow the way of good and to leave evil and polytheism. Even though, He still grants them all of those blessings, responds to their supplications, removes them from harm, and treats them kindly in the face of their disbelief, idolatry and evil. How much praise and wisdom belongs to Allah for all of that.

And He becomes beloved to His servants and they recognize His perfection. It is in the *Sahih* [of Muslim] that the Prophet (peace be upon him) said,

لَا أَحَدَ أَصْبَرُ عَلَى أَذًى يَسْمَعُهُ مِنَ اللهِ عَزَّ وَجَلَّ إِنَّهُ يُشْرَكُ بِهِ وَيُجْعَلُ لَهُ الْوَلَدُ ثُمَّ هُوَ يَرْزُقُهُمْ

"No one is more patient to the harm he hears than Allah. They claim He has a son while He provides for them."

And it is also in the *Sahih* [of al-Bukhari] that the Prophet (peace be upon him) related from the Lord,

قَالَ اللهُ عَزَّ وَجَلَّ كَذَّبَنِي ابْنُ آدَمَ وَلَمْ يَكُنْ يَنْبَغِي لَهُ أَنْ يُكَذِّبَنِي وَشَتَمَنِي ابْنُ آدَمَ وَلَمْ يَكُنْ يَنْبَغِي لَهُ أَنْ يَشْتُمَنِي أَمَّا تَكْذِيبُهُ إِيَّايَ فَقَوْلُهُ إِنِّي لَا أُعِيدُهُ كَمَا بَدَأْتُهُ وَلَيْسَ آخِرُ الْخَلْقِ بِأَعَزَّ عَلَيَّ مِنْ أَوَّلِهِ وَأَمَّا شَتْمُهُ

$$\text{إِيَّايَ فَقَوْلُهُ اتَّخَذَ اللَّهُ وَلَدًا وَأَنَا اللَّهُ الْأَحَدُ الصَّمَدُ لَمْ أَلِدْ وَلَمْ أُولَدْ وَلَمْ يَكُنْ لِي كُفُوًا أَحَدٌ}$$

"Allah has said, 'The son of Adam insulted me, and he had no right to do so. And he denied Me and he had no right to do so. As for his denying Me, it is his saying, 'He will not remake me as He made me in the first place.' And the initial creation is no easier for me than the remaking. As for his reviling Me, it is his saying, 'Allah has taken for himself a son,' while I am the One, the Everlasting, I beget not nor was I begotten. And there is none similar to Me.'"[1] Even with this reviling and denying, Allah still provides for the unbelievers in this world. He even cures them when they are ill. He even calls them to the way of paradise. He accepts their repentance when they repent. He changes their evil deeds into good deeds [at that time]. He is gentle with them at all times. He has made them qualified for accepting His message. He orders them to be soft in their speech and gentle. Al-Fadhl ibn Iyaadh said, "There is no night in which there is darkness except that Allah says, 'Who is greater in generosity than Me? The creatures disobey Me and I protect them in their beds as if they did not disobey Me. And I prolong their protection as if they did not commit sins. And I guard them as if they did not commit sins. I am generous with my providence to the sinner. And I give graciously to the one who commits evil. 'Is there one who calls me and I do not turn to him? Is there one who asks me and I do not give to him? I am the generous and from Me is generosity. And I am the noble and from Me is Nobility. From my nobility is that I give the slave whatever he asks from Me. And I give him what he did not ask for. And from my nobility is that I give the repenting one as if he did not disobey Me. Where can the creation flee from Me. And where from My gate can the sinners turn away to?'"

There is a narration from the Lord saying, "Me and the humans and the jinn are in a great affair: I created them and they worship other than Me. I provide for them and they thank someone else."

---

[1] The wording that the author al-Ashqar stated is actually that of al-Nasaai and not of al-Bukhari. However, al-Bukhari has something very similar to the above.—JZ

In a good report, the following is stated: "Son of Adam, you have not been just towards Me. My blessings are being descended to you and your evil is being raised to Me. How many blessings have I given you to make Me beloved to you and I am not in need of you. And how many times have you made Me angry with you by sins while you are in need of Me. The noble angel never stops coming to Me from you with your terrible deeds."[1]

In a *sahih* hadith it states,

لَوْ لَمْ تُذْنِبُوا لَذَهَبَ اللَّهُ بِكُمْ وَلَجَاءَ بِقَوْمٍ يُذْنِبُونَ فَيَسْتَغْفِرُونَ اللَّهَ فَيَغْفِرُ لَهُمْ

"If you were not to commit sins, Allah would take you away and replace you with a people that would make sins and seek Allah's forgiveness and He would forgive them."[2]

## Allah created His creation in order to show the decrees of His names and attributes and their effects

Because of Allah's complete love for His own names and attributes, He decided by His wisdom to make a creation that would demonstrate their excellence and effect. Out of His love for clemency, He created those who deserved clemency. Out of his love for forgiveness, He created those who He forgives and is gentle and patient with and who He does not punish immediately. In fact, He loves His guardianship and respite.

---

[1] According to al-Hindi, thi
Hindi, *Kanz al-Ummaal fi Sunan al-Aqwaal wa al-Afaal* (Beirut: Muasassah al-Risaalah, 1989), vol. 15, p. 800.] Unfortunately, this translator could not find it in its expected place in the published edition of al-Dailami's work. However, the general principle is that if a hadith is recorded only by al-Dailami from among all the works of hadith, the hadith is considered suspect unless shown to be acceptable. Ibn al-Qayyim's statement that it is a "good report" may mean that the meaning is good and not necessarily that the hadith is of the level of *hasan*. Allah knows best.—JZ
[2] Recorded by Muslim.—JZ

Out of His love for His own justice and wisdom, He created those who demonstrate His justice and wisdom.

Out of His love for generosity, kindness and piety, He created those who respond to Him with evil deeds and disobedience while He treats them with forgiveness and kindness. If He did not create those people who respond to Him with disobedience, then this greatness and kindness and its multiple related benefits would have been loss. Blessed be Allah, the Lord of the Worlds, and the Most Just of the Rulers, the One of Infinite Wisdom, and countless blessings, whose Wisdom is as great as His ability. In every action He is full of clear wisdom in the same way that in every action He demonstrates His Infinite abilities.

## Resulting from the creation of this accursed being is a wisdom that leads to the love of Allah

How many things come about due to the creation of this one, who has earned Allah's wrath, that lead to what is beloved to Allah, the Blessed and Most High? It reaches in what is beloved to Him more than what comes about of what is disliked to Him. The Wise One is the One who attains the more beloved affair to Him by bearing the thing He dislikes and hates if that is the path that leads to the thing He loves. It is not possible for the condition to exist without its necessary components. If the creation of Iblees and his army leads to some evil and harm, how much of what Allah loves, such as jihad in His way and denying one's desires, results from his existence and the existence of the army that follows him? People undertake hardships seeking His love and pleasure. The most beloved thing to the one who loves Allah is to bear hardships and harm out of love for his beloved and to show the sincerity of his love. [As is said in lines of poetry,] "Because of you, I have made my cheek an earth— for every gloating and envious person until You are pleased with me."

And there is a narration from the Lord stating, "What I desire is what the bearers can bear for Me." There is nothing more beloved to Allah than His servants bearing the harm of His enemies for His sake and for His pleasure[1]; that harm will benefit them greatly as will the praise that they will give Him for their final result, as well as what they will gain from the honor of being His beloved and those whom He is especially pleased with. But it is forbidden for the one who rejects the love of the Lord to smell that fragrance or to enter from that door or to taste that drink.

"Say to the one who cannot see the sun, there are eyes
others than yours that can see it during sunset and sunrise
Forgive the desperate who is not qualified for that love
It is not good to be too devoted in every matter."

If that creation (Satan) angers the Lord, then He is still pleased with His messengers, prophets and servants because of it. And that pleasure far outweighs that displeasure. If He is displeased by the actions of the disobedient, then He is even more pleased by the repentance of His slaves than the one who has lost his camel with all of his food and drink upon it and then finds them later. If He is displeased by what Satan does to His Prophets and Messengers, He is even more pleased by the battlig, opposing, angering of him and striving against Iblees and the final victory that they have against him. That pleasure is greater in His sight and more righteous than what would have come about if that displeasing thing did not occur and those beloved results would not have happened.

If He was displeased with Adam eating from the tree, then He was more pleased with his repentance, submission, humility and his return unto Allah.

If He was displeased by the Prophet (peace be upon him) being expelled from his native Makkah by the disbelievers, then he was even more pleased by the Prophet's final return.

If He is displeased by the killing and the spilling of the blood of His servants on the earth, then He is more pleased with the new life that He will grant them— the most gracious, blessed and pleasant life possible— close to Allah.

---

[1] This point needs some justification from either the Quran or sunnah. It implies that bearing hardship could be in itself a goal. Unfortunately, this translator could not trace the hadith that ibn al-Qayyim mentioned. From the way he mentioned it, it does not seem to be a strong narration. Allah knows best.—JZ

If He is displeased with the disobedience of His slaves, He is more pleased by the witness of His angels, messengers, prophets and servants of His forgiveness, clemency, kindness, nobility, generosity; as well as the praise and magnification for all of those attributes. All of that is more beloved to Him than what has been lost by the sin of the sinner.

One should know that praise is the great source of all of that. It is by it that the creation and the order stands. And for the Lord is all of the Praise for all that He does and enacts. He did not create anything or decide anything except that due to it He is to be praised, a praise that reaches as far as his creation and rule. A true praise that guarantees the love for Him and being pleased with Him and glorifying of Him and accepting of His Infinite Wisdom in everything that He created or ordered. Denying his Wisdom is not denying His praise. As if he cannot be but Praiseworthy, than He cannot be but full of Wisdom. His praise and Wisdom is like His knowledge and power. His life is a necessity of His being and one cannot deny any of His attributes or names and what they imply as that would lead to a shortcoming that would deny His perfection, greatness and magnificence.

## He loves to be the Protector and the Refuge for His patrons

On this point, ibn al-Qayyim wrote: From the attributes of being perfect and the owner of praise and glorification, He is generous, beneficent and giving. Similarly He also gives refuge, support and aid. In the same way that He loves for people to seek His protection, He loves to give refuge to those who seek refuge in Him. People even take refuge in the kings such as what Ahmad ibn Hussein al-Kindy said in a kings' praise,
"O, the one in whom I seek protection for what I want,
    and the one I seek refuge from what I am cautious about
People will not mend a bone that you broke
    and they cannot break what you mend."
If he had said that about his Lord and Creator, he would have been the happiest of all creation.

The point is that the Master of all of the Dominions loves for His slaves to seek protection in Him and seek refuge in Him as He ordered His Prophet to seek refuge in Him from the accursed Satan on more than one occasion in His Book. That makes apparent His complete blessings on His servants that He gives them refuge from their enemies. His giving of refuge and protection is not from the lesser blessings and Allah loves to complete his blessings upon His believing slaves by letting them see His succor for them against their enemies as well as His protection for them and His giving victory to them. And from these blessings for them, their pleasure and blessings are made complete and justice against his enemies and opponents are made apparent.

"There is none of the two except therein is wisdom that all who ponder cannot possibly completely comprehend."

# The wisdom behind leaving Satan until the end of time

Ibn al-Qayyim has also addressed this question in *Shifa al-Aleel*. The points he makes are the following:[1]

## A trial for the servants

From the points that ibn al-Qayyim makes is that Allah has left Satan in order to use him as an instigator and test for His servants: to distinguish between them, to see which are the good and which are the evil. Therefore He has allowed him to remain forever. If Satan were to die, this purpose of Satan's original creation would vanish. Similar is the case with His decision to always have unbelievers on the earth that would be a test for His devoted slaves. If He were to remove all of them, many wise points and benefits would be done away with. In the same way that the father of the humans was tested by Satan, his offspring shall

---

[1] Ibn al-Qayyim, *Shifa al-Aleel*, pp. 327f.

also be tested. Those who disobey Satan and fight against him will be happy and those who follow him will be leading themselves to their own destruction.

## He leaves Satan as a reward for his previous deeds

From the wisdom of leaving Satan to live is that, since according to His law Satan will not have any good portion in the Hereafter although Satan used to worship Allah along with the angels, all of his reward for his good deeds shall come in this life. Therefore, Allah left him until the day of judgment as a reward for his past deeds and Allah does not do injustice to anyone. As for the believer, he will get his goodly portion in this life and in the Hereafter. As for the unbeliever, he will get all of the reward for his good deeds in this life and he will receive no goodly portion in the hereafter, as is confirmed in *sahih* hadith.

## He is left to increase his sins

Satan has been left until the day of judgment, but this is not due to the honor of his creation. In fact, if he were to die it would be better for him. This would lessen his punishment and the number of his evil deeds. But he made his sin great by continuing to refuse to submit to the Lord and he swore to himself that he would mislead mankind until the day of judgment and keep them away from worshipping their Lord. Thus, his punishment was the greatest punishment. He, therefore, has been left to live in order for him to increase his sins as he will receive the greatest punishment in the hereafter. It is just that he should receive a punishment that is not matched by any other. He is the leader of evil and disbelief. Since he was the foundation of every evil, he should also get the punishment of every evil in the Hereafter. Every punishment in the Hereafter will start with him and then move on to those who followed him in those deeds. This is clearly just and infinitely wise.

## He has been left to be the patron and ally of the evildoers

Part of the decree to leave him until the day of judgment comes from his statement in dispute to the Lord,

$$\text{أَرَءَيْتَكَ هَـٰذَا ٱلَّذِى كَرَّمْتَ عَلَىَّ لَئِنْ أَخَّرْتَنِ إِلَىٰ يَوْمِ ٱلْقِيَـٰمَةِ لَأَحْتَنِكَنَّ ذُرِّيَّتَهُۥٓ إِلَّا قَلِيلًا}$$

"(Satan) said, 'Do you see this creature that you have honored above me? If you give me grace until the Day of Judgment I verily will seize his seed, save a few'" (*al-Israa* 62). Allah was aware that from Adam's progeny there would be many who do not deserve to live in paradise, so He granted Satan his respite. He told Satan, by the tongue of pre-ordainment, that such evildoers would be his companions and friends and that Satan can wait in lurk for them. Every time one of them passed by, it would be Satan's affair. However, if the person were deserving of Allah's pleasure, Allah would prevent Satan from him for He protects the righteous. Allah said that they are deserving of Him while for Satan is only the criminals and evildoers, who refused Allah's protection and did not desire His pleasure.

$$\text{إِنَّهُۥ لَيْسَ لَهُۥ سُلْطَـٰنٌ عَلَى ٱلَّذِينَ ءَامَنُوا۟ وَعَلَىٰ رَبِّهِمْ يَتَوَكَّلُونَ ۝ إِنَّمَا سُلْطَـٰنُهُۥ عَلَى ٱلَّذِينَ يَتَوَلَّوْنَهُۥ وَٱلَّذِينَ هُم بِهِۦ مُشْرِكُونَ}$$

"Lo! He has no power over those who believe and put their trust in their Lord. His power is only over those who make a friend of him, and those who ascribe partners unto Him" (*al-Nahl* 99-100).

But the prophets and messengers die. However, this is not a type of disgrace for them. In fact, it gives them a rest from this worldly life and from their enemies and it gives them honor. And Allah sends messengers after them. And their deaths are better for themselves and their nations. As for themselves, they leave this lowly life and join the companions on high in the greatest of pleasure. This is one of the greatest things that could happen to them and one of the reasons why Allah always gave them a choice between staying in this life or dying. And their nations know that they must not only obey them while they are alive but also after they are dead; but if they obey them they are not worshipping them, but are worshipping Allah instead. For Allah is the Living who never dies. Therefore, how many are the benefits and wisdom for them and their nations in their deaths? Furthermore, they are humans and Allah did not decree for any human everlasting life without death. Furthermore it leads to the succession of the people in this world. If Allah did not allow them to die, the benefits of them having successors would be lost and the earth would be filled by them. Death is the completion for every believer. If there were no death, the people of earth would never have any good life and pleasure. The wisdom behind death is similar to the wisdom behind life.

## To what extent will Satan be successful in misleading humans?

When Satan refused to bow down to Adam, Allah threw him out of His mercy, paradise and pleasure and became angry with him and cursed him. Satan then took an oath upon himself in front of the Lord to mislead and seduce mankind. He promised himself,

لَعَنَهُ ٱللَّهُ وَقَالَ لَأَتَّخِذَنَّ مِنْ عِبَادِكَ نَصِيبًا مَّفْرُوضًا ۝ وَلَأُضِلَّنَّهُمْ وَلَأُمَنِّيَنَّهُمْ

"Surely I will take of Your servants an appointed portion, and surely I will lead them astray and surely I will arouse desires in them" (*an-Nisaa* 118-119).

$$قَالَ أَرَءَيْتَكَ هَٰذَا ٱلَّذِي كَرَّمْتَ عَلَيَّ لَئِنْ أَخَّرْتَنِ إِلَىٰ يَوْمِ ٱلْقِيَٰمَةِ لَأَحْتَنِكَنَّ ذُرِّيَّتَهُۥٓ إِلَّا قَلِيلًا$$

"Do You see this creation that you have honored over me. If you give me grace until the day of Resurrection I verily will seize his seed, save a few" (*al-Israa* 62).

To what extent will he be able to fulfill his wish with respect to the children of Adam? If one takes a cursory glance at the history of humans, one will find humans being misguided and denying the messengers and the books and Allah and making partners with Allah from among His creation. Allah says,

$$وَمَآ أَكْثَرُ ٱلنَّاسِ وَلَوْ حَرَصْتَ بِمُؤْمِنِينَ$$

"And though you try much, most men will not believe" (*Yusuf* 103). Therefore, they have earned the anger and punishment of Allah.

$$ثُمَّ أَرْسَلْنَا رُسُلَنَا تَتْرَا كُلَّ مَا جَآءَ أُمَّةً رَّسُولُهَا كَذَّبُوهُ فَأَتْبَعْنَا بَعْضَهُم بَعْضًا وَجَعَلْنَٰهُمْ أَحَادِيثَ فَبُعْدًا لِّقَوْمٍ لَّا يُؤْمِنُونَ$$

"Then We sent Our messengers one after another. Whenever its messenger came unto a nation they denied him; so We caused them to follow one another (to disaster) and We made them [the subject] of narrations. A far removal for folk who believe not" (*al-Muminoon* 44).

The one who ponders over what is happening will see the servants of Satan swarming all around us. They are raising their banners and calling others to it. They are punishing the servants of Allah. This proves that Satan certainly has been given respite and that he is taking the offspring of Adam and leading them to the hell-fire. And the proportions have been stated, "[Out of every one hundred] ninety-nine to the hell-fire and one to heaven," and in another version, "[Out of every one thousand] nine hundred and ninety-nine in the fire and one in paradise."

This confirms what Satan thought about the offspring of Adam who did not consider what happened to their father or the other preceding generations. This cursed one has remained to lead them to their own destruction. Sometimes they even race him to the hell-fire.

There is nothing worse than having one's enemy's expectations about you come true.

$$\text{وَلَقَدْ صَدَّقَ عَلَيْهِمْ إِبْلِيسُ ظَنَّهُ فَاتَّبَعُوهُ إِلَّا فَرِيقًا مِّنَ ٱلْمُؤْمِنِينَ}$$

"And Satan indeed found his calculation true concerning them, for they follow him, all save a group of true believers" (*Saba* 20). It is terrible for mankind to fulfill this expectation of Satan and to follow that enemy and disobey their Lord, the Merciful. But it has reached an unbelievable and unimaginable degree. There are groups in Iraq and elsewhere who call themselves "the worshippers of Satan," and in their books they swear by what they call, "the rights of Satan." What can be more astonishing?

## Do not think too much about the great number that are being destroyed

The mind should not worry about this great number that is being destroyed as quantity is not important in the measure of Allah. All that matters there is truth and justice, even though the survivors of this measure may be few.

So be among those who follow the truth, are pleased with Allah as their Lord, with Islam as their religion and with Muhammad as their messenger. They are the ones who recognize Satan and the followers of Satan and fight against them with hatred in their heart, speech, and writings, and by doing the works of truth and by fighting against the devils with evidence, proofs, swords and speech. Before that, one should turn to the Merciful and cling to His religion.

$$\text{يَٰٓأَيُّهَا ٱلَّذِينَ ءَامَنُوا۟ ٱدْخُلُوا۟ فِى ٱلسِّلْمِ كَآفَّةً وَلَا تَتَّبِعُوا۟ خُطُوَٰتِ ٱلشَّيْطَٰنِ ۚ إِنَّهُۥ لَكُمْ عَدُوٌّ مُّبِينٌ ۝ فَإِن زَلَلْتُم مِّنۢ بَعْدِ مَا جَآءَتْكُمُ ٱلْبَيِّنَٰتُ فَٱعْلَمُوٓا۟ أَنَّ ٱللَّهَ عَزِيزٌ حَكِيمٌ}$$

"O you who believe! Come, all of you, into submission (unto Him); and follow not the footsteps of Satan. Lo! he is an open enemy for you. And if you slide back after the clear proofs have come unto you, then know that Allah is Mighty, Wise" (*al-Baqara* 208-209). We ask Allah to make us, by His grace and generosity, among those who enter into Islam completely and who do not follow the footsteps of Satan. And the peace and blessings of Allah be upon His slave and Messenger Muhammad.

## Author's References

1. *Ighaatha al-Luhfaan* by ibn al-Qayyim.[1]
2. *Al-Imaan bi-l-Malaaikah* by Ahmad ibn Izz al-Deen al-Bayaanooni.
3. *al-Bidaayah wa al-Nihaayah* by ibn Katheer.
4. *Tafseer ibn Katheer.*
5. *Talbees Iblees* by ibn al-Jauzi.
6. *Jaami al-Rasaail* by ibn Taimiya.
7. *Daairah al-Maarif al-Hadeethah* by Ahmad Atiyah.
8. *Al-Roohiyyah al-Hadeethah* by Muhammad Muhammad Hussain.
9. *Sharh al-Aqeedah al-Tahaawiyyah.*
10. *Shifaa al-Aleel* by ibn al-Qayyim.
11. *Sahih al-Jaami* by Naasir al-Deen al-Albaani.
12. *Al-Aqaaid al-Islaamiyyah* by Sayyid Saabiq.
13. *Al-Furqaan bain Auliyaa al-Rahmaan wa Auliyaa al-Shaitaan* by ibn Taimiya.
14. *Lawaami al-Anwaar al-Bahiyyah (Aqeedah al-Safaareeni).*
15. *Majmoo al-Fataawa Shaikh al-Islaam ibn Taimiya* - collected by ibn Qaasim.
16. *Al-Waabil al-Sayyib min al-Kalim al-Tayyib* by ibn al-Qayyim.
17. The Kuwaiti newspaper *al-Qubus.*
18. The Kuwaiti newspaper *al-Watn.*

---

[1] Unfortunately, in the published work, al-Ashqar did not provide the publisher or year of publication for the works he cited. The references here are exactly as presented in the published edition of the work in Arabic.—JZ

# Translator's References

al-Albani, Muhammad Naasir al-Deen. *Dhaeef al-Jami al-Sagheer wa Ziyadatuhu.* Beirut: al-Maktab al-Islami. 1988.

-----*Sahih al-Jaami al-Sagheer.* Beirut: al-Maktab al-Islami. 1986.

-----*Sahih Sunan Abi Dawud.* Riyadh: Maktab al-Tarbiyyah al-Arabi li-Duwal al-Khaleej. 1989.

----- *Sahih Sunan al-Tirmidhi.* Riyadh: Maktab al-Tarbiyyah al-Arabi li-Duwal al-Khaleej. 1988.

Al-Arnaoot, Shuaib and Adil Murshid. *Musnad al-Imaam Ahmad.* Beirut: Muasassah al-Risaalah. 1997.

Al-Darweesh, Abdullah. *Bughyat al-Raaid fi Tahqeeq Majma al-Zawaaid wa Manba al-Fawaaid.* Beirut: Dar al-Fikr. 1992.

al-Hindi, Alaa al-Din. *Kanz al-Ummaal fi Sunan al-Aqwaal wa al-Afaal.* Beirut: Muasassah al-Risaalah. 1989.

Ibn al-Atheer, Majd al-Din. *al-Nihaaya fi Ghareeb al-Hadith.* N.c.: al-Maktab al-Islami. n.d.

Ibn Taimiya, Ahmad. *The Criterion between the Allies of the Merciful and the Allies of the Devil.* Birmingham, England: Idarah Ihya-us-Sunnah. 1993.

Maroof, Bashaar and Shuaib al-Arnaoot. *Tahreer Taqreeb al-Tahdheeb.* Beirut: Muasassah al-Risaalah. 1997.

Al-Munaawi, Abdul Rauf. *Faidh al-Qadeer Sharh al-Jaami al-Sagheer.* Beirut: Dar al-Marifa. 1972.

Al-Nasaai, Ahmad. *Sunan al-Nasaai.* Beirut: Ihyaa al-Turaath al-Arabi. n.d.

al-Tabaraani, Sulaimaan. *al-Mujam al-Ausat.* Riyadh: Maktabah al-Maarif. 1985.

Zarabozo, Jamaal al-Din. "Innovations and Islam I: The Meaning of *Bida.*" *al-Basheer.* Vol. 1, No. 4. November 1987.

# Index of Quranic Verses Cited

*al-Faatiha (surah)*: p. 136
*al-Baqara* 101: p. 48
    102: p. 48, 121-122
    168: p. 172
    169: p. 75
    207: p. 127
    208: p. 171
    208-209: p. 243
    255: p. 25, 34, 134, 207, 210
    257: p. 92
    268: pp. 79-80
    275: p. 87
*ali-Imraan* 36: p. 83, 181
    126: p. 224
    159: p. 163
    175: pp. 95-96, 113
    179: p. 227
*al-Nisaa* 43: p. 119
    51: p. 162
    76: p. 14, 38, 95
    117-118: p. 78
    118-119: p. 240
    119: p. 71, 92
    120: p. 104
*al-Maaidah* 8: p. 206
    79: p. 165
    90: p. 20
    90-91: pp. 117-118
    91: p. 75
    105: p. 98
*al-Anaam* 68: p. 111
    121: pp. 94-95
    130: pp. 53-54
    153: pp. 170-171
*al-Araaf* 14-15: p. 24, 70, 89
    15-16: p. 70
    16-17: p. 76
    20: p. 114
    21: pp. 105-6
    23: p. 202
    27: p. 5, 71, 94
    37: p. 54
    48: p. 105
    54: p. 192
    54-57: p. 189
    128: p. 117
    130: pp. 57-58, 206
    175-176: pp. 42-43
    179: p. 54
    199-200: p. 173
    201: p. 201
    202: p. 202
*al-Anfaal* 48: p. 32, 33, 93
*Yunus* 29: p. 9
*Hood* 6: p. 117
*Yusuf* 42: p. 112
    53: p. 213
    100: p. 124
    103: p. 241
*Ibraheem* 22: p. 40, 94
    35-36: p. 120
*al-Hijr* 9: p. 123

26-27: p. 7
27: p. 6
39-40: p. 39, 96-97
42: p. 39
*al-Nahl* 63: pp. 98-9
98-99: p. 177
99-100: p. 239
100: p. 40
*al-Israa* 15: p. 206
27: p. 202
53: p. 204
62: p. 72, 239, 241
64: p. 90
65: p. 38
85: p. 152
88: p. 49, 59
*al-Kahf* 20: p. 16
24: p. 112
36: p. 105
50: p. 17, 92
63: p. 111
103-104: p. 99
*Maryam* 83: p. 40, 90, 203
*Taha* 66: p. 122
69: p. 162
82: p. 117
102-104: p. 215
115: p. 111
120: p. 100, 128
*al-Hajj* 52-54: p. 116
*al-Muminoon* 44: p. 241
98-99: p. 173
112-114: p. 215
*al-Shuaraa* 210-212: p. 49
*al-Naml* 39-40: p. 29
*al-Room* 21: p. 22
*al-Sajdah* 13: p. 54
*Saba* 12-13: pp. 31-32, 46
14: p. 159

20: p. 96, 242
20-21: p. 39
40-41: p. 79
54: p. 117
*Faatir* 6: p. 71, 72-73, 93
*al-Saaffaat* 1-10: p. 189, 193
62-65: p. 27
158-159: p. 57
*Saad* 35: p. 46
36-38: p. 45
41: p. 83
82-83: p. 66
*al-Zumar* 42: p. 152
*Fussilat* 25: p. 91, 99
*al-Shoora* 11: p. 229
*al-Zukhruf* 36: p. 91
37: p. 99
*al-Ahqaaf* 29-32: p. 60
30: p. 58
35: p. 215
*al-Dhaariyaat* 56: p. 53
*al-Rahmaan* (*surah*): p. 62
15: p. 6
26-28: p. 23
33-35: pp. 50-51, 189
46-47: p. 54
56: p. 23
60: p. 20
*al-Mujaadalah* 10: p. 95
19: p. 112
*al-Hashr* 16: p. 73, 110
21-24: p. 189
*al-Saff* 5: p. 110
*al-Jinn* 1: p. 11, 61
1-2: pp. 59-60
6: p. 11, 137, 176
8-9: p. 30
11: p. 65
14-15: p. 65

26-28: p. 160
*al-Naaziaat* 46: p. 215
*al-Fajr* 27-28: p. 213
*al-Ikhlaas* (*surah*): p. 136

*al-Falaq* (*surah*): p. 180
*al-Naas* (*surah*): p. 180
4-5: p. 128

# Table of Contents

**INTRODUCTION** ................................................................... 1

**1 IDENTIFICATION AND CLARIFICATION** ........................... 5

WHAT ARE THE JINN? ................................................................ 5
   *Their Origin* ........................................................................... 5
   *When were they created?* ...................................................... 6
   *The Names for the Jinn in the Arabic Language* ................... 7
   *Types of Jinn* ......................................................................... 7
THERE IS NO ROOM FOR THE DENIAL OF THE EXISTENCE OF THE JINN ....... 8
   *Not possessing knowledge concerning them is not a type of proof* ........... 9
   *The truth of the matter* ......................................................... 9
   *Proofs for the correct position* ............................................ 10
   *Donkeys and Dogs see the jinn* .......................................... 13
SATAN AND THE JINN ............................................................... 13
   *Satan, the created* .............................................................. 14
   *His origin* ........................................................................... 15
   *Was Satan the origin of the Jinn or was he just one of them?* ........... 17
THE FOOD AND DRINK OF THE JINN ......................................... 17
   *Do the jinn marry and procreate?* ..................................... 20
   *Marriage between the jinn and humans* ............................ 22
   *Do the devils die?* .............................................................. 23
   *The residence of the jinn and their places and the times that they can be found* ........... 24
   *The places where the devils sit or gather* .......................... 25
   *The animals of the jinn* ...................................................... 25
   *Specific animals that the devils accompany* ..................... 26
   *The ugliness of Satan* ........................................................ 27
   *Satan has two horns* .......................................................... 27
THEIR ABILITY AND STRENGTH ................................................ 29
   *They preceded mankind in matters related to space* ........ 29
   *Superstitions during the period of ignorance* .................... 30
   *Their knowledge in building and other crafts* ................... 31

*Their ability to take on other shapes* ............................................... 32
*The jinn of the houses* ............................................................. 34
*Important notes* ................................................................... 36
*Satan is able to flow in the descendants of Adam like blood flows through a vein.* ............................................................................ 37
THEIR WEAKNESSES AND INABILITIES ................................................. 38
*They have no power over the pious worshippers of Allah* ............................. 38
*He has power over the believers due to their sins* ................................. 41
*Satan's fear and fleeing from some of the slaves of Allah* ......................... 43
*The jinn were made subservient to Solomon* ......................................... 45
*The Jews lied about Solomon* ....................................................... 47
*They are incapable of performing miracles* ......................................... 48
*They are not able to appear like the Prophet (peace be upon him) in a vision or dream* ................................................................... 49
*They are not able to go beyond the limit set for them in the skies* ................ 50
*They are not able to open the closed doors that have had the name of Allah mentioned over them* ................................................................ 51

## 2 RESPONSIBILITY FOR THEIR ACTIONS ............................................. 53

THE ULTIMATE PURPOSE OF THEIR CREATION ............................................ 53
*They are responsible according to their own specific standard* ..................... 55
*A Misconception and its Reply* ..................................................... 56
*There is no relationship between the jinn and Allah, the Glorious* ................. 56
*How does Allah's revelation reach them?* ........................................... 57
*The message of Muhammad (peace be upon him) is for both jinn and humans* .......................................................................... 59
*The delegation from the jinn* ...................................................... 61
*The jinn preaching to the humans* .................................................. 63
*Their order to do good deeds and being witnesses for Muslims* ...................... 64
*They are at different levels of good and evil* ..................................... 65
THE NATURE OF SATAN ................................................................ 65
*Can a devil embrace Islam?* ........................................................ 66

## 3 THE ENMITY BETWEEN SATAN AND MANKIND ......................................... 69

THE REASON BEHIND THE ENMITY, ITS HISTORY, AND ITS SEVERITY ...................... 69
*Allah's warning to us concerning Satan* ............................................ 71

| | |
|---|---|
| THE GOALS OR THE AIMS OF SATAN | 72 |
|    Long-term Goal | 72 |
| SHORT-TERM GOALS | 73 |
|    1. To get the slave involved in disbelief and idolatry | 73 |
|    2. If he is not able to lead them to disbelief, he leads them to sins | 74 |
|    3. Blocking the slave from obeying Allah | 75 |
|    4. Ruining the Acts of Obedience to Allah | 77 |
|    Every disobedience to the Merciful is obedience to Satan | 78 |
|    Conclusion | 79 |
|    5. Psychologically and physically harming humans | 80 |
| THE LEADER OF THE BATTLE | 88 |
| THE SOLDIERS | 89 |
|    His soldiers from the jinn | 90 |
|    Every human has a "partner" | 90 |
|    His patrons from among the humans | 91 |
|    He deceives and disappoints his patrons | 93 |
|    Satan uses his patrons as troops to serve him and to help him in his battle against the believers | 94 |
| THE WAYS OF SATAN IN LEADING HUMANS ASTRAY | 96 |
|    (1) Making evil look good | 96 |
|    Giving pleasing names to forbidden things | 100 |
|    (2) Going to extremes | 100 |
|    (3) Satan hinders the slave from acting by means of procrastination and laziness | 102 |
|    (4) Promises and hopes | 104 |
|    (5) Satan appears as a sincere advisor to humans | 105 |
|    (6) He uses a step-by-step approach to misguide mankind | 110 |
|    (7) The slave of Allah is made to forget what is good and best for him | 110 |
|    (8) Making the believers fear his supporters | 112 |
|    (9) He gets to the person through what the person loves or desires | 113 |
|    (10) Casting doubts in the person's mind | 114 |
|    (11-14) Alcohol, games of chance, idols and divining arrows | 117 |
|    Divining Arrows | 120 |
|    (15) Magic | 121 |
|    Is magic real? | 122 |
|    The spell of the Jew on the Prophet (peace be upon him) | 122 |

| | |
|---|---|
| *(16) Human weaknesses* | *123* |
| *(17) Women and the love of this world* | *125* |
| *(18) Singing and music* | *125* |
| *(19) Making Muslims lackadaisical in fulfilling what they have been ordered to do* | *126* |
| HOW DOES SATAN GET TO THE SOULS OF HUMANS? | 128 |
| *The secret whispering* | *128* |

## 4 [THE CAPABILITIES OF SATAN] .................. 131

| | |
|---|---|
| THE FORMS DEVILS CAN TAKE | 131 |
| *Those who are served by the devils get close to them by way of sinful acts* | *135* |
| *"Invisible men"* | *136* |
| *The Ruling about being served by the jinn* | *138* |
| MAKING THE SPIRITS APPEAR [THROUGH SEANCES AND CHANNELING] | 140 |
| THE USE OF THE JINN AND DEVILS | 142 |
| *Making the spirits appear is an ancient claim* | *142* |
| *A modern day experience* | *143* |
| *The beginning of the experience* | *143* |
| *How did the deception begin?* | *144* |
| *The situation develops* | *145* |
| *Who were those visitors?* | *145* |
| *The beginning of my vigilance* | *146* |
| *The reality becomes uncovered* | *147* |
| *Conclusions* | *148* |
| *The gravity of this call* | *149* |
| *Is it possible to make the spirits appear?* | *151* |
| *A conjecture and a reply* | *153* |
| THE DEVILS LEAVE THOSE WHO FOLLOW THEM | 154 |
| *The beginning of his plight* | *154* |
| *What did an eyewitness say?* | *156* |
| *Our Comments to this Event* | *157* |
| *The Jinn and the Knowledge of the Unseen* | *158* |
| *Fortune tellers and diviners* | *159* |
| *Questioning the diviner for the purpose of testing him* | *161* |
| *Astrologers* | *161* |

| | |
|---|---|
| *A Misconception*............................................................ | *162* |
| *The soothsayers are the messengers of Satan* ................. | *163* |
| *The Obligation of the Muslim Nation Towards Them* ...... | *164* |
| JINN AND UNIDENTIFIED FLYING OBJECTS ....................... | 165 |
| *After the above, we can conclude the following*............... | *166* |

## 5 THE WEAPONS OF THE BELIEVER IN HIS WAR AGAINST SATAN............................................................... 169

| | |
|---|---|
| 1. CAUTION AND CARE.................................................. | 169 |
| 2. STICKING TO THE BOOK AND THE SUNNAH ................. | 170 |
| 3. TAKING REFUGE AND SHELTER IN ALLAH..................... | 172 |
| *Seeking refuge upon entering bathrooms* ...................... | *174* |
| *Seeking refuge during the time of anger* ....................... | *175* |
| *Seeking refuge during the time of sexual intercourse*..... | *176* |
| *[Seeking Refuge Upon Entering a Valley or a Strange Land]* ............. | *176* |
| *Seeking refuge in Allah from Satan upon hearing the braying of a donkey*................................................................ | *177* |
| *Seeking refuge in Allah before reciting the Quran*........... | *177* |
| *Invocations for one's children and family* ..................... | *180* |
| *The best of invocations are the last two surahs of the Quran*............. | *180* |
| *A great understanding*................................................. | *181* |
| *A Misconception*......................................................... | *181* |
| 4. BEING BUSY WITH THE REMEMBRANCE OF ALLAH....... | 182 |
| 5. STICKING TO THE MUSLIM COMMUNITY....................... | 195 |
| 6. UNCOVERING DESIGNS AND PLANS OF SATAN ........... | 196 |
| 7. DIFFERING FROM SATAN ........................................... | 197 |
| *The transportation of the devils and their lodging* ......... | *198* |
| *Haste is from Satan* .................................................... | *200* |
| *Yawning*..................................................................... | *200* |
| 8. REPENTANCE AND SEEKING FORGIVENESS ............... | 201 |
| 9. TO PUT AN END TO THE SUSPICIOUS ASPECTS AND THE QUESTIONABLE MATTERS BY WHICH SATAN ENTERS INTO THE SOUL...................................... | 203 |
| THE CURE FOR BEING POSSESSED.................................... | 204 |
| *The causes of being possessed* ..................................... | *204* |
| *Our obligation towards them* ....................................... | *205* |
| *Prohibition of killing the snakes of the houses*................ | *206* |

*Abusing the jinn and striking them* .................................................. 207
*Using dhikr and Quranic reciting as help against the jinn* ............... 207
*The Messenger (peace be upon him) drove away the jinn from the possessed* ............................................................................................. 208
*Imam Ahmad ordered the jinn to leave and they responded* ............ 210
*What the Healer Must Be Like* .......................................................... 210
*Incantations and invocations* ............................................................. 211
*Conciliation to the jinn* ....................................................................... 212
THE REALITY OF THE STRUGGLE .................................................. 212
*How can a person make his heart observant during the prayer?* ........ 221

# 6 THE WISDOM BEHIND THE CREATION OF SATAN ............. 225

*1. The effects of fighting against Satan and his supporters leads to the perfection of worship* ............................................................................ 225
*2. By the existence of Satan, the slaves of Allah become fearful due to their sins* ....................................................................................................... 225
*3. Allah has made him a lesson for those who reflect* ........................ 226
*4. Allah has made Satan a test and trial for His slaves* ...................... 226
*5. The creation of Satan demonstrates the complete ability of Allah to create opposites* ................................................................................... 227
*6. Opposites show the virtues of their opposites* ................................ 228
*7. Trials are a way to the actualization of thankfulness* ..................... 228
*8. In the creation of Iblees rests many aspects of worship* ................ 228
*9. The creation of Satan makes Allah's signs clear as well as the wonderfulness of His power* ............................................................... 229
*10. Iblees' creation from fire is a sign* ................................................ 229
*11. Iblees' creation makes apparent the meaning of many of Allah's names* .................................................................................. 229
*12. The creation of Satan makes apparent Allah's complete rule and control over the affairs of this creation* ............................................. 230
*13. Iblees' existence is from the completeness of Allah's wisdom* ........ 230
*14. Praise to Allah for what He has hindered and subdued* ............... 230
*15. By Iblees' creation, Allah shows His servants His calmness and patience* ............................................................................................... 231
*Allah created His creation in order to show the decrees of His names and attributes and their effects* ................................................................... 233

*Resulting from the creation of this accursed being is a wisdom that leads to the love of Allah* .................................................................................................. *234*
*He loves to be the Protector and the Refuge for His patrons* .................. *236*
THE WISDOM BEHIND LEAVING SATAN UNTIL THE END OF TIME .................... 237
*A trial for the servants* ........................................................................ *237*
*He leaves Satan as a reward for his previous deeds* .............................. *238*
*He is left to increase his sins* ................................................................ *238*
*He has been left to be the patron and ally of the evildoers* .................... *239*
*To what extent will Satan be successful in misleading humans?* ............ *240*
*Do not think too much about the great number that are being destroyed* ...................................................................................... *242*

**AUTHOR'S REFERENCES** ........................................................................ **244**

**TRANSLATOR'S REFERENCES** ................................................................ **245**

**INDEX OF QURANIC VERSES CITED** ...................................................... **246**

**TABLE OF CONTENTS** ............................................................................ **249**

# ORDER FORM

To order any of the books published by Al-Basheer Company, simply copy or tear out this page, fill in the order form below and send it with a check or money order for the appropriate amount to: Al-Basheer Company, 1750 30$^{th}$ St. PMB #440, Boulder, CO 80301

| Qty | Title | Price | Amount |
|---|---|---|---|
| | *Marital Discord* – Saalih Sadlaan | $6.00 | |
| | *He Came to Teach You Your Religion* – Jamaal Zarabozo | $11.00 | |
| | *The World of the Jinn and Devils* – Umar al-Ashqar | $11.00 | |
| | *Words of Remembrance and Words of Reminder* w/ tape – Saalih al-Sadlaan | $9.00 | |
| | *The Fiqh of Marriage in the Light of the Quran and Sunnah* - Saalih al-Sadlaan | 10.00 | |
| | *How to Approach and Understand the Quran* - Jamaal Zarabozo | 16.00 | |
| | *Fiqh Made Easy* by Dr. Saalih al-Sadlaan | 11.00 | |
| | *Commentary on the Forty Hadith of al-Nawawi* (3 volumes) - Jamaal Zarabozo (Special Shipping Charge = $8.00) | 80.00 | |
| | | **Subtotal** | |
| | **CO Residents add 7.41% Sales Tax** | | |
| | Postage for inside U.S.: $3.75 for first book, $1.00 for each additional book; for orders of over $100 pay only 10% as shipping charge | | |
| | | **TOTAL** | |

Name _____

Address _____

City _____ ST _____ ZIP _____

Phone number _____

# ORDER FORM

To order any of the books published by Al-Basheer Company, simply copy or tear out this page, fill in the order form below and send it with a check or money order for the appropriate amount to: Al-Basheer Company, 1750 30$^{th}$ St. PMB #440, Boulder, CO 80301

| Qty | Title | Price | Amount |
|---|---|---|---|
| | *Marital Discord* – Saalih Sadlaan | $6.00 | |
| | *He Came to Teach You Your Religion* – Jamaal Zarabozo | $11.00 | |
| | *The World of the Jinn and Devils* – Umar al-Ashqar | $11.00 | |
| | *Words of Remembrance and Words of Reminder* w/ tape – Saalih al-Sadlaan | $9.00 | |
| | *The Fiqh of Marriage in the Light of the Quran and Sunnah* - Saalih al-Sadlaan | 10.00 | |
| | *How to Approach and Understand the Quran* - Jamaal Zarabozo | 16.00 | |
| | *Fiqh Made Easy* by Dr. Saalih al-Sadlaan | 11.00 | |
| | *Commentary on the Forty Hadith of al-Nawawi* (3 volumes) - Jamaal Zarabozo (Special Shipping Charge = $8.00) | 80.00 | |
| | | **Subtotal** | |
| | **CO Residents add 7.41% Sales Tax** | | |
| | Postage for inside U.S.: $3.75 for first book, $1.00 for each additional book; for orders of over $100 pay only 10% as shipping charge | | |
| | | **TOTAL** | |

Name _____

Address _____

City _____ ST ____ ZIP _____

Phone number _____

# ORDER FORM

To order any of the books published by Al-Basheer Company, simply copy or tear out this page, fill in the order form below and send it with a check or money order for the appropriate amount to: Al-Basheer Company, 1750 30th St. PMB #440, Boulder, CO 80301

| Qty | Title | Price | Amount |
|---|---|---|---|
| | *Marital Discord* – Saalih Sadlaan | $6.00 | |
| | *He Came to Teach You Your Religion* – Jamaal Zarabozo | $11.00 | |
| | *The World of the Jinn and Devils* – Umar al-Ashqar | $11.00 | |
| | *Words of Remembrance and Words of Reminder* w/ tape – Saalih al-Sadlaan | $9.00 | |
| | *The Fiqh of Marriage in the Light of the Quran and Sunnah* - Saalih al-Sadlaan | 10.00 | |
| | *How to Approach and Understand the Quran* - Jamaal Zarabozo | 16.00 | |
| | *Fiqh Made Easy* by Dr. Saalih al-Sadlaan | 11.00 | |
| | *Commentary on the Forty Hadith of al-Nawawi* (3 volumes) - Jamaal Zarabozo (Special Shipping Charge = $8.00) | 80.00 | |
| | | **Subtotal** | |
| | **CO Residents add 7.41% Sales Tax** | | |
| | Postage for inside U.S.: $3.75 for first book, $1.00 for each additional book; for orders of over $100 pay only 10% as shipping charge | | |
| | | **TOTAL** | |

Name _____

Address _____

City _____ ST _____ ZIP _____

Phone number _____